PERSPECTIVES ON INTERNATIONAL BUSINESS
Theories and Practice

Adonis & Abbey Publishers Ltd
St James House
13 Kensington Square,
London, W8 5HD
United Kingdom

Website: http://www.adonis-abbey.com
E-mail Address: editor@adonis-abbey.com

Nigeria:
Suites C4 & C5 J-Plus Plaza
Asokoro, Abuja, Nigeria
Tel: +234 (0) 7058078841/08052035034

British Library Cataloguing-in-Publication Data
A catalogue record for this book is available from the British Library

ISBN: 978-1-909112-55-1

PERSPECTIVES ON INTERNATIONAL BUSINESS
Theories and Practice

Edited by

John Kuada

ADONIS & ABBEY
PUBLISHERS LTD

Table of Contents

Foreword

Welcome to the International Business Centre (IBC) at Aalborg University. The International Business Centre (IBC) was established in 1984 and celebrated its 30 years anniversary in 2014. From a modest beginning, IBC has grown in to a comprehensive centre that runs three graduate programmes, one in International Business (started in 1984), the second in International Marketing (started in 2008), and the third in Innovation Management (started in 2012 in Beijing). The Centre also has a PhD programme as well as a research programme that engages around 20 scholars. Over the years, we have also built solid collaboration with the local and international business community. Furthermore, IBC has an open door policy and enjoys having guest professors and Adjunct Professors from different parts of the world as collaborating partners. You can read more about us on www.ibc.aau.dk

The centre has just adopted "IBC Strategy 2020" aimed at responding effectively to the challenges of a dynamic global business community and making us an attractive partner for students, researchers and businesses. This book is the first in a series of books that the centre plans to publish as a means of communicating our research output to our stakeholders.

We are mindful of the fact that the field of international business is wide in scope. Geographical dimensions are frequently used as a dominant defining characteristic of the field. But other scholars focus attention on selected topics, as well as firms and institutional characteristics in their research. In line with these defining characteristics, IBC scholars have decided on the following themes for their research:

- Internationalization of Companies and Global Strategies
- Culture, Inter-Cultural Management & Leadership

- International Marketing, Global Branding and Consumer Behaviour
- Global Innovation, Knowledge Management and Organisation
- Global Industrial Dynamics and Value Chains in Institutional Context
- E-business in an International Perspective

The research presented in this volume covers the first five of the themes. We hope that the discussions initiated in the book will motivate you sufficiently to contact the Centre or any of the individual researchers to explore opportunities for collaboration. Enjoy your reading,

Olav Jull Sørensen
Professor of International Business
Head of the International Business Centre
Department of Business and Management
Aalborg University

CHAPTER ONE

Introduction

International Business Challenges in the 21 Century – Some Key Issues and Research Opportunities

John Kuada

Globalization has brought with it game-changing events that produce opportunities and challenges to which governments and businesses have to respond – sometimes with unfamiliar models. On the positive side, it has encouraged increased economic integration, mobility of skilled labour, improved capital investment in research and development, as well as favourable externalities that lower overall costs of transactions in the developed countries. It has also offered the developing countries some improved opportunities to kick-start their economies. But globalization brings with it some short-term negative challenges that societies and their key decision makers must continuously be mindful of. These include growing wage gaps between the educated and uneducated segments of the populations and increased social liabilities (African Union and Economic Commission for Africa, 2009).

At firm level, empirical studies have shown that firms adopt a wide variety of successful approaches to internationalization. It has been noted that approaches that may be found by scholars to be intuitively appealing, may be considered inappropriate by some firms in some contexts (Osarenkhoe, 2009). Their choices of strategy tend to depend on a variety of factors including home country and host country contexts and conditions, the nature of industry in which a firm operates, the nature of product and services they offer, cost considerations and possibilities of compensating for disadvantages through the deployment of a combination of tangible and intangible set of resources (Madsen, 1989; Leonidou and Katsikeas, 1996). It is therefore not surprising that several scholars have decried the lack of unified frameworks in international business research (Toyne and Nigh, 1997; Hambrick and Chen, 2008). The individual chapters in this volume draw attention to the diversity of challenges, opportunities as well as the policy and strategy options that governments and businesses face.

In chapter two, George Tesar and Hamid Moini provide a historical perspective on managerial activities leading to internationalization of smaller manufacturing enterprises. They explore some of the dominant environmental forces that shaped the internationalization of such enterprises as well as the corporate framework suitable for their internationalization. The studies reviewed have been characterized as fragmented and do not produce a consistent, meaningful, and comprehensive framework. They therefore suggest that future research needs to be guided by dynamic models which describe entire internationalization process of small enterprises.

Arnim Decker discusses the role of social capital in the internationalization process of small entrepreneurial firms in chapter three. He sees social capital at three levels: (1) as attributes of individuals in their relationship with others, (2) as an inherent property of networks, into which smaller firms and entrepreneurs are embedded, and (3) as a defining characteristic of relationships between nations. He argues that all three levels of social capital can be actively deployed by entrepreneurs as resources that facilitate the internationalization process of their enterprises. Thus, researchers' awareness of social capital and the manner in which they are operationalized can improve insight into the success or otherwise of the internationalization processes of small firms.

John Kuada provides an integrated conceptual framework for the internationalization process of firms in developing countries in chapter four. He draws a distinction between downstream and upstream aspects of internationalization. In his view, downstream internationalization assumes that all firms initiate their internationalization process with export and proceed in a path-dependent manner towards the location of production activities abroad. In contrast, upstream internationalization focuses attention on imports of both tangible and intangible resources into firms in order to facilitate their operations in a domestic market. His main argument is that firms may adopt one or a combination of four routes of internationalization: upstream only, downstream only, sequential upstream-downstream, and/or concurrent upstream-downstream routes. It is therefore strategically misleading to examine internationalization of firms in terms of either downstream or upstream processes only.

Yimei Hu discusses globalization of innovation from a network organizational perspective in chapter five. She explains network organization from (1) a narrow, and (2) a broad perspective. In a narrow perspective network organizations represent forms of internal organizational design aimed to promote innovation strategy through encouraging more interaction between business units, introducing market mechanism to optimize internal resource allocation, and reducing hierarchies. In a broad sense, they may appear in the form of inter-organizational innovation networks such as strategic technological partnerships, joint ventures, value, networks and technological outsourcing and licensing. To her the adoption of network perspective as a research method will enable researchers to analyze organizations and business contexts in terms of the nodes and ties that provide frameworks for innovation.

In chapter six Daojuan Wang and Hamid Moini discuss performance assessment in cross-border mergers and acquisitions with special focus on motives, valuation practices, and performance. The study is based on an online survey conducted among the chief financial officers of 131 Danish firms. The results showed that five primary motives underscore the formation of these mergers and acquisition: - i.e. 1) geographic expansion, 2) achieving more rapid growth, 3) expansion or improvement of product mix, 4) gaining economies of scale/scope, and 5) acquiring technical knowledge/expertise. Discounted cash flow models are typically used in the valuation process. Almost half of the respondents in the study had no metrics to assess the outcomes of the mergers and acquisitions.

John Kuada examines aspects of the competitiveness of nations and firms in a global context in chapter seven. The focus of his contribution is on the human side of national and firm-level competitiveness in a dynamic global business environment. He introduces the concept of *human capability development* into the business economics literature, arguing that competitiveness depends on the overall capability of people, not only in a technical sense of having required work competencies and applying them efficiently. He therefore suggests a broader perspective of human capability development, defining the construct in terms of the following four sets of factors - (1) the *cultural and civil societal characteristics*, (2) the overall *institutional capabilities* of the nation, (3) *leadership and governance capabilities*, and (4) the *global orientation* of individuals, organisations and the society as a whole (as well as the integration of firms and institutions within the global family). In his view competitiveness can only be sustained if an appropriate balance is maintained between these factors.

Andreea Iacob provides a review of the contemporary literature on country-of-origin effect on brand perception in chapter eight. Her literature review covered the period between 1993 and 2013 and included 77 papers from leading journals on the subject. The results suggest that the existing knowledge of the impact of the country-of-origin effect on brand perception has some conflicting views and therefore calls for further research.

She suggests that consumer behaviour studies need to be undertaken in the following areas: relationships between multiple countries of origin and brand perception; consumer ethnocentrism and brand perception; country-of-origin effect and brand evaluation, and country-of-origin effect, purchase intention and brand perception.

In chapter nine, Jeanne S. Bentzen and Andreea Iacob extend the knowledge of the effect of brand familiarity on how country-of-origin influences brand perception in a developed country. They use a 2x2 factorial experimental design to test the effects of country-of-origin with two levels of sourcing location – Czech Republic and Romania- on a technological complex product (cars), represented by 2 brands, one familiar brand (Skoda) and one unfamiliar brand (Dacia). The findings suggest that country-of-origin has a significant positive impact on the consumers' perception of the Czech manufactured Skoda Fabia, representing the familiar brand, and a significant negative impact on the consumers' perception of the Romanian manufactured Dacia Sandero, representing the unfamiliar brand.

In chapter ten, Li Thuy Dao revisits the question of how much culture has an impact on the operation of international joint ventures and provides an integrative approach to studying the subject. She argues that current discourse on the topic is generally split into two opinions: one views culture as differences that exert some negative influence on joint venture performance, while the other views culture-as-emergence in the joint venture's working processes. In her view, the former stream of research still lacks consensus on the degree of impact, and the latter (stream of research) provides no clarity on how culture emerges through the different processes in the post-formation phase. She presents a critical review of the two perspectives, argues for the need of an integrative approach based on a dynamic view of culture.

Marita Svane discusses the concepts of strategizing and organizing from a multicultural, pluralistic perspective. Building on this perspective, the chapter discusses the role of fragmented cultures and cultural dynamics in the strategizing and organizing processes. She illustrates her discussions with a specific multi-cultural merger, leaning on the Heideggerian lifeworld ontology.

Evidently, insights provided by the chapters in this volume do not, by any means, exhaust the research domains of international business. But they build on earlier accomplishments in the field and provide pointers at new areas of research. As such, they offer a useful basis for current and future researchers. The contributions are diverse and have been guided by different meta-theoretical lenses. They also illustrate how changes within the macro and micro economic space will continuously provide new challenges and opportunities for research.

References

African Union and Economic Commission for Africa (2009) *Growth and Social Development in Africa in 2008 and Prospects for 2009* (Economic Report on Africa)

Hambrick, D. C. & Chen, M.-J., (2008) "New academic fields as admittance-seeking social movements: The case of strategic management" *Academy of Management Review*, 33: 32-54.

Leonidou, Leonidas C., and Constantine S. Katsikeas (1996), 'The Export Development Process: An Integrative Review of Empirical Models', *Journal of International Business Studies*, 27(3), pp. 517–51.

Madsen, T. K. (1989), 'Successful Export Marketing Management: Some Empirical Evidence', *International Marketing Review*, 6 (4), pp. 41-57.

Osarenkhoe, Aihie (2009) "An integrated framework for understanding the driving forces behind non-sequential process of internationalisation among firms" *Business Process Management Journal* Vol. 15 No. 2, pp. 286-316

Toyne, B., & Nigh, D., (1997) *International business: An emerging vision* (Columbia: University of South Carolina Press).

CHAPTER TWO

Historical Dimensions and Perspectives about Managerial Activities Leading to Internationalization of Smaller Manufacturing Enterprises

George Tesar and Hamid Moini

Abstract

This chapter examines some of the antecedents to internationalization of smaller manufacturing enterprises (SMEs), explores some of the dominant environmental forces that shaped their internationalization, and looks at the corporate framework suitable for such internationalization. A review of past research suggests that the results of much research concerning SMEs' internationalization cannot be logically integrated into a consistent, meaningful, and comprehensive domain. Researchers responsible for most of the studies examined components of the internationalization process among SMEs, but not the entire process. This chapter suggests that because the circumstances in which SMEs attempt to internationalize their operations change considerably over the years, it may be necessary to start thinking about developing dynamic models which describe their entire internationalization process.

Introduction

The objective of this chapter is to present a series of historical dimensions and perspectives concerning managerial activities leading to internationalization of smaller manufacturing enterprises (SMEs). The chapter places the main emphasis on early stages of SMEs activities leading to internationalization of their strategic and operational managerial activities. More specifically, it will examine the long term evolution of private and public efforts to internationalize SMEs for the primary purpose of reducing countries' trade deficits, creating jobs, and generating sustainable tax revenue. As a part of this study, a vast amount of literature was reviewed along with studies and research cases that remain in the main stream of the research on topic of SMEs' internationalization as the topic is conveniently titled today.[1]

The seminal academic and managerial literature that began to focus on issues of internationalization emerged in the late 1950s when academic, managerial, and administrative thinking became concerned with the emergence of foreign operations among large and small industrial enterprises in Europe, North America, and Australia. In the academic and managerial literature, the concept of internationalization evolved sequentially with an emphasis on different aspects of managerial activities such as the orientation of top managers, their planning activities, and an identification of perceived differential advantages. In the beginning, the evolution of the internationalization concept pertaining to SMEs focused almost exclusively on their export operations. Governmental agencies in a number of countries very early on attempted to promote and stimulate development of export operations among their SMEs by offering a variety of direct managerial assistance and financing opportunities. At the same time, some of the seminal studies concerning export promotion, stimulation, and development were in the form of masters or doctoral theses, later followed by formal studies dealing with the strategic managerial considerations of SMEs. However, the initial ideas and thoughts about potential internationalization of SMEs had been discussed extensively among academics, management consultants, bankers, and governmental administrators, among others, for at least sixty years.

The stream of research dealing with the concept of internationalization has progressed from relatively simplistic studies by today's standards, to complex experimental research that examines internationalization from the perspectives of

---

[1] "Internationalization" as a process of managing SMEs operations in several countries at the same time is a relatively new concept that was introduced in academic and managerial research as early as the 1960s. The authors of this chapter find it difficult to clearly establish when and, by whom, the term "internationalization" was first used. Historian Robert L. Heilbroner used it in *The Great Ascent: The Struggle for Economic Development in our Time*, published in 1963. The search for this determination is ongoing (see for example: Czinkota, Michael R. and George Tesar, *Export Management: An International Context*, New York: Praeger Publishers, 1982).

entrepreneurial innovation, technology transfer, resource allocation theories, and theories of organizational behavior to mention just a few. This stream of research has produced a broad assortment of studies and research approaches that focus on export promotion, stimulation, and development as part of the internationalization of SMEs. However, the environmental conditions in which SMEs function today are significantly different from those that existed, in one form or another, over the past sixty years or so. The external business environment in which SMEs function constantly changes and, over the past sixty years, SMEs have evolved into much more complex organizations than ever before. Organizations today are managed by better educated and more experienced managers; these managers are much more aware of environmental dynamics than were their predecessors. Consequently, SMEs today view their internationalization efforts as a totally different process than their predecessors did. Many SMEs' managers today tend to view internationalization as a question of intense competition and survival.

Because of the dynamics of the external business environment in which SMEs attempt to internationalize their activities, it is important to evaluate some of the antecedents that have been found relevant to internationalizations of SMEs, to examine some of the dominant environmental forces that helped to shape such internationalization, and to examine corporate frameworks suitable for internationalization. The research in this chapter is based on an extensive literature survey and social science case research approaches to attempt to understand internationalization as a concept among SMEs. This research has been combined with research cases that serve as examples of contemporary internationalization challenges found today among SMEs. A descriptive conceptual model outlining some essential elements of internationalization is delineated at the end of the chapter.

Historical Dimensions of Internationalization

Although this chapter focuses on internationalization research among SMEs, the concept of internationalization, among a variety of enterprises, has been studied from many different perspectives since the notion of international trade was introduced. As pointed out by Meier and Baldwin (1957) the classical and neo-classical economists emphasized the mutually beneficial nature of trade very early in the history of economics. The majority of the literature (Kindleberger, 1968; Snider, 1967) concerned with internationalization (more specifically at this point with countries' exports and imports) is found in trade theory and deals with theoretical concepts of internationalization in general (export promotion, stimulation, and development) and does not include day-to-day operations of individual enterprises. On a macro-economic level, the important developments in the theory of the product life cycle (Vernon, 1966) in international trade are useful for developing a fundamental understanding of the general working concepts regarding contemporary exports.

Some of the internationalization studies, especially those focusing on export performance, have been generally descriptive and only marginally representative of the important underlying issues of internationalization as a valid research topic in economics or in the social sciences and eventually in management studies. Nevertheless, studies concerned with the international operations of SMEs have increased over the past sixty years or so. However, these studies often lack conceptual integration and focus on peripheral issues in the internationalization process. These studies tend to ignore the impact of the external business environment on the decision of SMEs to internationalize. Even in the absence of conceptual integration, there appears to be a continuation and succession of theoretical and conceptual underpinnings of international trade theory, economic development, industrial stimulation, and internationalization of industrial and manufacturing enterprises.

It is important to note that international trade theory provides a sound foundation for the theory of economic development with a strong focus on regional and country development. Economic development in turn provides a theoretical foundation for industrial stimulation with a strong emphasis on country and regional development (within each country region). Industrial stimulation focuses primarily on development of industries and industry clusters. Industrial stimulation provides a platform for internationalization of industrial and manufacturing enterprises. Since the mid-nineteen sixties the integration between economic development, industrial stimulation, and internationalization (with emphasis on export promotion, stimulation, and development) has been significant (Bilkey, 1970) and research in these areas is increasing.

Approaches to export performance

During the integration process between economic development and industrial stimulation, internationalization, export promotion, stimulation, and development became the focal points. Researchers focused on several issues concerning integration and export promotion, stimulation and development. For example, Mintz (1967) conducted an empirical investigation of the fluctuations in U.S. exports and their relation to American business cycles over the period 1879 to 1961. Mainzels (1965) analyzed the long-term relationship between industrial growth and international trade in manufactured goods. Cooper and others (1970) were concerned with identifying the factors that affected export performance of a number of industries between 1958 and 1966. Other economists and social scientists (Maddison, 1964) compared the economic growth of the advanced industrial countries of Western Europe and North America over the past century. The results of these studies provided a fundamentally sound platform for additional research. Most of the studies, however, were based in economic theory or had a comparative economics perspective to them.

Less comprehensive studies concerning international trade, economic development, industrial stimulation, and internationalization outside the so-called "Western World" were also completed during this period. For example, Blumenthal (1972) examined the relationship between exports and economic growth in post Second World War Japan. The importance of internationalization in developing countries also became an issue early on and was examined by Maddison (1970) and Heilbroner (1963) among others. At about the same time Stabler (1968) studied the impact of internationalization (exports) on regional evolution and change. None of these studies, however, were concerned with individual enterprises and their internationalization in development of their export opportunities.

During this period, the product life cycle model developed by Vernon was perhaps the most important and significant contribution to the theory of internationalization (Wells, 1972a). The model differs from traditional concepts of international trade and internationalization (exports). The product life cycle model suggests that certain kinds of products go through a cycle that has four fundamental stages: (1) the United States is initially an exporter with a monopoly position, (2) foreign production begins to displace American exports in some markets, (3) foreign goods become competitive in third markets and further reduce American exports, and (4) foreign goods become competitive in the United States (Wells, 1972b). The product life cycle model was a major contribution to internationalization research because it provided a conceptual and theoretical foundation for such research. The product life cycle model spread rapidly.

Antecedents to internationalization

The studies listed above produced insufficient understanding of how individual enterprises, especially SMEs, internalized and managed their own internationalization processes. In order to answer such questions, researchers generated studies that attempted to describe the internationalization process from the standpoint of individual enterprises. For example, Yoshino (1965) studied marketing orientation in international business operations and concluded that the strategies of foreign market penetration were often poorly conceived and executed. Poor initial exposure of export performance could totally discourage any further exploration of foreign marketing opportunities. McMahon and others (1968) evaluated the actual experiences of individual enterprises in foreign markets and their conclusions were that manufacturing and agricultural enterprises were more dependent on foreign markets than any other enterprises.

Subsequently, Zenoff (1971) was the first to point out that internationalization of an enterprise (exporting to a foreign country) normally represents a means of entry into "new" markets in a manner that normally minimizes the assets risked and personnel committed by the enterprise. However, even earlier, Robinson (1967) had attempted to contrast a decision to market a product domestically to a decision to market a product in a foreign market. He observed that (1) there are more variables involved in the foreign decision, (2) the external pressures on the enterprise to enter into a foreign market are greater than the internal pressures, (3) the decision is more likely to be the result of a superficial analysis of a limited number of perceived factors than a systematic market study, and (4) the decision to enter a foreign market (internationalize) is less quantitative than a domestic decision.

Export studies among SMEs

In the mid-1960s researchers started to focus their research on individual enterprises and their involvement in foreign markets—most of them were SMEs. The studies dealing with export operations among these enterprises were generally concerned with only those enterprises that exported their products. Analysis was attempted of those factors that were somewhat characteristic of export operations. The studies did not attempt to compare exporting and non-exporting enterprises on some common basis. Most of these studies lacked fundamental statistical sophistication and they were typically completed outside of any framework that might exist or be characteristic of the enterprise being examined.

One of the first studies focusing on export policy within an enterprise was formulated by Kaye (1961). It focused on fifty-one enterprises in four industries: industrial machinery, construction machinery, chemicals, and metals. The objective of that study was to learn how these export policies contribute to more competitive U.S. exports. He concluded that export management and the related policies did not constitute a realistic answer to expansion of U.S. exports. This was perhaps the first study that addressed the issue of internationalization from the perspective of the strategic importance of exports.

The seminal research that focused on small exporters was undertaken by Neidell (1965) in his master's thesis. He attempted to identify the strategies utilized by successful small exporters and assumed that, by examining several countries and industries, he would be able to define successful and unsuccessful common export practices. The study examined American and Scandinavian enterprises. At the time, the intuitively obvious conclusion was that American exporters were significantly inferior to Scandinavian exporters.

Two additional pieces of research influenced the beginning of international research in the mid-1970s. Simpson (1973) attempted to construct a model of export decision-making of small and medium-sized manufacturing enterprises. He focused on fifty exporting and seventy non-exporting enterprises and his objective was to examine both internal and external stimuli and their impact on both types of enterprises. A number of environmental variables were identified, mostly related to the personalities of the managers interviewed. Weinrauch and Rao

(1975) presented a paper concerning obstacles to and the challenges of internationalization, as managers of small enterprises perceived them. They concluded that many small enterprises in their study wanted to export but did not have adequate background information to make any serious attempt. Both conclusions were consistent with the results of previous studies.

Internationalization research and business history

Regardless of what the stream of internationalization research concerning individual enterprises has produced, the historical and more recent observed performance of enterprises tends to be much more complex and is embedded in an individualistic decision-making process among the top managers of individual enterprises. Historians such as Boorstin (1965) and Durant, W. and Durant, A. (1968) suggest that environmental circumstances force entrepreneurs and their enterprises into foreign markets. Internationalization is not a new socio-economic phenomenon to the historians. In his writing Boorstin describes how the New Englanders successfully exported ice to India in exchange for spices and textiles in colonial times. The Durants (1968) discuss the importance of trade and trade routes throughout the centuries. In his writings, Braudel (1979) examined the history of internationalization (exports) from a world perspective with an emphasis on economics, trade, and consumption. Historians tend to view internationalization of enterprises as a necessary socio-economic phenomenon of their times.

Business historians tend to view internationalization of enterprises in a similar fashion. Internationalization is an inevitable venture into foreign markets, partnerships, alliances, cooperative agreements and other types of commercial endeavors. Wilkins (1974, 1970) describes in several of her books how American business expanded abroad by establishing subsidiaries before 1892 (Thomson-Houston Electric Company which later became the General Electric Company); how Aluminum

Company of America, later Alcoa, responded to European business practices in the late 1880s; and Wilkins and Hill (1964), describe how Ford Motor Company, as a small family business in the early stages of its operations, expanded abroad.

Histories of several well-known international companies also illustrate how they established their presence in foreign markets. Companies such as Honda, Sony, Nokia, and Nestlé's are well known in academic research circles. In virtually every industrialized country there are examples of successful small enterprises that grew into major international corporations. They all proceeded through their own unique process of internationalization at an appropriate time, in a changing business environment, and with suitable levels of resources.

One such example is the story of the Bata Shoe Company that has the dubious honor of being labeled as the first "displaced multinational corporation" (Cekota, 1968). The Bata Shoe Company was established in the Austro-Hungarian Empire in 1894; later, when the Empire was disassembled after World War I and Czechoslovakia was established, the Bata Shoe Company became one of the most important enterprises in Czechoslovakia. Again because of changes in the socio-political system (when Czechoslovakia was taken over by communists), the Bata Shoe Company moved its offices to Canada. Throughout its existence it followed a process of ongoing internationalization with operations in over ninety countries.

Similar accounts can be told about Svend Olufsen and Peter Bang, founders of B&O, a well known international enterprise and stereo equipment manufacturer; and Swedish telephone manufacturer Ericsson. Each enterprise proceeded on its own unique path of internationalization early in its commercial life. They all started out as SMEs and they all grew into large international enterprises.

By the early 1990s over two hundred research studies, mostly quantitative, focusing on export promotion, stimulation, and development were completed. The published results focused on managerial issues, some strategic and some operational, concerning internationalization of SMEs through export transactions. The early 1990s became a transitional period for substantial and robust research studies; it was also a period when the next level of internationalization among SMEs began due to the new concepts of outsourcing and value chain management.

A dozen or so books also focused on the internationalization process and related issues. Eight major monographs were published between 1968 and 1988 by various governmental agencies and trade associations. Some of the researchers specializing in export promotion, stimulation, or development studies also generated a number of unpublished papers, reports, and briefings for presentation at government sponsored meetings and conferences such as the United States Department of Commerce or the International Chamber of Commerce in Washington, D.C. Over thirty of these are still considered to have significant research value (Tesar, 1992).

It is interesting to note that a search of publications on Google Scholar reveals that the export development part of internationalization clearly dominates (see Table 1). It would be interesting to closely examine the types of publications that are cited. A cursory examination suggests three sources for these publications—academic, consulting, and governmental.

Table 1
Search of Literature
Export Promotion, Stimulation, and Development

Types of export activities	Approximate number of hits
Export promotion	1,870,000
Export stimulation	2,610,000
Export development	4,870,000

Source:*Google Scholar, January 20, 2014, search criteria: (1) export promotion, (2) export stimulation, and (3) export development.*

From a historical perspective, it is also interesting to examine publications based on the types of international activities—internationalization, multinationalization, transnationalization, and globalization—quoted in academic literature since the late 1970s and early 1980s. A Google Scholar search suggests that internationalization and globalization are the most researched topics by far (see Table 2).

Table 2
Search of Literature
Types of Internationalization

Types of internationalization	Approximate number of hits
Internationalization	312,000
Multinationalization	2,010
Transnationalization	15,400
Globalization	1,320,000

Source: *Google Scholar, January 20, 2014, search criteria: (1) internationalization, (2) multinationalization, (3) transnationalization, and (4) globalization.*

These somewhat unscientific findings are important—over a longer period of time, academic researchers apparently were not very much interested in the concept of 'multinationalization' or 'transnationalization' which were popular academic terms in the period between the late 1970s and the early 1980s and were very much parts of contemporary textbooks on the subject (Robock et al, 1977; Keegan, 1980).

Academic researchers, and their findings, began to take different directions in the late 1980s and in the first half of 1990, both in terms of the breadth and depth of studies. Much of the research took on much more narrow and sometime seemingly unrelated concepts, theories, and generalizations in their explanation of the internationalization of SMEs. Several leading researchers from Europe started moving away from managerial-focused research and started moving into areas of social research and used common qualitative social research tools, primarily case research techniques. In many instances, and in contrast to the North American quantitative research practices, these tools are still being used today.

Present Approach to Internationalization

As suggested above, interest in internationalization, as a stream of academic research, started in the late nineteen sixties and was motivated by several events. Many economically advanced and economically challenged countries realized that they faced growing trade deficit problems and needed policies to stimulate exports of domestically produced goods and commodities. In the U.S., the major motivating factor was a rapidly growing trade deficit. In all cases governmental agencies sought better and more efficient approaches to stimulate exports (internationalization) among their manufacturing enterprises. The above overview of previous research suggests that relatively little empirical research was focused on the role of exports in individual firms (as antecedents to internationalization).

By the late nineteen sixties, the entire academic research community had begun using advanced organizational theories combined with better survey techniques and robust statistical methods which made it possible to conduct large scale surveys designed to study large samples of SMEs in order to generate a better understanding of their strategies and operations. In North America, the use of quantitative research became common in academic research. At the same time, methodologies evolving in qualitative research were also used, mostly to provide theoretical and conceptual foundations for quantitative research.

For example, Johanson and Wiedersheim-Paul (1975) examined internationalization in four Swedish enterprises and developed a platform for additional research by identifying the course of their internationalization. Later, using the same sample, Johanson and Vahlne (1977) presented another model concerning the internationalization process. Another excellent qualitative study was completed by Wiedersheim-Paul, Olson, and Welch (1978) that examined pre-export activity as the first step in internationalization. These and additional studies are part of the so called Uppsala School of research in the internationalization literature.

Researchers in North America developed the more quantitative approach to the stream of internationalization research. For example, Bilkey and Tesar (1977) introduced the concept of stages of exporting; followed by Cavusgil, Bilkey, and Tesar's (1979) attempts to develop profiles of exporters using the same data set as in the previous study. These are just some of the studies that were done at the University of Wisconsin. Other quantitative studies (Czinkota and Tesar, 1982) also contributed to the advancement of internationalization research.

Although the quantitative research concerning internationalization of SMEs has produced a large number of studies in today's rapidly changing international business environment, none of these studies sufficiently answers all the questions regarding why SMEs are still reluctant to internationalize their operations. Many recent studies using various research approaches, including internationalization from perspectives of entrepreneurial innovation, technology transfer, resource allocation and organizational behavior theories, to mention a few, do not take into consideration the necessary variables that potentially could explain the entire internationalization process among SMEs.

Potential Factors Leading to SMEs Internationalization

The following is an attempt to present a list of relevant factors that have been found in the literature as factors contributing to internationalization of SMEs. The factors are divided into three categories: (1) environmental forces shaping the internationalization process of SMEs, (2) antecedents to approaches to internationalization of SMEs, and (3) a selected approach to internationalization of SMEs based on a corporate model.

Table 3 lists the environmental factors that have shaped the internationalization processes of SMEs over time. These are important factors, especially for SMEs in economically challenged countries. A comprehensive assessment of these environmental factors needs to be made in order to understand the relationship between these factors and the internationalization process. A two-stage research approach should be used. First a qualitative approach should be used to specify the importance of these factors to the internationalization process followed by quantitative research formulated to define their level of importance.

Table 3
Environmental Forces Shaping the Internationalization Process of SMEs

1. **Economic forces:**
   Gross domestic product
   Rate of inflation
   Exchange rates
   Disposable income
   Discretionary income
   Consumer debt

2. **Technological forces:**

Rate of innovation
R&D investments
Diffusion of innovation
Technology growth
Market acceptance

3. Life style forces:
Standard of living
Market trends
Consumerism
Consumption patterns
Social class structure

4. Societal forces:
Ethical issues
Political issues
Legal issues

5. Ecological forces:
Environmental awareness
Renewable resources
Recycling
Energy conservation
Environmental consumption

Owners and managers of SMEs in various national or regional business environments indicate that the business environment has a great deal of influence on their decision to establish and manage their operations. Much internationalization research suggests that the degree to which SMEs will internationalize, and more specifically expand their exports, depends on the openness and changes that the external business environment allows. The external business environments that are closely administered by governmental agencies or even a 'benevolent dictator' find it very difficult to allow their SMEs to internationalize and maintain contacts with customers outside of their external business environment.

Some antecedents to approaches to internationalization among SMEs are presented in Table 4. All of the antecedents relate directly to individual SMEs and have been used in both qualitative and quantitative studies to determine internationalization tendencies among SMEs.

Table 4
Antecedents to Approaches to Internationalization of SMEs

1. **Managerial issues of SMEs concerning the key decision-maker and related decision-making style:**
   Craftsman
   Promoter
   Rational manager

2. **Future orientation and planning activities:**
   New product development
   New market development
   Market share expansion
   Greater national distribution
   Development of foreign markets
   Diversification into other businesses

3. **Perceived competitive advantages by key decision-makers:**
   Adequate assets
   Competitive price
   Dynamic sales force
   Efficient distribution
   Efficient marketing techniques
   Efficient production methods
   Proximity to the market
   Strong management
   Technology
   Unique product

4. **Types of performance goals:**
   High profit rate on investment
   High growth rate
   Security of investment
   Development and security of markets
   Contribution to the development of local, national, or regional economy

5. **Size (last year averages):**

Annual sales volume
Annual average employment
Total capital investment

6. **Internationalization (export operations) decision-making:**
   Exports
   Indirect
   Direct agent/distributor
   Direct branch/subsidiary
   Contractual entry modes
   Licensing
   Franchising
   Technical agreements
   Service contracts
   Management contracts
   Construction/turnkey contracts
   Contract manufacture
   Co-production agreements
   Investment entry modes
    Sole direct investment
   Sole acquisition
   Joint venture
   Cross-activity agreements
   Cross-selling
   Cross-distribution
   Cross-marketing
   Cross-manufacturing

7.**Fixed policy regarding internationalization (export operations):**
   Yes
   No
   Flexible

8. **Formal structure for evaluating internationalization options (export operations):**
   Yes
   No
   Flexible

9. **Perceived obstacles to internationalization (export operations):**
   Determination of foreign opportunities
   High cost of doing business
   Product standards

Service is difficult
Adequate representation
Foreign business practices are difficult
Shipping documentation

A sample of how some individual SMEs approach the internationalization process is presented in Table 5. This approach has been adapted from a combination of the experience of a large international enterprise and by observation research (Owens, 2006; Tesar and Moini, 1998). This is a stage approach to internationalization that considers a broad number of factors and combinations of theories. Both the approach itself and the number of factors involved need to be included in a large quantitatively based study in order to closely examine the relevance of this approach among a large sample of SMEs

Table 5
Selected Approach to Internationalization of SMEs Based on A Corporate Model and Observation Research

Approach I:
Up to date product design
Latest technology
Up to date product production

Approach II:
Lower costs
High productivity
Lean manufacturing principles
Increase use of robotics
Increase the level of automation
Focus on just in time delivery

Approach III:
Focus on people
Workforce training
Education
Nurture competitive spirit

Approach IV:

Turn outward
Compete on world market
Focus on international competition
Focus on globalization
Increase operational and strategic efficiency

The implicit idea in an examination of research findings that concern internationalization of SMEs centers on the notion of perpetual changes in the external business environment and the ongoing re-examination of socio-economic values internationally, including some international trade theories. The fundamental argument may be that SMEs do not and cannot internationalize their operations in non-stable conditions. That is why internationalization research must keep up with current developments. However, it is also important to understand the basic foundation of this research and its history.

The following are three cases representing real SMEs that were recently faced with internationalization as integral steps of survival, integration in a supply network, or a decision concerning potential growth issues. They are only a sample of representative problems encountered almost daily by SMEs. These are real cases. Comprehensive research designed to assist these small enterprises is needed to assure their survival in an internationally dynamic and highly competitive marketplace.

Alpha: **European Distribution A.B.**

The Marketing Research and Information Processing department of European Distribution, A.B. (ED), located in a small rural part of German- speaking Switzerland, is faced with a serious problem. Several months ago Hans Zimmer, the Chief of the department, convinced the General Director of ED to develop an Internet website and list all of its products that ED distributes in Europe for its clients from the United States, Canada, Japan, and Australia along with all product specifications and wholesale prices. At that time that was a great idea, Hans reminisces, as he thinks back about the decision.

A few days ago, the General Director called a staff meeting to discuss the results and consequences of this decision and, in a way, confront Hans. The General Director complained about the number of inquiries ED received over the Internet, the quality of these inquiries, and the unreasonable demands that some potential customers were placing on ED, not to mention the fact that some of them are not even located in Europe. Even more aggravating to the General Director was the fact that some of their clients in the United States and Canada had reviewed ED's web page and were complaining that ED is attempting to "sell outside of their original agreement."

ED's Director for Sales and Marketing took the position that since Hans created the problem, Hans should also be able to solve the problem. Johan Diemal, who is the Senior Applications Engineer for ED, argued that this was not Hans' fault, but the fault of the Internet; anybody anywhere can access it. If the North American clients do not understand that, perhaps ED should renegotiate its sales and distribution agreements.

Beta: **DataTest Advantage e-Com**

DataTestAdvantage e-Com is an Internet-based high technology company that wants to specialize in providing competitive and marketing data and information to larger, globally focused, industrial manufacturers such as United Technologies, Siemens, Sharp Electronics, or General Electric among others. Its Internet web page is impressive. The web page lists all kinds of useful information about potential services to be offered along with impressive resumes of its research specialists. Over the period of the last three months or so, DataTestAdvantage e-Com sent out hundreds of messages to potential customers, but did not receive any significant responses.

In response to one of the messages, a potential customer from the United Kingdom sent the following message: "...we are interested in your services, we have looked up your web page and reviewed some of the resumes of your specialists ... but, we cannot determine where you are located or what it is that you actually do ...?"

The Founder and President of DataTestAdvantage e-Com, John Jones, was shocked! How could this be? In the age of the Internet, why would anyone need to know the street address? After Mr. Jones reread the message and regained his composure, he called a staff meeting to review the entire situation. You are the marketing person who designed the web site. What should you say in the meeting if Mr. Jones should happen to ask you about the web site?

Gamma: **Alfa Packaging a.s.**

Alfa Packaging a.s. has been operating as an independent subsidiary of a large paper manufacturer in the Czech Republic for over eight years and specializes in fabrication of mechanical packaging machinery to clients' specifications. Recently, a large Western manufacturer of industrial products (mass produced electrical components for the automobile industry) entered the Central European market. The products are low volume high-density products that require a great deal of care in transportation and handling. The Western firm has approached Alfa Packaging a.s. to design a package for these components, and engineer and fabricate the necessary packaging machinery needed for automated packaging of these components.

The management of Alfa Packaging a.s. has never had a request such as this before. In fact, Alfa Packaging a.s. has never designed a package for any product, nor has it ever designed a packaging machine. It has only somewhat limited experience in fabricating packaging machines from clients' blue prints (outputs from CAD systems). Karel Nový, the Chief engineer at Alfa

Packaging a.s., insists that "there is nothing to it." The Operating Director, Aleš Kopecký, pointed out that the income from this proposition is badly needed, but insisted that Alfa Packaging a.s. should not take on this job because it does not have the necessary experience in this field. You are a Swedish consultant that has been hired by Alfa Packaging a.s. for another assignment. Mr. Kopecký called you to his office because he wants your opinion on (1) the "Western" ethics of taking the job and (2) prospects for the future reputation of Alfa Packaging a.s. if the job does not work out.

Conclusion

Examining the historical evolution of research on internationalization of SMEs from a socio-economic perspective using a social science research approach and an assessment of some present developments, plus a tentative look to the future suggests that this stream of research has produced inconclusive results. Results of much of the research concerning internationalization of SMEs cannot be logically integrated into a consistent, meaningful, and comprehensive domain. Researchers responsible for most of the studies have examined parts and components of the internationalization process among SMEs, but not the entire process.

Since the circumstances in which SMEs attempt to internationalize their operations change rapidly, it might be necessary to start thinking about developing dynamic models, which describe the entire internationalization processes. Information technology today is able to provide continuous quantities of data from a variety of sources for researchers to design such dynamic models. Experiences provided by the data mining industry suggest that it might be possible to design dynamic models of internationalization processes among SMEs.

In the future SMEs' decisions to internationalize might be made routinely on the basis of the outcomes of a series of calculations made using a stream of data sent to an individual SME over its information generating channels. This might be particularly the case for those SMEs, which are members of supply chains, industrial networks, or other collective arrangements. A great deal of quantitative research focusing on the information necessary to design and build these models will be needed along with a sound understanding of the theoretical and conceptual constructs of the entire internationalization process among SMEs.

References

Bilkey, W.J. and Tesar, G. (1977) 'The Export Behavior of Smaller Sized Wisconsin Manufacturing Firms,' *Journal of International Business Research,* 8 (Spring/Summer), 93-8.

Bilkey, W.J. (1970) *Industrial Stimulation* (Lexington, Massachusetts: D.C. Heath and Company).

Blumenthal, T. (1972) 'Exports and Economic Growth: The Case of Postwar Japan,' *Quarterly Journal of Economics,* LXXXVI (November), 617-31.

Boorstin, D.J. (1965) *The Americans, The National Experience* (New York: Random House).

Braudel, F. (1979) *The Wheels of Commerce: Civilization & Capitalism 15th-18th Century,* Volume 2 (New York: Harper & Row Publishers).

Cavusgil, T.S., Bilkey, W.J. and Tesar, G. (1979) 'A Note on the Export Behavior of Firms: Export Profiles,' *Journal of International Business Studies,* 10 (Spring/Summer), 91-7.

Cekota, A. (1968) *Entrepreneur Extraordinary: The Biography of Tomas Bata* (Rome: University Press of the International University of Social Science).

Cooper, R.A., et al. (1970) *Export Performance and the Pressure of Demand* (New York: Humanities Press).

Czinkota, M.R. and Tesar, G. (1982) *Export Management: An International Context,* edited by Michael R. Czinkota and George Tesar (New York: Praeger Publishers).

Durant, W. and Durant, A. (1968) *The Lessons of History* (New York: Simon and Schuster).

Heilbroner, R.L. (1963) *The great Ascent: The Struggle for Economic Development in our Time* (New York: Harper Torchbooks, Harper & Row, Publishers).

Johanson, J. and Wiedersheim-Paul, F. (1975) 'The Internationalization of the Firm—Four Swedish Cases,' *Journal of Management Studies* (October), 305-22.

Johanson, J. and Vahlne J.E. (1977) 'The Internationalization Process of the Firm—A Model of Knowledge Development and Increasing Foreign Market Commitment,' *Journal of International Business Studies,* 8 (Spring/Summer), 23-32.

Kaye, R.A. (1961) 'Study of Export Traffic Management Policy of Selected Manufacturing Firms,' (unpublished Ph.D. dissertation, The George Washington University).

Keegan, W.J. (1980) *Multinational Marketing Management* (Englewood Cliffs, New Jersey: Prentice-Hall, Inc.).

Kindleberger, C.P. (1968) *International Economics,* 4th edition (Homewood, Illinois: Richard D, Irwin, Inc.)

Maddison, A. (1970) *Economic Progress and Policy in Developing Countries* (New York: W.W. Norton and Company, Inc.)

Maddison, A. (1964) *Economic Growth in the West* (New York: W.W. Norton and Company, Inc.).

Mainzels, A. (1965) *Industrial Growth and World Trade* (Cambridge, United Kingdom: University Press).

McMahon, R.O., et al. (1968) 'Organizing for International Marketing,' *Northwest Business Management* (Winter), 20-33.

Meier, G.M., Baldwin, R.E. (1957) *Economic Development: Theory, History, Policy* (New York: John Wiley & Sons, Inc.), 136.

Mintz, I. (1967) *Cyclical Fluctuations in the United States since 1879* (New York: Columbia University Press).

Neidell, L.A. (1965) 'Comparative Export Practices of Small Firms in the United States and Scandinavian' (unpublished M.S. thesis, Massachusetts Institute of Technology).

Owens, J. (2006) 'Embrace Globalism,' *The Wall Street Journal*, April 17, A17.

Robock, S.H., Simmonds, K. and Zwick, J. (1977) *International Business and Multinational Enterprise* (Homewood, Illinois: Richard D. Irwin, Inc.).

Simpson, C.L. Jr. (1973) 'The Export Decision: An Interview Study of the Decision Process in Tennessee Manufacturing Firms (unpublished Ph.D. dissertation, Georgia State University).

Snider, D.A. (1967) *Introduction to International Economics*, 4th edition (Homewood, Illinois: Richard D. Irwin, Inc.).

Stabler, J.C. (1968) 'Exports and Evolution: The Process of Regional Change,' *Land Economics*, XLIV (February), 11-23.

Tesar, G. and Moini, H. (1998) 'Longitudinal Study of Exporters and Nonexporters: A Focus on Smaller Manufacturing Enterprises,' *International Business Review*, 7, 291-313.

Tesar, G. (1992) 'Export Promotion, Stimulation, and Development: Studies and Writings,' dated March 16, 1992, revised April 10, 1992 is available on request from George Tesar, gtesar@chorus.net.

Vernon, R. (1966) 'International Investment and International Trade in the Product Cycle,' *Quarterly Journal of Economics*, LXXX (May), 190-207.

Weinrauch, J.D. and Rao, C.P. (1975) 'small Business Marketing: Obstacles and Challenges in Developing Foreign Export Businesses,' paper read at Southwestern Marketing Association, Houston, March 6 to 8.

Wells, L.T. Jr., editor (1972a) *The Product Life Cycle and International Trade* (Boston: Harvard University, Division of Research, Graduate School of Business Administration), 5-6.

Wells, L.T. Jr. (1972b) 'Test of a Product Cycle Model of International Trade: U.S. Exports of Consumer Durables,' in

The Product Life Cycle and International Trade, edited by L.T. Wells, Jr. (Boston: Harvard University, Division of Research, Graduate School of Business Administration), 55-6.

Wiedersheim-Paul, F.; Olson, H.C. and Welch, L.S. (1978) 'Pre-Export Activity: The First Step in Internationalization,' *Journal of International Business Studies* (Spring/Summer), 47-58.

Wilkins, M. (1974) *The Maturing of Multinational Enterprise: American Business Abroad from 1914 to 1970* (Cambridge, Massachusetts: Harvard University Press), 146-7.

Wilkins, M. (1970) *The Emergence of Multinational Enterprise: American Business Abroad from Colonial Era to 1914* (Cambridge, Massachusetts: Harvard University Press), 86-7.

Wilkins, M. and Hill, F.E. (1964) *American Business Abroad: Ford on Six Continents* (Detroit, Michigan: Wayne State University Press), 4-6.

Yoshino, M.Y. (1965) 'Marketing Orientation for International Marketing,' *MSU Business Topics* (Summer), 58-64.

CHAPTER THREE

Levels of Social Capital in Internationalization: A View on Smaller Firms and Entrepreneurs

Arnim Decker

Abstract

This contribution introduces the notion of social capital and discusses integration into the studies on internationalization of smaller firms and entrepreneurs. Integrating social capital into the resource based perspective we categorize social capital at three levels: first, social capital can be attributed to individuals, affecting their relationship with the external environment. Second, social capital is an inherent property of networks, into which smaller firms and entrepreneurs are embedded. Third, social capital exists at the macro level, where its characteristics and availability varies between environments and nations. This contribution attempts to fascilitate the operationalization of social capital in order to improve our understanding of processes of internationalization of smaller firms and entrepreneurs.

Notion of social capital

Social capital is a complex and now widely applied concept that is broadly used for example in organizational studies (Yli-Renko et al., 2001, Nahapiet and Ghoshal, 1998, Tsai and Ghoshal, 1998). The OECD defines social capital as "networks together with shared norms, values and understandings that facilitate co-operation within or among groups" (Cote and Healy, 2001). As a relatively new term, social capital has only started to be employed within the last thirty years. During this period, however, it has experienced dramatic success and rapid ongoing development. It is gaining a more solid foothold within the area of firm studies, from here on influencing the further development of other already established concepts. It is mainly scholars like Coleman (1994), Putnam (1993), Bourdieu (1986), Portes (2000) who are credited with the establishment of social capital as a concept to analyze social network structures. Having started out from sociological studies, they take the view of seeing social capital mostly as as a key element of communities, supporting family relations and providing individuals with resources. In studies conducted by these scholars, social capital has been found to be a useful concept to study social mobility, psychology, political participation or competitive advantages of organizations (Lin and Erickson, 2008). For Bourdieu and Wacquant (1992) social capital is a resource that can be drawn upon by individuals, communities or specific entities like firms through the existence of networks. Social capital is connected to networks and varieties of social relations. Bourdieu (1986) and Coleman (1994) see social capital as rooted in individuals as well as in relationships which can occur in various forms. For them, the network is the primary unit of analysis. Individuals and groups move within these networks, at the same time as they benefit from being part of them. Putnam (1995), in turn, takes a different view by concentrating on social activities and association as a generator of social capital. However, between these there is a general agreement that social capital derives from and is created as a result of human interaction and connections between individuals.

Social capital as a term resembles similar notions like financial capital, human capital or cultural capital. What distinguishes social capital from other forms of capital is the fact that it does not decrease with use, instead, the more it is used the stronger it becomes. A second important difference, in particular in comparison to financial capital, resides in its near non- fungibility. In other words, social capital may be difficult to trade and can only partly be transferred.

The glue and the oil

Social capital has two faces: on the one hand it acts as a bonding mechanism (Woolcock and Narayan, 2000), allowing for a shared understanding between actors in a networks where it feels comfortable to share ideas and understanding of the world

(De Carolis and Saparito, 2006). As a bonding mechanism, social capital can lead to *closure*, meaning that social groups have strong interior cohesion that could in the worst case lead to isolation and rejection of outside information and knowledge. The second aspect of social capital is the function of *bridging*, which, contrasting to closure mechanisms, allows wider spanning connections between more dispersed groups. Actors, for example individuals or smaller firms, can utilize bridging social capital to reach farther out to access more diverse information including more varied and promising arbitrating opportunities. Bridging activities that create new relationships between groups open new opportunities to innovate (Oh et al., 2006). Anderson and Jack (2002) note that social capital resembles a paradox in that it can act as a lubricant and can also take on the properties of glue. Social capital has two contradictory roles: as a lubricant, social capital helps to get things done, as a glue it provides social stability and coherence (Anderson and Jack, 2002, Powell and Smith-Doerr, 1994). Just as social capital is important for the success of individuals, it is also of important significance in facilitating economic exchanges (Anderson and Jack, 2002, Nahapiet and Ghoshal, 1998, Adler and Kwon, 2002, Yli-Renko et al., 2001, Zhou et al., 2007). Social capital generates returns both for individuals and collectives and provides them with the ability to access resources that are embedded in complex network relationships.

Social capital as a resource base

The resource based view forms the basis for an understanding of competitive advantages of firms. The resource base view sees firms as a bundle of heterogeneous resources that are mostly immobile in their nature. Combined in the right way, these resources can be a valuable base that forms the competitive advantage of firms. Small firms frequently suffer from the disadvantage that comes as a result of scarcity of resources, forcing them to find ways to compensate for these deficiencies. Through utilizing social capital, SMEs can attract resources they need to maintain themselves within their environments. According to Barney (1986), superior performance of firms rests on resources that are valuable, rare, inimitable and sufficiently organized. A firm is a bundle of valuable resources that are tangible or intangible. They form a pool of heterogeneous and not perfectly mobile resources that enable a firm to gain competitive advantage and generate superior profits. Resources are considered as residing mainly within the firm. Although internal resources are significant for building up competitive advantage, a singular focus on the internal side does not always offer a complete picture of a firm's resource base. Depending on the nature of the venture, firms show varying capabilities with regards to finding sources of competitive advantage outside their internal environment. The effective governance of inter- organizational relationships through social capital strengthens exchange mechanisms (Dyer and Singh, 1998), and increases firm performance in a variety of ways through for example increased effectiveness (Yli-Renko et al., 2001, Zahra et al., 2000).

In a knowledge-based society, intangible resources like knowledge, reputation and social relationships are an increasingly more important part of a firm's resource base. Intangible resources need to be drawn from the external environment, in particular when firms are not large in size (Kristandl and Bontis, 2007). Competition between firms matters, but equally important are outside relationships of cooperative nature which firms maintain through trading practices, strategic alliances or other kinds of cooperations. While the resource based view (Barney, 1991) predominantly considers the internal circumstances of firms, they can also utilize external connections as part of their resource base (Lavie, 2006). Dyer and Singh (1998) argue that firms can achieve rents through access to relation-specific assets, sharing of information and knowledge, complementary resources and what they call *effective governance* of outside relationships. In his analysis Lavie (2006) argued for conceptually including the resources that firms tap on by utilizing their external firm networks. He showed that the nature of relationships matters more than the nature of resources, which underline the significance of social capital for network formation and the resources that a firm can dispose of.

It is thus generally accepted that physical and financial assets are important constituents of the resource base of a firm. As we see, some scholars have extended this perspective to include the notion of social capital as a resource that can be the basis for the competitive advantage of firms. Social capital can be integrated as an essential component of the resource base view and is helpful to strengthen the analytical power of the resource based view. Including social capital into the resource based view helps to gain an understanding of the nature of inherent resources of firms. Likewise, Chisholm and Nielsen (2009) argue that social capital can form an essential part of the intangible side of firms' resources. With sufficient presence of social capital as an important and in some cases even most prominent part of the intangible resource base, firms can obtain competitive advantage for increased profits. Through the existence of external networks, smaller firms can compensate for the lack of internal resources. Utilizing the analytical lenses of the social capital concept with respect to the internal perspective of firms, firstly it helps to understand the nature of the firm's organization. Secondly, the concept is useful to understand the position of firms vis-à-vis their external environment. Smaller firms can compensate for the lack of internal resources by relying on inter-firm networks, which serve as an alternative to transactions conducted within spot markets or with hierarchies coordinated by a single centralized authority. The existence of external social capital can be essential for the survival and growth of firms. Small and newcoming firms have to overcome the obstacles that are in the way to accessing external resources which they need to assure their survival and growth.

These arguments have found widespread acceptance. For example, Stieglitz (2000) points to the importance of social capital for structures and functions of organizations. He argues that the market value of firms typically considerably exceeds the value physical assets and human capital accumulated in a firm. It is the excess value of firms - also called *good will* by accountants- that explains the existence of social capital as a sort of tacit knowledge. Thus at can be argued that social capital is an important part of the resource base of a firm.

Networks and social capital in small firms internationalization

The ongoing dramatic changes within the global business environment are opening new opportunities for smaller firms including for international and international/ transnational entrepreneurs. While in earlier days trade at the international level was mainly an activity of larger firms, the picture has in the last couple of decades changed considerably. Due to technological developments, deregulation and reduction of trade barriers transaction cost of conducting cross border activities have significantly decreased. The emergence of transnational structures such as the European Union and different other trade blocs reduced the role of economic politics at the national level. The role of the nation-state around which all macro-economic activity is centered, organised and conducted has partly decreased in importance. Likewise, the stand- alone firm is no longer the principal unit of production; instead it is increasingly replaced by networks and similar structures into which individual firms are connected (Dana and Wright, 2004). As a result the opportunities connected with eased access to international markets become more accessible for smaller businesses and entrepreneurs. Through identifying and exploiting market and technology niches, smaller firms and entrepreneurs now find it more feasible to make use of opportunities that international markets can offer. It seems that smaller firms including entrepreneurs are profiting disproportionally from the new circumstances: Reynolds (1997) noted that larger firms do not correspondingly expand their business in the process of globabisation, instead, the new spaces were rather taken by smaller companies. However, despite the increased accessibility of global markets, smaller firms still face considerable hurdles that need to be overcome.

Small firms (SMEs) often suffer from the disadvantage that comes as a result of scarcity of resources. New firms have to overcome the obstacles that are in the way to accessing external resources which they need to assure their survival and growth. This often means that firms have to deal with a set of significant disadvantages, which do not affect larger firms in the same way. Firstly they need to overcome the *liability of smallness*, the fact that they are small, and frequently constrained by resource limitations. When small firms initialize their internationalization process (Johanson and Vahlne, 1977, 1990, 2009, Knight, 1996, Chetty and Campbell-Hunt, 2004), they are confronted with liability of newness and foreignness (Stinchcombe, 1965, Dunning, 1988, Zaheer, 1995). Just as the ability to access and built up new social capital is important for an individual, smaller companies can rely on social capital to overcome resource constraints.

Smaller firms are frequently constrained by reduced economies of scale, scope, experience and learning, which limit their ability to internationalize (Nooteboom, 1993). *Liability of smallness* amplifies *liabilities of foreignness* in foreign environments. However, small firms can compensate resource constraints through building social network structures. The possession of relevant social capital to support bridging processes is significant for success. The ability to develop social capital in useful way helps to enable them to gain information about foreign markets (Senik and Sham, 2011). When small firms initialize their internationalizing process, they are confronted with a number of difficulties that larger companies do not have to cope with. Firstly, as they are usually young their resource base is fragile anyway; they need to find the resources which are necessary to be successful in international markets. This adds an additional dimension to the problem that smaller firms already have to overcome in the first place. They need to learn how to do things in a different environment, but at the same time have to deal with the complexity and uncertainty because the foreign environment is unknown to them (Johanson and Vahlne, 1990). Learning about how to do business and act in the foreign environment will mostly take place through connecting to sources of knowledge which firms find in external networks. Successful acquisition of external knowledge should then have a positive advantage on the success of a firm. While it has been largely acknowledged that knowledge and learning play are important for the success of smaller firms, there is less knowledge about *how* knowledge inputs are achieved (Autio et al., 2005). These may be done through building up and utilizing social capital in existing networks. This is a difficult task, in particular for smaller companies with limit knowledge and experience. A foreigner coming to a new country needs to be able to adapt to new sets of circumstances: culture and language, rules and norms are also different. Additionally, foreigners do not enjoy the same degree of networks embeddedness compared to indigenous firms (Freeman, 1979). However, in terms of knowledge, network connections or reputation, they can bring resources with provides them with legitimacy. What may not be available in the host country can be bought from the home country, thereby creating in one way or the other certain competitive advantages. These could come from special knowledge, country image or other legitimizing factors that may in this form not be available to indigenous firms in the host country.

To summarize, there is an increasing awareness that usage of social capital can be a vehicle to overcome these constraints that small firms typically face. This point is underlined by Tolstoy and Agndal (2010), who demonstrated that SMEs profit from the ability to combine and find arbitration opportunities within their networks connections which helps them to be successful in international markets. They also demonstrate that the nature of these activities impacts the way firms combine their resources. Some firms broadly use their social network connections to find new combinations for redefining markets and products, other firms take a narrower approach and use their network resources to expand gradually and in less radical ways. In this sense, entrepreneurs and managers of SMEs use networks and embedded social capital that are critical for international growth. Social capital that spans accross international boundaries give international- oriented founders of SME an advantage over those that not previously developed such types of links. SMEs use a combination of large numbers of weak ties and a few strong ties, which serve as information channels to define internationalization strategies. Indirectly, the embeddedness in a structure of weak and strong ties (Han, 2006) impacts the performance on internationalizing SMEs. Also, Zhang et al. (2012) showed that different forms of social capital support the internationalization of Chinese SMEs. Social capital is dynamic in nature- over time, it can grow but it can also deteriorate. Multinational background of owners and key managers is helpful in facilitating the internationalization process. By investigating the dynamics that underly the development of social capital, Prashantham and Dhanaraj (2010) showed that founders with a migration background or experience in MNEs have a higher stock of social capital.

It is both the strong and weak ties that impact the internationalization of SMEs (Ruzzier and Antoncic, 2007). For example, with a focus on born global type companies, Smith et al. (2012) showed that Irish TV entertainment production firms use strong and weak connectors within their international network for their expansion into new markets. Social capital is not static; during the process of internationalization, the nature of entrepreneur's social capital changes as they expand their operations (Kontinen and Ojala, 2012). Social capital is one of the instruments that enable SMEs to find their way into foreign markets, through business associates, personal efforts and institutions. Also pointing to the volatile nature of social capital, Agndal et al. (2008) analyzed the development of SMEs' social capital and found that at the beginning stages SMEs employ direct social capital ties that are useful for achieving their immediate goals. Later however, indirect social capital links and serendipity become more prevalent. Adding the geographic dimension, Agndal et al. (2008) also found that the economic dimension of social capital is not affected by geographical distance. But contrary to this, distance affects the structural dimension of social capital. Stieglitz (2000) sees a similar picture: in the initial phases of a firm's startup, available social capital mainly depends on the founder/ owner, particularly in the form of strong ties. Because of scarcity of resources that lead to inherent uncertainty, security given by strong ties is important. In later stages, when the problem of resources is alleviated as a result of accumulation, firms gain more scope for risk acceptance and experimentation. Then, a firm becomes less reliant on strong ties, it becomes more beneficial to build up and strengthen ties of weaker nature. Agndal et al. (2008), Kontinen and Ojala (2012) show that firms put significant efforts into developing network ties and aim for high quality network closures. According to them, social capital based on weak ties and intermediary relationships leads to serendipity. Bonding capital and associability of entrepreneurs help entrepreneurs to develop new networks ties to drive their internationalization. The existence of a few previous ties abroad serves as a motivating driver to continue the search for international contacts abroad. This is happening for example through visiting trade fairs and international exhibitions (Kontinen and Ojala, 2011).

In general, the above cited scholars build on previous work of colleagues from the field of sociology, who conceptualized and described the nature of direct and indirect links in social networks. For example, with a view on internationalization, (both from an egocentric and socio- centric perspectives), Portes et al. (2002) showed how immigrant entrepreneurs use their individual social capital to gain a foothold in their host country by arbitrating existing links with their home country through economic and social connections to establish new firms (varying from each other both in scale and scope).

Knowledge and learning

The ability to draw on external knowledge through social capital and for learning and identification of opportunities creates benefits for entrepreneurs and SMEs. Smaller firms with constrained resources use social capital to generate profits by exploiting relational capital to gain knowledge about export markets (Roxas and Chadee, 2011), or how to directly act in external markets. As discussed above, possession of internal and in particular external social capital is an integral part of the resource base of firms. For smaller firms that struggle with resource constraints, the availability of external social capital is of even higher importance. There is a broad consensus on the significance of social capital for smaller firms' internationalization. The existence of social capital influences the mode of internationalization of firms (Chetty and Agndal, 2007). While knowledge as a driver for internationalization is embedded in knowledge-based assets (both in the external environment and in the internal firm's structures), processes that enable transfer efficiently need to be put in place. As a resource, small firms rely on knowledge-based assets which they derive from widely scattered international network of relationships and active management (Prashantham, 2006). Management needs to implement the adequate means for enabling knowledge transfer, for example through developing channels for transmission of information, or mechanism for facilitating motivation and socialization (Gooderham, 2007). Knowledge can be transfered as information about for example opportunities or advice by third parties. The ability of firms to develop their networks and the way how they do it have significant impacts on the diffusion of knowledge and in this way also the internationalization patterns of firms. Knowledge which upcoming firms are in need of to overcome their resource limitations can be obtained through managerial practices and collaboration to enhance competitiveness. For owners and other key personal of SMEs the use of national and international social networks can be useful in gathering intelligence. Finding collaborating partners can help them integrate their operations and enhance competitiveness through social settings, for example by jointly innovating their marketing practises (Sepulveda and Gabrielsson, 2013) or technological improvements, and also process innovations. In dynamic international and global environments firms need to be able to cope with radical uncertainty. Saarenketo et al. (2004) point out that many times windows of opportunities are not open for longer than short periods, and there is not enough time for entrepreneurs and SMEs to go through prolonged learning processes. Smaller companies can accelerate their learning process in several ways, each of them requiring to some degree the involvement of social capital: a) learning through imitating what others do, for example from those companies that already enjoy a high degree of legitimacy in a foreign market, b) grafting by acquiring resources for example personal or other types of resources (thereby facilitating new sources of social capital, and c) searching in proactive ways including through utilizing existing social capital. And finally, there is also the possibility to acquire new sources of knowledge through d) usage of networks, an activity that per se involves the employment of social capital. Entrepreneurs need the ability to initiate new *variation generating* activities which open up for new opportunities (Saarenketo et al., 2004). These abilities can be found through social capital sourced from networks at the national and international levels. There is a positive relationship between success in international markets and the degree of availability of social capital a firm can draw upon. Challenged by resource constraints, the ability to explore external knowledge is therefore important for entrepreneurs and SMEs (Desouza and Awazu, 2006).

Levels of social capital

The underlying idea of this contribution is an attempt to operationalize the concept of social capital for research in international entrepreneurship. In this contribution, for an improved understanding of the role of social capital in the internationalization process of smaller firms, we suggest to divide the notion of social capital into three different levels. At the first level, social capital is a construct that is connected to individuals. Through possession of different forms of human capital, an individual gains certain abilities that are helpful in achieving desired outcomes. Secondly, social capital exists at the level of interpersonal connections, networks, and communities an individual can draw upon. Thirdly, social capital existing at the macro level is closely connected to institutional factors that may differ from country to country. From here on we will discuss the proposed differentiation of social capital in relation to internationalization of smaller companies. In this sense, analysis of social capital can be undertaken from two fundamentally different positions. Both, however, assume that persons as social beings are embedded into networks of social relationships. Networks can thus be analyzed both from the egocentric and the socio- centric perspective. The egocentric perspective takes the individual as the unit of analysis. The socio- centric perspectives' point of departure, in turn, is the network of relationships and its structure. From there individuals are seen as a part of the whole structure. Thirdly, within the model which we develop in this contribution, we include the notion of social capital at the macro level. The connection to internationalization comes from circumstances related to institutionally determined condition which influences the state of social capital in different nations. These background conditions on the influence of social capital have an impact at the individual and at the network levels.

The individual embedded in a network- egocentric view

With a view on the individual, social capital is an attribute that can be connected to a single person which however in our view is not completely free of problems (van der Gaag and Snijders, 2005). Firstly, the reason is that social capital can be attributed to an individual, but it will only become useful when the individual is entering into interaction with others. Although conceptualization at the individual level is rather unproblematic, operationalization seems to be more problematic due to the complexity of the concept (van der Gaag and Snijders, 2005). It is difficult to decide on which criteria measurement should take place, and the how to transfer the results into useful data. One way to proceed could be to link individual social capital to human capital as a property of the individual, for example education and formal qualifications. It could also be other personal properties, for example even the possession of humor (Gundelach, 2009), a characteristic that is difficult to measure but may be significant for an individual. Humor can be helpful to overcome cross- cultural differences and support the creation of other forms of social capital. Some scholars (Ostrom and Ahn, 2009) see the element of trust that is attributed to an individual as the central cornerstone of social capital. They offer a different perspective on social capital by differentiating between 1) trustworthiness, 2) networks, and 3) formal and informal rules of institutions. Trust resides with the individual that is seen as trustworthy, through its existence trust facilitates actions between groups and individuals. Trust is seen as the link that connects social capital to collective action. Trust is enhanced by institutions that reward honest behavior and sanction opportunism. When trust exists, it becomes easier to facilitate the problem solving process within social settings. The two scholars see trust that an individual possesses in relation to other actors as a transmitting device for various other forms of social capital. An individual can, however, only possess trust when others regard this individual as trustworthy. In this sense, it is similar to beauty as a desirable but also subjective attribute of persons, because it can only rest in the eyes of the beholder. Ronald (1992) asserts that an individual cannot have individual rights to social capital- it comes as a result of human interaction.

Business researchers have shown ongoing efforts to relate social capital to individuals. For example, Useem and Karabel (1986) write that career prospects of individuals depend on their level of education. An academic degree from a prestigious school increases the chances of climbing higher on the corporate carrier ladders. Furthermore, if an individual has a background in a family with a high social status, his or her career prospects will be likely to increase further. With a similar perspective on large corporations, Belliveau et al. (1996) showed that the social capital available to CEOs had a significant impact on their payment level. Seen from this position, social capital adheres to person at the individual level, and it is an effect of family descent, quality of education etc. Through personal attributes, an individual improves his position within a network, a community or as it is discussed here within the corporate hierarchy. By studying the benefits of social capital - instead of its forms- Sandefur and Laumann (1998) focus on the concept from the individual's perspective- the egocentric view. Other research shows that at their founding stages, successful entrepreneurs had a large number of structural holes in their networks. Then, they expanded their operations instead of consolidating their networks. These successful entrepreneurs create new network links and closures to generate fresh opportunities through continously bringing new structural holes into being (Kontinen and Ojala, 2012). Individuals can enhance their position by arbitrating weak and strong ties, also in internationalized contexts. Individuals who possess relevant social capital are in a better position to navigate in heterogeneous cultural, economic and institutional environments (Hampden-Turner, 2000). These observations are confirmed by a number of scholars, see for example Portes et al. (2002), Zhou (2004), Levitt and Jaworsky (2007) in the field of transnational entrepreneur ship, or Oviatt and McDougall (2005), McDougall and Oviatt (2000), Jones and Dimitratos (2004), Kontinen and Ojala (2011), Jones et al. (2011), Mejri and Umemoto (2010) in the field of international entrepreneurship, or Moen (2002), Smith et al. (2012), Sharma and Blomstermo (2003), Rasmussen and Madsen (2002), Sepulveda and Gabrielsson (2013) on research on born global firms.

Social capital embedded in networks- sociocentric view

Departing from the egocentric network view, Sandefur and Laumann (1998) identify three main benefits that an individual can obtain through individual social capital that is in turn facilitated by a certain position in a network: information, influence and control, and social solidarity. The second view is taken by Burt (1997, 2000 and 2004) who sees the social networks in its entirety, and then positions the individual within these structures. Individuals alone cannot own social capital from this perspective, because social capital is embedded within the links that exist *between* single persons.

This perspective started gaining currency after a seminal article written by Granovetter (1973), who was the first to describe the *strength of weak ties*. Opposed to what he calls strong ties, weak ties are less intensive relationships between individuals, which can for example be of temporary character. It is often out of *weak ties* that new ideas and opportunities emerge. In turn, strong ties are strongly integrated connections between individuals or groups, for example family ties or other close friendships. They provide for solidity, but are less frequently the source of new ideas, inspirations, innovations, and so on.

Burt then contributed by developing this concept further by introducing the the notion of *structural holes* which come into existence because of voids or less populated spaces that often exists within network structures. Burt (1992) himself speaks of *separation of redundant contacts* which he calls *structural holes*. To illustrate the concept, it is useful to imagine individuals who are firmly embedded within the center of their own networks where they maintain intensive contacts but do not reach further out. In contrast, those individuals who are located at the boundary of the network can reach out to establish new contacts with more remote networks, thereby closing the gap over what Burt (1992) calls structural holes. This enables individuals to participate in the diffusion of information, at the same time as they control the process. Social capital which underlies structural holes provides individuals with valuable opportunities for brokerage and gives competitive advantage over other individuals who do not have access to structural holes.

Burt (2000) compares structural holes with insulators that isolate components of a structure from each other. Insulators prevent electrical flow from passing between one component and another, just as structural holes prevent the flow of information between one group and another. The ability to cross the gap between structural holes thus provides an individual with brokerage opportunities. Structural holes give control advantages, because individuals can link otherwise disconnected parts of the overall network with each other. These brokers between groups have access to different sets of information and more timely information, which makes them a valuable source of information and which they can use to their advantage. For example, they can simply transfer information between network segments or transfer best practices, facilitating value creation processes. Being a broker between structural holes allows for increased creativity and innovation and enables the individual to be a catalyst for structural change helping the individual to improve her own situation.

Social capital in institutional settings

Institutional arrangements affect for example consumer behavior, privacy, or structure of distribution channels. Knowledge about different conditions is often tacit in character which can best be acquired through interaction in social networks (Tate, 2001). For societies and communities, social capital is an important resource. This is not only in general recognized in scholarly circles, politicians also actively aim to pursue strategies that foster generation of social capital at the level of larger societies. Citizens profit from the availability of social capital accompanied by norms such as trust and reciprocity. As Putnam (2001) discusses, citizens that generate social interactions through forming associations and networks show more ability to solve problems and conflicts. While individuals profit from social capital, the benefit becomes visible at the macro level resulting in economic stability and growth. However, social capital is also a complex concept which is used for many purposes. Other countries seem to dispose of substantial social capital that is beneficial for societies at large. Some authors connect society level social capital to the availability of trust (Hooghe and Stolle, 2003). With time, the existant level of trust within societies is subject to change. Institutionally determined factors can be beneficial for the creation of trust, but not always: for example the Italian Mafia or Columbian drug cartels are high on internal social capital, providing their members with certain benefits, but have negative implications for the overall society. The level of trust is typically lower in poorer societies, where school education is not widely available and poverty related problems persist. Just like trust and social capital in richer soocienties changes over time, within poorer nations there are changes for the better or the worse. As we pointed out above, trust can be high within families and clan structures, but its may be low outside these groups. Citizens in those environments- as not connected long as there are not socially connected within these structures- mutually regard themselves as to be as untrustworthy. As Rose (2000) notes, in certain societies there is a distinction between what he denominates as *Binnenmoral* "inner morals", and *Aussenmoral* "outer morals". "Inner morals" represents what an actor actually believes, but "outer morals" is what a person would claim about her convictions and beliefs in public. These discrepancies can be a challenge for management of SMEs or entrepreneurs as they increase the costs of conduction transactions in foreign environments (Gupta and Malhotra, 2013). The diversity of institutional arrangements affects consumer behavior, privacy, or structure of distribution channels; just to name a few examples. Knowledge and understanding of environmental conditions is often tacit in character, the best way of immersing is through interaction in social networks (Tate, 2001). What makes the difference are laws, regulations including the ways they are handled, cultural settings, including standards which may vary from country to country. All these aspects matter to support learning processes at individual and collective levels, and serve as devices to facilitate monitoring and benchmarking (Tate, 2001). Standards, if they are applied on a larger scale, serve as a base to achieve economies of scale, and improve efficiency by fascilitating collaboration. Standards are the base of tacit understanding between actors at the individual or group level. We observe, for example, that through establishment of standards for digital cooperation, transactions costs can be substantially reduced, also when cultural settings are diverse. From a general perspective, in liberal market economies, standards may provide opportunities for coordination which helps to gain economies of scale and scope. They can also serve as a means to create transparency. However, achieving economies of scale and scope is often a game that larger companies are good at. If they are not able to keep up, smaller companies and entrepreneurs are then forced in niche markets where standardized transactions are not the rule and larger firms cannot play out their competitive advantages. In these circumstances, there is a need for closer collaboration and the availability of useful social capital becomes important as a means to smoothen transactions.

Conclusion and outlook

This contribution identified three basic dimensions that the concept of social capital can play for an improved understanding of smaller firms and entrepreneurs in the process of internationalization. Firstly, we identified social capital at the level of the individual which is closely related to human capital. While the latter is based on individual characteristics of the individual, for example as forms of professional qualifications and knowledge embedded within the individual, social capital is derived from the social relations that the individual is in possession of. Although the social capital is extracted from existing networks and social relations, it is still a form of capital that is in possession of an individual. The individual can control its usage, at least to a partial degree, as well as making use of it with the aim to increase personal benefits.

Secondly, from the socio- centric view, social capital is attached to the network structure. The socio- centric view moves the center of attention away from the individual towards the network structure as a whole. Social capital is embedded within networks structures, so that there can be networks where the degree of embedded social capital can be different from case to case. Naturally, in the end it is individuals that profit from the existence of social capital. Thirdly, social capital is embedded in national and transnational institutions. As soon as SMEs and entrepreneurs start venturing into globalized markets they are confronted by the need to deal with variations in terms of social capital when institutional settings change (DiMaggio and Powell, 1983, Powell and DiMaggio, 2012). A wide range of literature deals with these topics, ranging from cultural differences at the micro and meso level to questions of institutional analysis. Within these discourses, the notion of social capital clearly has a place and should not be ignored.

To summarize, while there has been substantial research for an improved internationalization processes, the notion of social capital opens up new and interesting perspectives for understanding internationalization from a different angle. In particular, as was pointed out in this contribution, the connection of social capital with social networks helps to understand how smaller firms and entrepreneurs can overcome substantial limitations on several dimensions to make a mark in global business.

References

Adler, P. S. and Kwon, S.-W. (2002). Social capital: Prospects for a new concept. *Academy of management review*, 27(1):17–40.

Agndal, H., Chetty, S., and Wilson, H. (2008). Social capital dynamics and foreign market entry.*International Business Review*, 17(6):663–675.

Anderson, A. R. and Jack, S. L. (2002). The articulation of social capital in entrepreneurial networks: a glue or a lubricant? *Entrepreneurship & Regional Development*, 14(3):193–210.

Autio, E., Sapienza, H., and Arenius, P. (2005).International social capital, technology sharing, and foreign market learning in internationalizing entrepreneurial firms.*Advances in Entrepreneurship, Firm Emergence and Growth*, 8:9–42.

Barney, J. (1991). Firm resources and sustained competitive advantage. *Journal of management*, 17(1):99–120.

Barney, J. B. (1986). Organizational culture: can it be a source of sustained competitive advantage? *Academy of management review*, 11(3):656–665.

Barney, J. B. (2002). Gaining and sustaining competitive advantage.

Belliveau, M. A., O'Reilly, C. A., and Wade, J. B. (1996). Social capital at the top: Effects of social similarity and status on ceo compensation. *Academy of Management Journal*, 39(6):1568–1593.

Bourdieu, P. (1986). The forms of capital.*Handbook of theory and research for the sociology of education*, 241:258.

Bourdieu, P. and Wacquant, L. J. (1992).*An invitation to reflexive sociology.*University of Chicago Press.

Burt, R. S. (1992). The social structure of competition.*Networks and organizations: Structure, form, and action*, 57:91.

Burt, R. S. (1997). The contingent value of social capital.*Administrative science quarterly*, pages 339–365.

Burt, R. S. (2000). The network structure of social capital.*Research in organizational behavior*, 22:345–423.

Burt, R. S. (2004). Structural holes and good ideas.*American journal of sociology*, 110(2):349–399.

Chetty, S. and Agndal, H. (2007).Social capital and its influence on changes in internationalization mode among small and medium-sized enterprises.*Journal of International Marketing*, 15(1):1–29.

Chetty, S. and Campbell-Hunt, C. (2004). A strategic approach to internationalization: a traditional versus a "born-global" approach. *Journal of International Marketing*, 12(1):57–81.

Chisholm, A. M. and Nielsen, K. (2009).Social capital and the resource-based view of the firm.*International Studies of Management and Organization*, 39(2):7–32.

Coleman, J. S. (1994). *Foundations of social theory*.Harvard University Press.

Cote, S. and Healy, T. (2001).The well-being of nations.*The role of human and social capital. Paris: Organisation for Economic Co-operation and Development*.

Dana, L. P. and Wright, R. W. (2004).Emerging paradigms of international entrepreneurship. In Dana, L. P., editor, *Handbook of social capital: The troika of sociology, political science and economics*. Edward Elgar Publishing.

De Carolis, D. M. and Saparito, P. (2006). Social capital, cognition, and entrepreneurial opportunities: A theoretical framework. *Entrepreneurship Theory and Practice*, 30(1):41–56.

Desouza, K. C. and Awazu, Y. (2006). Knowledge management at smes: five peculiarities. *Journal of knowledge management*, 10(1):32–43.

DiMaggio, P. J. and Powell, W. W. (1983). The iron cage revisited: Institutional isomorphism and collective rationality in organizational fields. *American sociological review*, pages 147–160.

Dunning, J. (1988). The eclectic paradigm of international production: a restatement and some possible extensions. *Journal of international business studies*, 19(1):1–31.

Dyer, J. H. and Singh, H. (1998). The relational view: cooperative strategy and sources of interorganizational competitive advantage. *Academy of management review*, 23(4):660–679.

Freeman, L. C. (1979). Centrality in social networks conceptual clarification.*Social networks*, 1(3):215–239.

Gooderham, P. b. (2007). Enhancing knowledge transfer in multinational corporations: A dynamic capabilities driven model. *Knowledge Management Research and Practice*, 5(1):34–43.

Granovetter, M. (1973).The strength of weak ties.*American journal of sociology*, 78(6):l.

Gundelach, P. (2009). Homour. In Svendsen, G. T. and Svendsen, G. L. H., editors, *Handbook of social capital: The troika of sociology, political science and economics*. Edward Elgar Publishing.

Gupta, S. and Malhotra, N. (2013). Marketing innovation: A resource-based view of international and local firms. *Marketing Intelligence and Planning*, 31(2):111–126. cited By (since 1996)0.

Hampden-Turner, C. (2000). *Building cross-cultural competence: How to create wealth from conflicting values.*Yale University Press.

Han, M. (2006).Developing social capital to achieve superior internationalization: A conceptual model.*Journal of International Entrepreneurship*, 4(2-3):99–112.

Hooghe, M. and Stolle, D. (2003).*Generating social capital: Civil society and institutions in comparative perspective*. Palgrave Macmillan. SC at the macro level.

Johanson, J. and Vahlne, J.-E. (1977). The internationalization process of the firm—a model of knowledge development and increasing foreign market commitments. *Journal of international business studies*, 8(1):23–32.

Johanson, J. and Vahlne, J.-E. (1990). The mechanism of internationalisation. *International marketing review*, 7(4).

Johanson, J. and Vahlne, J.-E. (2009). The uppsala internationalization process model revisited: From liability of foreignness to liability of outsidership. *Journal of international business studies*, 40(9):1411–1431.

Jones, M. V., Coviello, N., and Tang, Y. K. (2011). International entrepreneurship research (1989–2009): a domain ontology and thematic analysis. *Journal of Business Venturing*, 26(6):632–659.

Jones, M. V. and Dimitratos, P. (2004). Emerging paradigms in international entrepreneurship: a synopsis. *Emerging paradigms in international entrepreneurship*, page 3.

Knight, G. (1996).Born global.*Wiley International Encyclopedia of Marketing*.

Kontinen, T. and Ojala, A. (2011).Social capital in relation to the foreign market entry and post-entry operations of family smes.*Journal of International Entrepreneurship*, 9(2):133–151.

Kontinen, T. and Ojala, A. (2012).Social capital in the international operations of family smes.*Journal of Small Business and Enterprise Development*, 19(1):39–55.

Kristandl, G. and Bontis, N. (2007). Constructing a definition for intangibles using the resource based view of the firm. *Management Decision*, 45(9):1510–1524.

Lavie, D. (2006). The competitive advantage of interconnected firms: An extension of the resource-based view. *Academy of management review*, 31(3):638–658.

Levitt, P. and Jaworsky, B. N. (2007). Transnational migration studies: Past developments and future trends. *Annu. Rev. Sociol.*, 33:129–156.

Lin, N. and Erickson, B. H. (2008).Theory, measurement, and the research enterprise on social capital.pages 1–24. Oxford University Press.

McDougall, P. P. and Oviatt, B. M. (2000). International entrepreneurship: the intersection of two research paths. *Academy of management Journal*, 43(5):902–906.

Mejri, K. and Umemoto, K. (2010). Small- and medium-sized enterprise internationalization: Towards the knowledge-based model. *Journal of International Entrepreneurship*, 8(2):156–167.

Moen, Ø. (2002). The born globals: a new generation of small european exporters. *International Marketing Review*, 19(2):156–175.

Nahapiet, J. and Ghoshal, S. (1998). Social capital, intellectual capital, and the organizational advantage.*Academy of management review*, 23(2):242–266.

Nooteboom, B. (1993). Firm size effects on transaction costs. *Small Business Economics*, 5(4):283–295.

Oh, H., Labianca, G., and Chung, M.-H. (2006). A multilevel model of group social capital.*Academy of Management Review*, 31(3):569–582.

Ostrom, E. and Ahn, T. (2009).The meaning of social capital and its link to collective action. In Svendsen, G. T. and Svendsen, G. L. H., editors, *Handbook of social capital: The troika of sociology, political science and economics*. Edward Elgar Publishing.

Oviatt, B. M. and McDougall, P. P. (2005). Defining international entrepreneurship and modeling the speed of internationalization. *Entrepreneurship theory and practice*, 29(5):537–554.

Portes, A. (2000). Social capital: Its origins and applications in modern sociology. *LESSER, Eric L. Knowledge and Social Capital. Boston: Butterworth-Heinemann*, pages 43–67.

Portes, A., Haller, W. J., and Guarnizo, L. E. (2002). Transnational entrepreneurs: An alternative form of immigrant economic adaptation. *American sociological review*, 67(2):278–298.

Powell, W. W. and DiMaggio, P. J. (2012).*The new institutionalism in organizational analysis.*University of Chicago Press.

Powell, W. W. and Smith-Doerr, L. (1994).Networks and economic life.*The handbook of economic sociology*, 368:380.

Prashantham, S. (2006).Foreign network relationships and the internationalisation of small knowledge-intensive firms.*International Journal of Entrepreneurship and Innovation Management*, 6(6):542–553.

Prashantham, S. and Dhanaraj, C. (2010).The dynamic influence of social capital on the international growth of new ventures.*Journal of Management Studies*, 47(6):967–994.

Putnam, R. D. (1993). The prosperous community.*The american prospect*, 4(13):35–42.

Putnam, R. D. (1995). Bowling alone: America's declining social capital. *Journal of democracy*, 6(1):65–78.

Putnam, R. D. (2000). *Bowling alone: The collapse and revival of American community.*Simon and Schuster.

Putnam, R.D. (2001). Social capital: Measurement and consequences. Canadian Journal of Policy   Research 8(1):41-51

Rasmussen, E. S. and Madsen, T. K. (2002).The born global concept.In *Paper for the EIBA   conference.*

Reynolds, P. D. (1997). New and small firms in expanding markets.*Small business economics*, 9(1):79–84.

Ronald, B. (1992). Structural holes: The social structure of competition. *Cambridge: Harvard.*

Rose, R. (2000). Getting things done in an antimodern society: social capital networks in russia. In Dasgupta, P. and Serageldin, I., editors, *Social capital: a multifaceted perspective.* World Bank Publications.

Roxas, H. and Chadee, D. (2011). A resource-based view of small export firms' social capital in a southeast asian country. *Asian Academy of Management Journal*, 16(2):1–28. cited By (since 1996)1.

Ruzzier, M. and Antoncic, B. (2007). Social capital and sme internationalization: An empirical examination. *Transformations in Business and Economics*, 6(1):122–138.

Saarenketo, S., Puumalainen, K., Kuivalainen, O., and Kyläheiko, K. (2004). Dynamic knowledge-related learning processes in internationalizing high-tech smes. *International Journal of Production Economics*, 89(3):363–378.

Sandefur, R. L. and Laumann, E. O. (1998).A paradigm for social capital.*Rationality and society*, 10(4):481–501.

Senik, Z. and Sham, R. (2011).Sme internationalization intelligence information and knowledge on international opportunities.*Gadjah Mada International Journal of Business*, 13(2):161–183. cited By (since 1996)0.

Sepulveda, F. and Gabrielsson, M. c. (2013). Network development and firm growth: A resource-based study of b2b born globals. *Industrial Marketing Management*, 42(5):792–804. cited By (since 1996)2.

Sharma, D. D. and Blomstermo, A. (2003). The internationalization process of born globals: a network view. *International business review*, 12(6):739–753.

Smith, A., Ryan, P., and Collings, D. (2012).Born global networks: The role of connectors.*European Journal of International Management*, 6(5):566–589.

Stieglitz, J. E. (2000). Formal and informal institutions. In Dasgupta, P. and Serageldin, I., editors, *Social capital: a multifaceted perspective*. World Bank Publications.

Stinchcombe, A. L. (1965). Social structure and organizations.*Handbook of organizations*, 142:193.

Tate, J. (2001). National varieties of standardization. In Hall, P. A. and Soskice, D., editors, *Varieties of capitalism: The institutional foundations of comparative advantage*. Oxford University Press.

Tolstoy, D. and Agndal, H. (2010).Network resource combinations in the international venturing of small biotech firms.*Technovation*, 30(1):24–36. cited By (since 1996)25.

Tsai, W. and Ghoshal, S. (1998). Social capital and value creation: The role of intrafirm networks. *Academy of Management Journal*, 41(4):464–476.

Useem, M. and Karabel, J. (1986).Pathways to top corporate management.*American Sociological Review*, pages 184–200.

van der Gaag, M. and Snijders, T. (2005). An approach to the measurement of individual social capital.

Woolcock, M. and Narayan, D. (2000). Social capital: Implications for development theory, research, and policy. *The world bank research observer*, 15(2):225–249.

Yli-Renko, H., Autio, E., and Sapienza, H. J. (2001).Social capital, knowledge acquisition, and knowledge exploitation in young technology-based firms.*Strategic management journal*, 22(6-7):587–613.

Zaheer, S. (1995).Overcoming the liability of foreignness.*Academy of Management journal*, 38(2):341–363.

Zahra, S. A., Ireland, R. D., and Hitt, M. A. (2000). International expansion by new venture firms: International diversity, mode of market entry, technological learning, and performance. *Academy of Management journal*, 43(5):925–950.

Zhang, X., Ma, X., and Wang, Y. (2012). Entrepreneurial orientation, social capital, and the internationalization of smes: Evidence from china. *Thunderbird International Business Review*, 54(2):195–210.

Zhou, L., Wu, W.-p., and Luo, X. (2007). Internationalization and the performance of born-global smes: the mediating role of social networks. *Journal of International Business Studies*, 38(4):673–690.

Zhou, M. (2004).Revisiting ethnic entrepreneurship: Convergencies, controversies, and conceptual advancements.*International Migration Review*, 38(3):1040–1074.

CHAPTER FOUR

Internationalisation of Firms in Developing Countries: An Integrated Conceptual Framework

John Kuada

Abstract

The last three decades have witnessed a substantial amount of research into the internationalisation process of firms. The focus of most of these studies have, however, been on the downstream aspects of internationalisation with the assumption that all firms initiate their internationalisation process with export and proceed in a path-dependent manner towards the location of production activities abroad. The present chapter challenges this perspective, arguing that internationalisation of firms may be initiated through either or both upstream and downstream activities. It therefore proposes an integrated conceptual model for internationalisation, encompassing both upstream and downstream activities. Building on this understanding, the chapter suggests that firms in general and developing country-based firms in particular, may adopt one or a combination of four routes of internationalisation: upstream only, downstream only, sequential upstream-downstream, and or concurrent upstream-downstream routes. The implications of these perspectives for policy, strategy and research are discussed.

Introduction

The contemporary literature on the internationalisation processes of firms reflects two dominant streams of research. One group of scholars have focused attention on understanding the processes that relate to firms' initial entry into foreign markets, including their motives of internationalisation, their choice of entry modes, as well as the strategies adopted to chart the path of their onward process of internationalisation and to improve their performance (Bilkey and Tesar 1977, Johanson and Vahlne 1977, Cavusgil

1980, Cavusgil and Nevin 1981, Leonidou and Katsikeas 1996). The theoretical premises of this body of research have been rooted in the seminal works of Uppsala scholars, now generally referred to as the *stages theory* of internationalisation.

The second stream of research focuses attention on the later stages in the internationalisation process of firms where many of them decide to locate parts of their production abroad or to internationally outsource some of their value creation activities. The theoretical foundations of these studies are found partly in Dunnings ecletic paradigm (Dunning 1988), Vernon's International Product Life Cycle studies (Vernon 1966), and studies of international value chains and production networks (Gereffi 1994, Gereffi et al. 2004).

The two strands of research, however, assume that the internationalisation process of firms is initiated at the sales and marketing end of the value chain. Decisions to locate production activities abroad and to outsource resources are therefore seen as consequences of deeper involvement in the international market operations. Thus both types of research are labelled as downstream internationalisation (Kuada and Sørensen 1999).

In contrast, a number of scholars have consistently drawn attention to the emergence of a hybrid of cross-border linkages initiated partly by local firms in order to strengthen their production processes and to leverage resources through joint tasks, input deliveries, as well as upgrading their technological and managerial capacities. Some of the firms involved in these cross-border linkages may sell their products only on the domestic markets and consider the linkages as prerequisites for their competitiveness at home. This approach is denoted as the upstream or input-side of internationalisation in the literature (Welch and Luostarinen 1993, Kuada and Sørensen 1999).

Although previous academic research has provided valuable insight into the internationalisation processes of firms, the upstream and downstream processes of internationalisation are not explicitly integrated into a single conceptual model. As such, the policy and strategy implications of both processes are most often analysed separately and their potential synergies are lost in the fragmented analyses. Furthermore, theoretical viewpoints that have informed studies of internationalization of firms in the developed market economies have not been effectively integrated into the developing country-based studies. These omissions pose a serious weakness particularly in studies of internationalisation process of firms in developing countries since it denies their governments and managers the benefits of an integrated policy and strategy formulation. The increasing involvement of these firms in the global economy makes the policy guidelines derived from such an integrated framework extremely valuable.

The contributions of this chapter to the contemporary literature are therefore three-fold: First, it explores the theoretical arguments in support of an integrated conceptualisation. Second, it proposes a framework for such an integration noting its implications for studying some of the key questions addressed in internationalisation studies, e.g. motives and modes of internationalisation. Third, it outlines four alternative routes of internationalisation for developing country firms, based on the integrated conceptualisation and suggests their implications for policy and strategy in the developing countries.

The remainder of the chapter is organised as follows: The next section provides an overview of the dominant theories of internationalisation and draws attention to their limitations with regards to the analysis of the internationalisation process of developing country firms. Based on these discussions, an alternative conceptual framework is presented. This is followed by a discussion of its implications for strategic decisions of firms as well as its impacts on business performance. The research implications of these conceptualisations are then discussed.

Downstream Internationalisation

A large proportion of the frequently cited publications on the internationalisation process of firms tend to view internationalisation as a downstream activity. The dominant models of internationalisation are predicated on the general assumption that firms proceed with their internationalisation in a gradual and sequential manner. That is, internationalisation increases in a step-like fashion, firms moving to the next stage only after sufficient experience has been acquired from the preceding stage and the uncertainty surrounding the next stage has been substantially reduced (Johanson and Vahlne 1977, Bilkey and Tesar 1977, Cavusgil 1984).

The Stages Theory of Internationalisation

This process of internationalisation has been popularised in the studies of Uppsala scholars and is generally referred to as the *stages theory of internationalisation.* As indicated above, the theory holds that the internationalisation process consists of a number of identifiable and distinct stages with higher-level stages indicating higher degrees of internationalisation. Varieties of the stages theory differ only in terms of the number of stages and the actual parameters that trigger the change (Bilkey and Tesar 1977, Cavusgil 1980).

Further, the stages theory sees knowledge acquisition as an essential requirement in the internationalisation process of firms. Knowledge is, however, acquired experientially, i.e. through reflections on individuals' actions as well as the collective actions of the firms. The experience gained at each stage provides management with the information to either adopt or reject the option of further international commitment.

Following Eriksson et al. (1997), international firms require three kinds of knowledge: (1) foreign business knowledge, (2) foreign institutional knowledge, and (3) internationalisation knowledge. They define the foreign business knowledge component to cover knowledge about suppliers, clients, competitors and the market. Foreign institutional knowledge covers knowledge about government policies, bureaucratic regulations, and culture (broadly defined to include business practices, as well as societal values norms and accepted rules of behaviour). Internationalisation knowledge describes the firm's general understanding of how to do business outside the home country and include an insight into the procedures that facilitate international operations. Furthermore, it is assumed that as the export experience of a firm increases, its managers gain better understanding of export mechanisms and are likely to perceive less uncertainty in their exporting activities. Thus, Cavusgil (1984) argues that non-exporting firms and marginally active exporters tend to be more pessimistic in their evaluation of risks, costs and profits than active exporters.

Some Limitations of the Analytical Power of the Model

The export literature has registered severe limitations in the stages theory. First, it has been argued that the importance attached to experiential knowledge constitutes both strength and weakness of the stages theory. Experiences are slow to build, shared and integrated within firms. Thus if firms base their international decisions largely on experiential knowledge, their internationalisation process will invariably be slow. This will be a major disadvantage in a dynamic economy where business opportunities quickly change. Second, it has been empirically demonstrated that the choice of entry strategies does not always correspond to the sequential step-by-step approach suggested in the stages theory. Some firms may enter a new market via a direct export route but may serve the same market subsequently through an indirect export route, depending on their assessment of the relative pay-offs of the two entry strategies (Turnbull 1987).Third, when firms enter a foreign market they will usually be disadvantaged vis-à-vis the indigenous firms in terms of familiarity with the local business environment. This unfamiliarity is labeled *'liability of foreignness'* (Zaheer 1995), and is presumed to raise the entrant firms' levels of operational uncertainty with regard to relations with local actors. This implies that some companies may experience serious difficulties in their internationalization process in some countries. Fourth, firms may overestimate the similarities between neighbouring countries. Even countries that share language, historical, and legal traditions, often have very different institutions that do not allow the simple transfer of business practices and attitudes across borders.

Coupled with the limitations listed above, the path-dependent trajectory of internationalization appears hardly tenable in developing countries due to the sizes, ownership structures, resource disadvantages and limited managerial capabilities of these firms. As Vernon-Wortzel et al (1988) argue some firms in developing countries may feel content with reaching the active export involvement stage in the internationalisation process and may hold no ambitions for further growth, since this may push them far beyond their optimal capacities.

In addition to this, the contention that most companies must have a strong domestic market base before venturing abroad runs counter to the operational conditions found in most developing countries. For one thing, the small sizes of the home markets of firms in most developing countries do not offer them opportunities to enjoy economies of scale and growth through the accumulation and use of domestic resources. Furthermore, the non-competitive nature of the home markets for certain products (e.g. agro-industrial products) do not offer developing country firms the challenges necessary to develop product characteristics suitable for the highly competitive markets.

It has also been suggested by some scholars that the dearth of managerial capabilities imposes severe limitations on the abilities of these firms to use the experiential approach to internationalization. The "liability of foreignness" (Zaheer 1995) is, therefore, likely to be experienced more strongly by developing country firms than their developed country counterparts.

The Network Perspective of Internationalisation

While proponents of the stages theory assume that firms stand alone in developing their market entry strategies, another group of researchers see business activities among firms as characterised by interactions and mutual interdependence. These scholars have worked mostly within the International Marketing and Purchasing (IMP) group and their studies constitute the core of what is now referred to as the *network theory of internationalisation*.

The main contribution of the network theory to an understanding of the internationalisation process of firms lies in the emphasis on relationship as an exchange governing mechanism. It describes industrial systems as networks of firms engaged in production, distribution and use of goods and services. Firms within this network usually establish lasting business relationships. Thus, the network perspective shifts the focus of the unit of analysis from the individual firms to their relationships.

For network scholars, successful international firms must have a network orientation. Having such an orientation encourages firms to identify the roles, strengths and resource configurations of other actors within the network. This helps them position themselves within the network. "Position" here is a rich term. By positioning themselves within the network of relationships, firms are able to design strategies that improve their access to resources controlled by other firms. The higher the number of contacts, the better it is for the firm as this means access to more networks and providing their managers with greater access to opportunities.

Networks exist both within and outside national boundaries. This implies that the internationalisation process of firms may be initiated by activities of other firms within cross-border networks. A popular taxonomy in the network literature groups international firms in terms of the degree of internationalization of individual firms on the one hand and the degree of internationalization of the markets in which they operate on the other. Firms with low degrees of internationalization and operating in markets with low levels of internationalization are described as *early starters*. Those with low degrees of internationalization but operating in highly internationalized markets are classified as *late starters*. Those with high degrees of internationalization but operating in markets with low levels of internationalization are classified as *the lonely internationals*, while those whose markets are highly international and have, themselves, high degrees of internationalization are classified as *international among others*.

Over the years, network scholars have drawn on the works of economic sociologists and on resource-based studies to broaden their perspective of the strategic opportunities inherent in networking. Building on sociological concepts of embeddeness and social ties, it has been argued that networks are embedded in the socio-cultural contexts of the nations in which firms operate. Distinction is therefore drawn between national nets and international nets.

Building further on the sociological arguments, it has been suggested by some scholars that a firm's position within a national net provides it an access to social relationships and social knowledge. With social knowledge, firms may be able to reduce their reliance on ownership as a means of control over their foreign operations (Sharma and Johanson 1987). In the same vein, Burt (1992) distinguishes between contacts that are duplicates and contacts that are complementary. Duplicate contacts give access to more or less similar networks, while complementary contacts add new networks and offer firms with opportunities for new, random and unexpected information. Said differently, firms placed centrally in a network receive more, better, and early knowledge than their competitors. This is a source of advantage and may exert influence on the internationalization of firms. From this perspective, firms with a large number of heterogeneous weak network ties enjoy an advantage over firms that are engaged in narrow and homogenous strong ties.

Global Production Chains

Parallel to the network studies, another body of literature has emerged to explain changing patterns of production and distribution of goods and services within the global economy. Similar to the network theory, these studies have also acknowledged the vertical linkages in industrial production processes, i.e. tracing it from the first batch of input suppliers within the production chain through to the final user of the product or service. Most of these studies have endorsed the value chain conceptualisation popularised in Michael Porter's work (Porter 1985) and highlight deliberate strategies of Transnational Corporations to select firms in different parts of the world to participate in the global value chain. The result of this internationalisation strategy is that production is increasingly fragmented across geographic space (Arndt and Kierzkowski 2001).

Porter's own conceptualisation of value chain is reminiscent of the assembly line view of industrial management popular in the beginning of the last century. The chain is perceived as composed of a discrete set of activities performed by independent and potentially rival group of firms, each pursuing its individual goals. Collaboration is seen as a necessity rather than a desire. The primary concern in the value chain management is therefore to ensure optimal performance of each member of the chain in terms of cost effectiveness. Stated differently, the optimilisation of task means that the appropriate inputs are in the right place at the right time and that the flow of products and processes are facilitated through the chain.

Gereffi (1994) introduced the concept of *Global Commodity Chains* (GCC) to describe the coordination systems in value chains dominated by Transnational Corporations. He argued that value chains found in capital intensive sectors such as the automotive and aircraft industry are driven by major producers and are therefore referred to as *producer–driven commodity chains.* Such industries are characterised by extensive international subcontracting, controls exercised by the administrative headquarters of Transnational Companies, and the reliance on economies of scale to reduce overall transaction costs. There is therefore a relatively high degree of centralisation within these chains and across nations. In industries where transactions and labour costs are important to competitive positioning, the key drivers are the major buyers within the industry. These chains are therefore referred to as *buyer-driven*[2] commodity chains. Prominent among such chains are those found in garment, footwear, toys, and consumer electronics. The key drivers in these chains focus their resources on research, design, sales and marketing while outsourcing other value added activities within the chain.

Chain drivers send signals of cost-efficiency through the chain. In buyer driven chain, dominant buyers demand that their merchandise producers should lower prices. This reinforces the pressure on their contractors down the chain to lower prices of inputs and components supplied. This may necessitate lower wages for employees and the adoption of other cost-cutting strategies within individual firms. The decision of some producers of footwear, garment and consumer electronics to locate their production units in countries with cheap but skilled labour can be partly explained by the systemic effects of cost-cutting pressure initiated by chain drivers. The investment decisions may result in shifts in positions of firms within the chain. Firms whose investments in countries with cheap labour accords them with temporary static efficiencies may become major suppliers as long

---

[2] Gereffi's use of the term "buyer-driven" creates some confusion from channel systems perspective. "Buyers" in his terminology refer to key retail customers rather than consumers who buy small consignments of good for their private use.

as these conditions remain important means of reducing costs within the industry.

It has been stressed in recent literature, however, that the relationship between chain drivers and members must be one of mutuality and reciprocity (i.e. win-win relationships in the value systems) rather than coercion by chain drivers and grudging compliance of other chain members. Seen from this perspective, the strategic task of chain drivers is the reconfiguration of roles and relationships of companies within the value creating system. Successful value chain management is therefore an outcome of a multiplex of economic transactions combined with varieties of organisational development strategies, knowledge flows, and institutional arrangements among stakeholders within a time-space stretch. In other words, the players within the value system must continuously re-assess and re-design their competencies and relationships in order to keep their value-creating systems flexible and responsive.

Developing Country Firms in Networks and Global Value Chains

Both the network and global value chain perspectives hold promising contributions to internationalisation policies and strategies for developing country firms. Through their inclusion in the network of value creating activities, developing country firms can leverage key resources and thereby bridge their resource gaps. But there are drawbacks to their inclusion in already established international networks and value chains. A major drawback is the power asymmetries within the network and how new comers can manage their dependence on established actors.

In business just as in any other social spheres of human endeavour, power is exercised through the possession of resources on which other actors depend for the attainment of their own objectives. Sociological studies suggest that power is not a static quantity but vary according to context and resource ownership. All actors in a relationship have some amount of resources to start with but these resources change over time in terms of their degrees of importance and value. Thus, over time, as network members interact, some of them emerge more powerful than the others due to changes in their resource configurations. This produces differentiation within the network when some actors become increasingly dependent on others for services required in reaching their objectives.

Until recently, the developing countries have been at the losing end of the relationships. Some positive changes have emerged, particularly in the Asian countries due partly to the relative ease with which some types of knowledge and resources migrate across countries. It has, for example, been noted that explicit knowledge has a higher rate of migration than tacit knowledge and therefore has become less confined to specific geographical location as it was half a century ago. Thus technical skill levels and engineering knowledge in several Asian countries are reaching or exceeding those of the developed countries of the West. This change in international resource configuration has made Asian firms highly attractive candidates for inclusion in the global value chains of many industries today.

In sum, three bodies of theory constitute the pivot of contemporary studies in internationalisation. All of them, however, focus on the downstream dimensions of the internationalisation process of firms. Some of them have, however hinted at the importance of the input and supply side of internationalisation but fail to explicitly articulate this perspective. We argue below that linking the upstream and downstream sides of internationalisation provides a more coherent frame for understanding the internationalisation process of firms.

Upstream Internationalisation

The concept of upstream internationalisation covers the strategic decision of firms to source parts or all of their inputs (including technology, knowledge and human resources) from foreign sources in order to raise or sustain their competitive positions in target markets (Welch and Luostarinen 1993, Kuada and Sørensen 1999). The literature has treated such activities under supply chain management, outsourcing and international strategic alliances ((Boryd and Jemison 1989).

The theoretical logic of upstream internationalisation is that no single firm possesses all resources and capabilities needed for creating value for customers in a rapidly changing economic environment. Thus, if a firm generates its entire added-value using domestic resources only, its export success will depend exclusively on the quality of the home-based resources only. This may limit its competitiveness in key export markets served by firms with superior local resource bases. It is therefore important for local firms to seek resources from dispersed sources.

The more varied their foreign resource leveraging opportunities, the greater their innovative (and therefore operational) capabilities. Upstream resource leveraging is therefore a necessary requirement for downstream international expansion. This thinking has informed strategies of many new international ventures (Zander 1997, Cantwell and Piscitello 2000). Firms whose internationalisation process has followed the conventional traditional stages approach have also found upstream internationalisation highly useful to their corporate resource leveraging strategies.

Some strands of the upstream internationalisation research have leaned on the resource based perspective of the firm to argue that where the resources required by a firm to generate its value-adding activities are of a general character, easily identifiable or substitutable, the firm may depend on the market to acquire them and may use them in-house to perform the value-added activities that form the core of its business. But if they are of intangible nature (e.g. tacit knowledge and firm capabilities) the attributes of such resources would render them nearly impossible to buy directly. It therefore enters into collaborative arrangements with other firms to supply it with the required resources.

Thus most upstream international arrangements are distinctively different from downstream approaches in the sense that they involve fairly long-term inter-firm relationship rather than episodic (and perhaps, opportunistic) transactions. The literature lists several advantages of upstream collaborative arrangements. Contributions to the literature draw on theoretical traditions such as the resource-based perspective on firms (Barney 1991, 2001), competence-based perspectives (Prahalad and Hamel 1990) and knowledge-based perspective (Nelson and Winter 1982, Grant 1996, Inkpen and Crossan 1995, Gulati 1998, Simonin 1996). These scholars argue that collaborations do not only provide access to tangible resources. They also enable partners to access the embedded knowledge of co-partners and/or facilitate new knowledge generation (Inkpen and Crossan 1995).

But access to knowledge does not always translate smoothly into usage within the collaborating firms. Receiving firms may find it difficult to comprehend the knowledge due to its inherent characteristics or its cultural peculiarities. Thus, knowledge usage has been found to depend on the capacity of firms tointernalise the accessed knowledge or what Huber refers to as "grafting" (Huber 1996). The lack of absorptive capacity of co-partners (Cohen and Levinthal 1990), arduousness of the relationship between the partnering firms (Szulanski 1996), and causal ambiguity (Simonin 1999) have been listed among knowledge transfer barriers.

The wisdom in upstream internationalisation has also informed discussions in the international supply chain management literature where the focus has been on the management of relations with suppliers in foreign countries and the coordination of an integrated network of business processes. In brief international supply chain management partly entails making sure that all firms and activities which are associated with the flow and transformation of goods from the raw materials stage to the final consumer stage are well synchronised. That is production scheduling at suppliers' end of the chain are combined with elaborate logistics arrangements to make this function. Here information and knowledge management play a key role. Information about resources, inventory, output and logistic plans all help improve decisions such as safety stock placement, order replenishment and transhipment in a supply chain.

Thus from an upstream perspective, a firm must be concerned about the selection of a supplier that possesses the best bundle of resources that would deliver the inputs, components and/or resources that it requires under optimal conditions for it to maintain or enhance its competitive position as required by its strategic objectives. The key question would be this: how can we be sure that the supplier does not misrepresent its resources and capabilities?

This question has received attention in supply chain management discussions, building on agency analytical frameworks. It has been argued that firms in upstream relationships face two types of vulnerability in their operations. The first is *adverse selection* which describes the condition under which the firm cannot be certain that competencies that the supplier claims to have are also those required to provide the inputs and resources that it need for the optimal performance of its own value-adding activities. The second is what is referred to in agency theory as *moral hazards*. Moral hazard is the condition under which the firm contracting for the inputs or resources cannot be sure if the supplier has put forth maximal effort (Eisenhardt, 1989).

Integration of Upstream and Downstream Perspectives on Internationalisation

The discussions above indicate that the works of international network scholars and writers on international value chains provide theoretical legitimacy for an integration of upstream and downstream routes of internationalisation. But these scholars have not explicitly attempted to build an integrated conceptual and analytical framework. We argue in this section of the chapter that an explicit conceptual integration carries both practical and academic gains. For companies, it emphasises the strategic importance of discussing both marketing and purchasing activities jointly and encourages the development of organisational structures that would facilitate joint actions in the two key functional areas in business. It would therefore remedy situations (prevalent in high-profiled international companies today) where marketing and purchasing activities are still treated as distinctly separate functions belonging to separate departments. As it were, the existing conceptual separation produces a situation in which tools developed to strengthen relationships with customers (e.g. customer relationship management tools) do not find relevance in purchasing departments. From a practical perspective, however, it makes economic sense for international firms to have both customer and supplier relationship management tools.

Four Routes of Internationalisation

The integration of upstream and downstream processes of internationalisation re-defines our conceptualisation of internationalisation of firms as such, particularly with respect to the routes and strategies of internationalisation, as well as resources required to support the internationalisation process. We suggest that an integrated framework produces four distinct routes of internationalisation for every firm. These are:

1. Internationalization by upstream activities only
2. Internationalisation by downstream activities only
3. Sequential upstream-downstream internationalization
4. Concurrent upstream-downstream internationalization

Internationalization by Upstream Activities Only

As argued earlier, upstream internationalisation has its theoretical legitimacy in the resource-based literature. In brief terms, the resource-based perspective holds that each firm consists of a bundle of resources. But those components of the resources that are valuable, rare, inimitable and non-substitutable enable the firm to bundle other resources together and to implement value-creating strategies that cannot be readily duplicated by other firms (Barney 1991, 2001). Such resources combine to form firms' dynamic capabilities, which enable their managers to demonstrate exceptional alertness in identifying changes within the operational environment and to take actions sooner than their competitors in order to take advantages of the opportunities and avert threats within their operational environments. Such resources include the knowledge management capabilities of the firm, i.e. abilities to learn continuously, to disseminate the knowledge to all organisational members and to ensure that the available stock of knowledge within the firm is effectively deployed to inform strategies and behaviour (Prahalad and Hamel 1990). Continuous learning is to forestall situations where firms are managed by a dominant logic that is out of tune with the environmental changes.

To the extent that upstream activities help channel resources (including knowledge) to developing country firms, they have a critical role to play in the defining of the overall strategies as well as tempo and direction of the internationalisation process of the firms that use them. But the decision of firms to base their inter-nationalization process on upstream activities will depend on their overall motives of internationalization and the prospects of finding suitable partners abroad.

Internationalization by Downstream Activities Only

Our earlier discussions justify the promotion of downstream internationalisation in all market economies. At the macroeconomic level, exporting contributes to foreign exchange reserves of nations, provide employment and foment forward and backward linkages within an economy. At the micro level, export marketing provides firms with new market opportunities and thereby raises their capacity utilization, improves their financial positions and overall competitive positions. The small size of local demand of most developing countries provides additional justification for their reliance on export-led growth strategies. Available experience from various developing countries suggests that export promotion is a useful economic growth policy instrument since export recovery does generate substantial gains quickly (Fafchamps, Teal and Toye 2001).

Three conditions allow some developing country firms to engage in downstream internationalisation without any prior or significant upstream activities. The first is their inclusion in the international value chains of lead firms. Research work on the electronics industry and contract manufacturing in Asian countries (Sturgeon 2002), the apparel industries in Asia (Gereffi 1994) and Africa (Gibons 2001) as well as the horticultural industry in Africa (Dolan and Humphrey 2000) provide empirical evidence of these forms of internationalisation through chain inclusion. Second, producers of ethnic products that have differential advantages due to unique design can target niche market in Europe and North America. Examples include *kente* from Ghana (Kuada and Sørensen 2000) and utilitarian handicrafts from different developing countries. Third, several developing countries have embarked on export-led growth strategies that provide special locational incentives to local firms as well as locally-based foreign firms in export zones to produce for export (Kuada 2005).

But due to a multiple set of reasons, developing country firms' downstream internationalisation processes are severely constrained and can be extremely slow at best. The export literature contains a long list of factors (both external and internal) that inhibit developing country firms' downstream internationalisation. The external factors include high relative cost of financing exports (Bilkey 1978, Czinkota and Ricks 1983), dealing with bureaucracy within public agencies (Rabino 1980, Cavusgil 1984) export documentation (Rabino 1980, Czinkota and Ricks 1983), lack of market information (Katsikeas and Morgan 1994), logistical constraints and high cost of transportation (Rabino 1980). The internal constraints include difficulties in meeting importers' quality standards (Rabino 1980) export packaging (Czinkota and Ricks 1983), lack of competent staff (Kothari and Kaynak 1984) and inability to self-finance exports (Bilkey 1978).

Foreign distributors may hesitate to buy from developing country firms due to constraints listed above. In addition to these, the literature has identified supply side constraints such as limited capacity of suppliers to fulfil pre-shipment value-adding requirements of distributors abroad as severely reducing the attractiveness of these firms as exporters to Europe and North America. For example, Dolan et al(1998) report from their study of the supply chain management of UK horticultural markets that the major super-markets and importers in the UK require their suppliers to possess a broad range of post-harvest competencies, such as the management of cooling and cold storage systems, on-site packaging and capabilities to ensure high quality and reliable deliveries if they are to have any chance of being listed as regular suppliers.

Sequential Upstream-Downstream Internationalization

Sequential upstream-downstream internationalization implies that upstream activities and relations precede the initiation of downstream transactions. The former relations are, however, not terminated when downstream internationalization begins. They may, in fact, increase in range and complexity in response to changing needs of the firm.

The downstream internationalization may either be deliberately planned to succeed the upstream internationalization process or it may be unintended, but seen as a logical consequence of successful upstream activities. In the first case, firms engaged in the upstream relationship do so intentionally to support their downstream internationalization process. The strategic goal of the upstream activities, in this regard, is to raise the competitive capacity of the focal developing country's firm in its chosen export markets. Therefore, the success of the upstream internationalization is measured by the success of the downstream internationalization. In the second case, the downstream internationalization becomes an emergent rather than a deliberate strategy. For one thing, doing business with international suppliers gives managers an international exposure. Information about market opportunities abroad may be generated through these contacts. Having a position within an international business network as a buyer, management finds it relatively easier to explore opportunities in these markets for its products. Thus market selection flows naturally from these initial contacts.

Where the focal firm aims at being a major player on the international scene, i.e. using upstream internationalization as a springboard for downstream internationalization, an incremental approach to change may not prove effective. Firms with very low levels of technological capacity relative to the major players in the target markets may require dramatic changes in their profile, i.e. in terms of technology, financial resources, technical skill and managerial competencies for them to compete successfully in the target markets. Technological and financial resources may also be sought outside the home country for similar reasons.

A debatable question is whether developing country firms should engage in upstream relations with a single foreign firm or with several firms. The decision on the number of foreign firms with which to cooperate would depend on the focal firm's internal capacity to coordinate, absorb, and transform varieties of ideas and resources from different foreign partners as well as its ability to honour the obligations that the various relationships impose. But above all, the number of foreign firms interested in engaging in relationships with the firm would depend on the latter's comparative attractiveness.

Concurrent Upstream-Downstream Internationalisation

Firms with substantial resources and government support may engage in upstream and downstream internationalisation simultaneously. The downstream international activities may be triggered by those conditions listed earlier, i.e. the production of uniquely designed ethnic products, inclusion in global production networks by lead firms or taking advantage of government export development policies. Again as noted above, for most developing country firms, upstream internationalisation requires linkages with foreign firms. On their own, they are generally not attractive candidates for international firms in search of partners abroad, except for the production of specific product categories where resource location provides a significant comparative advantage. Government is therefore required to facilitate upstream collaboration of these firms (Kuada and Sørensen 2005).

It is important to bear in mind that firms that intend to engage in upstream and downstream internationalisation processes simultaneously must have the capacity to absorb external resources from the upstream relations and at the same time be able to meet the needs of downstream customers. The main argument here is that external resources require internally available resources for them to be effectively transformed and used for value creation purposes. This may explain why only very few developing country-based firms can follow this route.

Some Research Implications

The implications of an integrated perspective on internationalisation can be discussed in terms of its impact on overall strategy formulation and performance of firms as well as the various decisions that managers make in relation to the internationalisation processes themselves.

Figure 1 provides a schematic illustration of the link between combined upstream-downstream internationalisation and business performance. The argument here is that the upstream decisions (i.e. cross-border input and resource leveraging decisions) combine with downstream (i.e. marketing decisions) to shape the overall international business strategy of firms. These would determine the extent to which a given firm can sustain its competitive position in its key markets. This would in turn determine its overall corporate performance. In other words, it would not make much sense to analyse international business performance of firms without analysing its upstream and downstream activities.

Figure 1: A Schematic Illustration of the Link between Upstream-Downstream Internationalisation and Business Performance

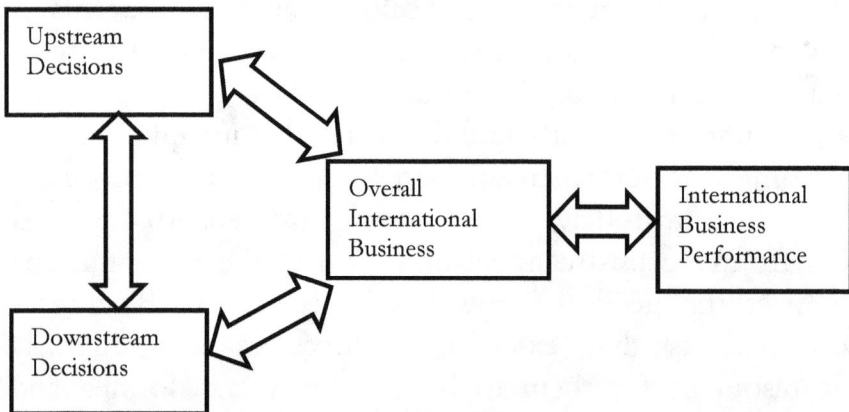

Arguably, this perspective should inform subsequent studies in internationalisation of firms, particularly for firms. Issues such as motives of internationalisation, market and partner selection decisions, choice of countries and modes of operation and governance in different markets must be studied jointly from both upstream and downstream perspectives. As noted above, earlier studies have focused on each dimension separately. The focus on downstream internationalisation only has produced partial insights into the complexity of internationalisation decision processes of firms. If, however, international business researchers were to design their research instruments with the understanding that firms engage in both upstream and downstream internationalisation (sequentially or concurrently), their research would likely produce other perspectives on the determinants and strategies of internationalisation of firms. For example, in the case of sequential upstream-downstream internationalisation process, foreign suppliers of key inputs might provide their partners with foreign market information that would ease their market selection and foreign market entry processes. Thus, upstream internationalisation might be seen as reducing the *liability of foreignness* of firms.

Furthermore, previous research has assessed the international business experience of firms (and therefore their reliability and trustworthiness as foreign partners) in terms of either their upstream or downstream engagements only. The pool of foreign experience existing in a company would be a lot different if one adds the experience purchasers of foreign inputs gain from their interactions with suppliers to those gained by employees from the export department. Pooling their international experience together provides a better basis for assessing the international business capacity of companies. The credibility of developing country firms as business partners would be assessed in a different light on the basis of such an analysis.

Conclusion

The aim of this chapter has been to review the contemporary theories of internationalisation of firms and explore their relevance in studying the internationalisation process of developing country-based firms. It has been argued that most previous studies have focused attention on the downstream aspects of internationalisation. Most scholars have adopted the stages theory as providing the most valid analytical framework for their studies. We have, however argued that the stages theory suffers severe weaknesses when applied to studying the internationalisation process of developing country firms. The contention in the stages theory that companies must have strong domestic market base before venturing abroad runs counter to the operational conditions found in most developing countries. First, the small sizes of the home markets of firms in most developing countries do not offer them opportunities to enjoy economies of scale and growth through the accumulation and use of domestic resources. Second, the non-competitive nature of the home markets for certain products do not offer developing country firms the challenges necessary to develop product characteristics suitable for the highly competitive markets in Western Europe and North America. Third, the sluggishness of economic growth in most of the developing countries makes it difficult for firms to acquire their first export experience from relatively similar market environments, - i.e. from nearby markets. In situations where the degree of competition within the domestic market increases due to trade liberalization, the local enterprises may be severely disadvantaged due to their relatively lower marketing experience and weaker resource bases.

The chapter further argues that analysing internationalisation process of firms exclusively from a downstream perspective provides only a partial insight into the degree of internationalisation of firms and the challenges and opportunities that internationalisation process produces. We have therefore suggested an integrated conceptualisation embracing both upstream and downstream processes as a more useful framework for analysis. This framework defines four routes for internationalisation: upstream only, downstream only, sequential upstream-downstream, and/or concurrent upstream-downstream routes.

We argue further that government policy interventions are required in developing countries to create an environment in which firms can adopt integrative upstream-downstream internationalisation strategies to stimulate rapid growth. Interventions must address binding constraints in both upstream and downstream dimensions of internationalisation. We believe that once the growth process is initiated with sufficient vigour, expectations of the private sector managers would change in a manner that supports growth.

References

Arndt S. and H. Kierzkowski (2001) *Fragmentation: New Production Patterns in the World Economy*, Oxford: Oxford University Press

Barney, J. B. 1991. Firm Resources and Sustained Competitive Advantage. *Journal of Management,* 17, pp.99-120.

Barney, J.B. (2001) "Resource-based theories of competitive advantage: A Ten-year Retrospective on Resource-based View" *Journal of Management* 27 pp: 643-650

Bilkey, W. J., and Tesar, G. 1977. "The Export Behavior of Smaller-Sized Wisconsin Manufacturing Firms". *Journal of International Business Studies,* 8, pp.93-98.

Bilkey, Warren J., (1978) "An attempted integration of the literature on the export behaviour of firms" *Journal of International Business Studies* Vol. 9 No. 1 33-46

Borys, B. and Jemison D.B. (1989) "Hybrid Arrangements as Strategic Alliances: Theoretical Issues in Organizational Combinations" *Academy of Management Journal* 14 (2): 234-49

Burt, R. S. (1992): The Social Structure of Competition. (In) Nohria, N. and R. G. Eccles, eds.: Networks and Organizations. Harvard Business School Press: Boston.

Cavusgil, S. Tamer (1984) "Organizational characteristics associated with export activity" *Journal of Management Studies* 21, 1

Cavusgil, S. Tamer and John R. Nevin (1981) "Internal determinants of export marketing behaviour: an empirical investigation" *Journal of Marketing Research* Vol. XVIII

Cavusgil, S.T. (1980): "On the Internationalization Process of Firms". *European Research*, Vol. 8 no. 4 pp: 273-281

Cohen, Westley M., & Levinthal, Daniel A. (1990), "Absorptive Capacity: A New Perspective on Learning and Innovation", *Administrative Science Quarterly*, 35: 128-152

Czinkota, Michael R. and D. A. Ricks (1983) "The use of a multi-measurement approach in the determination of company export priorities" *Journal of the Academy of Marketing Sciences* Vol. 11 No. 3 pp. 283 - 91

Dolan, Catherine and Humphrey, John and Harris-Pascal, Carla (1999) "Horticulture Commodity Chains: The Impact of the UK Market on the African Fresh Vegetable Industry" IDS Working Paper 96 University of Sussex, UK

Dunning, John H. (1988) "The eclectic paradigm of international production: a restatement and some possible extensions" Journal of International Business Studies, Spring, pp 1-31

Eisenhardt, Kathleen M. 1989 'Agency theory: An assessment and review'. *Academy of Management Review* Vol. 14 No.1: 57-74.

Eriksson, Kent, Jan Johanson, Anders Majkgård and D. Deo Sharma (1997) "Experiential knowledge and cost in the internationalization process" *Journal of International Business Studies*. Second quarter pp: 337 – 360

Fafchamps, Marcel, Teal, Francis and Toye, John Towards a Growth Strategy for Africa Centre for the Study of African Economies, University of Oxford REP/2001-06

Gereffi, G. (1994) 'The organization of buyer-driven global commodity chains: how U.S. retailers shape overseas production networks', in G. Gereffi and M. Korzeniewicz (eds) *Commodity Chains and Global Capitalism*, Westport: Praeger, pp. 95--122.

Gereffi, G. Humphrey, J., and Sturgeon, T. (2004) "The Governance of Global Value Chains" forthcoming in *Review of International Political Economy*

Gibbon, P. (2001) 'Upgrading primary products: a global value chain approach', *World Development* 29 (2): 345--63.

Gulati, Ranjay, (1998), Alliances and networks, *Strategic Management Journal*, vol. 19, p.293-317

Huber, George P. (1991). "Organizational Learning: The Contributing Processes and the Literatures." *Organization Science* Vol. 2 No. 1 pp: 88-115.

Johanson, J. and J.-E.Vahlne (1977). "The Internationalization Process of the Firm -- A Model of Knowledge Development and Increasing Foreign Market Commitments," *Journal of International Business Studies* 8 (1), 23-32.

Katsikeas, Constantine S. and Robert E. Morgan (1994) "Differences in Perceptions of Exporting Problems Based on Firm Size and Export Market Experience" *European Journal of Marketing* Vol, 28 No. 5

Kaynak, E., and V. Kothari (1984) "Export behaviour of small manufactures: a comparative study of american and canadaian firms" *European Management Journal* Vol. 2 summer pp: 41-7

Kuada, John and Olav Jull Sørensen (1999), "Upstream and Downstream Processes of Internationalization : Some Ghanaian Evidence" *The Journal of Euromarketing* Vol 7 No. 4 pp: 7-41

Kuada, John and Olav Jull Sørensen (2000) *Internationalization of Companies from Developing Countries:* (NY. The Haworth Press Inc.)

Leonidou, L. C. and C.S Katsikeas, (1996) "The Export Development Process: An Integrative Review of Empirical Models" *Journal of International Business Studies*, 27, pp.517-551.

Porter, Michael E. (1985). *Competitive Advantage – Creating and Sustaining Superior Performance*. New York: The Free Press.

Prahalad, C., & Hamel, G. (1990), The Core Competence of the Corporation, Harvard Business Review, May-June: 79-91

Rabino, S. (1980) "An examination of barriers to exporting encountered by small manufacturing companies" *Management International Review* Vol. 1 pp: 67-73

Sturgeon, T. (2002) 'Modular production networks: a new American model of industrial organization', *Industrial and Corporate Change* 11 (3): 451--496.

Szulanski, G. 1996. Exploring internal stickiness: Impediments to the transfer of best practice within the firm.*Strategic Management Journal*, 17 (Winter Special Issue): 27-43.

Turnbull, Peter W. (1987) "A challenge to the stages theory of the internationalization process" in P.J. Rosson and S.D. Reid (eds.) Managing Export Entry and Expansion (NY. Præger)   pp: 21-40

Vernon, Raymond (1966): International Investment and International Trade in the Product Cycle. *Quaterly Journal of Economics*, Vol. 80 No.2 pp 190-207

Vernon-Wortzel, H., Wortzel, L.H., and Deng, S (1988), "Do neophyte exporters understand importers?" Columbia Journal of World Business Vol. 23 No. 4 pp. 49-56

Welch, Lawrence S. and Luostarinen, Reijo (1993) "Inward-outward connections in internationalization", *Journal of Internaitonal Marketing*, Vol. 1, no. 1, 44-56.

Wiedersheim-Paul, F., H.C. Olson and L.S. Welch (1978) "Pre-export and activity: the first step in internationalization" *Journal of International Business Studies* 9 (1) 47-58

Zaheer, S. 1995 "Overcoming the liability of foreignness" *Academy of Management Journal* Vol. 38 No. 2 pp: 341-363

CHAPTER FIVE

Globalization of Innovation and the Rise of Network Organization

Yimei Hu

Abstract

In order to cope with the fierce global competition, more and more multinational corporations strive to gain and sustain their global competitive advantages through establishing a so-called network organization to facilitate global innovation. However, as a popular notion appearing in multiple theoretical streams, there exist distant and even highly debatable understandings of network organization. This chapter concludes with a three-level framework to facilitate our understanding of network organization. Firstly, a network organization can be an intraorganizational design to cope with a firm's innovation purposes. Such organizational structure is contrasted with traditional hierarchical organizational structure, and features - flexibility, market mechanism, internal trust, etc. Secondly, a network organization refers to various forms of interorganizational designs such as strategic alliances, strategic technological partnerships, value networks, joint ventures, industrial associations, etc. Moreover, some argue that the business context for global innovation by nature consists of overlapping networks, and under such network perspective, market and traditional hierarchical structures are just extreme forms of network. The main contribution of this chapter is in clarifying the contentious concept of network organization, and the final framework serves as a tool to bridge several distinct understandings towards network organization for global innovation.

The Era of Global Innovation

Globalization

Globalization, on the one hand, refers to the actual structural changes that broaden the geographical inter-linkages of markets, products and firms (Papaconstantinou, 1995); and on the other hand, globalization means the neo-liberal, free-market ideology of the globalization project (Dicken, 2011). With the ongoing trend of globalization, the world nowadays is flat (Freidman, 2005). Driven by multinational corporations (MNCs) seeking overseas markets and labor forces, the world is connected by massive material, financial and informational flows. It results in a growing world-wide integration and interpenetration of economic activities.

As we entered the new millennium, an even upgraded globalization version, namely Globalization 3.0 by (Freidman, 2006), arrived quickly and quietly, shrinking the world to a tiny one and leaving no business as an island (Håkansson, Ford, Gadde, Snehota, & Waluszewski, 2009; Håkansson & Snehota, 1989). Due to the revolution in information and communication technology, we can get in touch with friends who are thousands of kilometers away by clicking on keyboards; we may work with colleagues located in another continent seamlessly; and we are able to know the latest news as soon as it happens with the help of the World Wide Web. Individuals all over the world are connected by the information network. Nowadays, individuals, together with newly-emerged small and medium-sized enterprises (SMEs) are empowered to act globally and transnationally in a borderless world market, together with big global companies.

Since MNCs are facing a high-velocity market and a higher degree of complexities and uncertainties, they are firstly required to develop global competitiveness and worldwide learning through various forms of innovation, i.e. developing new products or services to adapt to customers' new needs, opening new markets, improving production processes, and designing new organizational forms. This makes critical and valuable knowledge resources as sources of competitive advantages. Therefore, global companies that are used to functioning in a market-seeking and labor force-seeking manner are now turning to knowledge-seeking with the purpose of enhancing their innovation capabilities and competitive stances. At the same time, due to the increasing risks and technological complexities related to innovation, especially R&D activities, companies usually discover that the needed knowledge resources often exceed national boundary. As a result, besides internationalization of production, we see an international expansion in R&D activities since the 1990s (Boutellier, Gassmann, & Von Zedtwitz, 2008; de Meyer & Mizushima, 1989; Zander, 1999).

Drivers of Internationalization of R&D

According to (Granstrand, Håkanson, & Sjölander, 1993), MNCs that centralize their R&D activities in home countries mainly have five reasons: 1. protecting firm-specific technology resources; 2. keeping strength in home market; 3. keeping economies of scale in R&D; 4. minimizing coordination cost of R&D activities; and 5. simply locating R&D activities on existing company premises. However, it is obvious in the past two decades that the trend of internationalization of R&D counterbalanced the above concerns for centralization of R&D.

Motivation, drivers and forces for internationalization and decentralization of R&D are well-established research areas, and there exist different categorizations. Table 1 summarizes some influential literatures discussing drivers of internationalization of R&D. According to Granstand et al. (1993), there are demand-oriented and supply-oriented forces for decentralization. Demand-oriented forces induce MNCs to locate their R&D activities to better support host countries' markets; while supply-oriented factors refer to those R&D related advantages that the host countries provide, such as accessing technical engineers, research institutions and lower costs. (Chiesa, 1996) further develops five sets of factors to explain the choice of R&D location, which were R&D related factors, input factor costs, transfer costs, organizational costs, and input resource quality. Gassmann and von Zedtwitz (1998) summarized five categories of drivers of R&D internationalization, which were input-oriented, output oriented, external, efficiency-oriented and political/ social-cultural factors. Based on different drivers and differentiating research and development activities, they further propose four archetypes of international R&D dispersion: national treasure, market-driven, technology driven, and global R&D (von Zedtwitz & Gassmann, 2002). Gassmann and Han (2004) summarize the motivations of internationalization of R&D into three categories: input-oriented motivations such as tapping into knowledge resources; performance-oriented motivations such as local market-specific development; and business-ecological motivations such as beneficial governmental policies and peer pressure.

Table 1: Drivers of internationalization of R&D: some main researches

Author & Year	Drivers and motivations of R&D Internationalization
Granstand, Håkanson, & Sjölander (1993)	• Demand-oriented forces E.g. To better support local markets or customers • Supply-oriented forces E.g. Assessing skilled technical labor forces, and research institutions
Chiesa (1996)	• Technology supply factors E.g. Accessing qualified technological personnel and technological centers of excellence • Demand factors E.g. Proximity to customers • Political factors E.g. Interacting with host country government • Enhancing image on international markets
Gassmann & von Zedtwitz (1998) **Table 1 continued**	• Input oriented E.g. Local infrastructure; insufficient home personnel; tapping into local networks • Output oriented E.g. Market and customer proximity • External E.g. Tax optimization, peer pressure • Efficiency-oriented E.g. Lower R&D personnel cost, utilizing different time zones • Political/social-cultural E.g. Patenting laws, governmental subsidies
von Zedwitz & Gassmann (2002)	• National treasure R&D: domestic research and development • Technology-driven R&D: dispersed research and

Table 1 continues		
		domestic development
	•	Market-driven R&D: dispersed development and domestic research
	•	Global R&D: dispersed research and development
Gassmann & Han (2004)	•	Input-oriented motivations E.g. Tapping into skilled personnel, networks and knowledge sources.
	•	Performance-oriented motivations E.g. Cost advantages; adaptation to local market and customer needs
	•	Business-ecological motivations E.g. Government policies; peer pressure

Sources: *based on Granstand, Håkanson, & Sjölander (1993); Chiesa (1996); Gassmann & von Zedtwitz (1998); von Zedwitz & Gassmann (2002); Gassmann & Han (2004)*

As shown in the above listed literature, we can summarize that the two major drivers of R&D internationalization are technology-related and market-related factors. Technology-related factors include access to technical resources such as skilled engineers and R&D resources in host countries; while market-related factors are related to local market adaptation, local production process improvement, proximity to customers, and enjoying preferential government policies.

The strategic role of global R&D subsidiaries

Driven by different motives, MNC's R&D subsidiaries and sites are now globally dispersed undertaking different roles and strategies. Subsidiaries' role and subsidiaries' strategies are always used interchangeably in the literature, yet as indicated by Birkinshaw and Morrision (1995), the two concepts have different focuses. R&D subsidiary strategy is part of subsidiary management, and assumes that the subsidiary has the autonomy to define and decide its own destiny; while roles of R&D subsidiaries or sites suggest a "designed" or "imposed" function by the MNC headquarter that the subsidiary is supposed to fulfill

(Birkinshaw & Morrison, 1995). TNC's R&D subsidiaries have the possibility of accessing resources from two distinct knowledge contexts: firstly, they enjoy the knowledge transferred from the TNC's internal networks; and secondly, they can utilize knowledge resources from local host countries (Papanastassiou & Pearce, 2009; Phene & Almeida, 2008). In this section, some influential typologies of R&D subsidiaries' roles will be discussed. These typologies are based on different functions and autonomy levels of R&D sites, and different relationships between global R&D sites and headquarter.

Two fundamental types of R&D sites are *home-base-augmenting site* and *home-base-exploiting site* (Kuemmerle, 1997; Kuemmerle, 1999). Accroding to Kuemmerle (1997, 1999), the major task of home-base-augmenting site is to explore and utilize global knowledge resources from host countries, which means that information mainly flows from foreign R&D site to the R&D headquarter. Home-base-exploiting site is established to facilitate host country production, adapt to local market needs, and to commercialize R&D result from home country to global markets. Therefore information mainly flows from R&D headquarter to local sites.

Birkinshaw and Morrison (1995) reviewed influential categorizations of subsidiaries' roles, and proposed a synthesized typology consisting three types: local implementer, specialized contributor, and world mandate. Among the three types, foreign subsidiaries' geographical scope enlarges from single country or single market to worldwide responsibility. In line with that, Nobel and Birkinshaw (1998) proposed a typology for global R&D sites, and suggested that R&D sites may act as local adaptor, international adaptor, and global/international creator (Nobel & Birkinshaw, 1998). *Local adaptor* is mainly a supportive R&D unit that is local in scope and limited in development mandate. The essential task of a local adaptor is to ease the technology transfers from R&D headquarter to local production site, and to facilitate local production site to utilize technology from the headquarters in a more efficient and effective way (Nobel & Birkinshaw, 1998; Ronstadt, 1977). *International adaptor* has broader scope in terms of responsibilities and geographical focuses. Rather than just facilitating local production site, an international adaptor has international scope, and may act as an innovator that develops improved products for foreign markets. Therefore, an international adaptor is strategically more important than a local adaptor, and thus owns more resources and decision making rights. Generally speaking, a local adaptor and an international adaptor are in line with what Kuemmerle (1995, 1997) conceptualized as "home-base-exploiting site". *Global creator* has global R&D responsibilities, rather than adaptation and improvement. Global creator sites are interdependent with other global R&D sites within a MNC, and are not necessarily linked with local production sites. The global creator concept is what Kuemmerle (1995, 1997) named as home-base augmenting site.

Rather than treating R&D activities as an integrated function, Medcof (1997) differentiated three types of technical work: research, development and technical support. Based on three dimensions, type of technical work (research, development, or support); functional works (marketing, manufacturing, marketing and manufacturing combined); and geographic area of collaboration (local, international), eight types of R&D sites are proposed (Medcof, 1997). The eight types are: local research, local development, local marketing support, local manufacturing support, international research, international development, international marketing support, and international manufacturing support.

It is worth noting that the strategic role of an R&D site is evolving rather than static, and it is highly possible that an R&D subsidiary has hybrid function, e.g. being both a local adaptor while having global R&D mandate. Besides, researches have shown that R&D subsidiaries are evolving from local support laboratory to international interdependent R&D subsidiary (Dicken, 2011; P. Reddy, 2011; Von Zedtwitz, 2004). The emergence of R&D sites with global responsibilities and the increasing interdependencies between them are thus making MNC's organization evolving from functional form to global matrix and network organization (Bartlett, 1986; Boutellier et al., 2008; Gassmann & Von Zedtwitz, 1999; C. C. Snow, Miles, & Coleman, 1992).

The Myth of "Network Organization" for Innovation

Transnational strategy and the rise of network organization for innovation

In the previous section, the globalization and internationalization of R&D are discussed. Along with the globalization and the R&D internationalization trend, the competitive landscape and global business environment are being reshaped. This brings about new challenges and requirements for companies in terms of both strategic and organizational changes. In order to keep a competitive position nowadays, a "transitional solution" emerges to be the strategic choice, and more and more companies evolve into TNCs and emerge to become main actors in global business (Bartlett & Ghoshal, 2002).

From Table 2, we can see that international, global, multinational and transnational corporations have different organizational characteristics in terms of the configuration of assets and capabilities, roles of overseas operations, and development and diffusion of knowledge (Bartlett and Ghoshal, 2002). Transnational organizations (TNC) evolve from their predecessors, i.e. the international, multinational, and global organizations, but have many different features. Ostensibly, transnational corporations (TNCs) are located within different national contexts and knowledge networks. One key task of TNCs' subsidiaries is to both exploit and explore knowledge resources from host countries. Within a TNC, each R&D subsidiary may have its own competitive advantages and specialties compared with other R&D sites. These R&D subsidiaries are interdependent on each other in terms of competencies and knowledge resources, and usually have global R&D responsibilities.

Table 2: Multinational, global and international companies.

Organizational Characteristics	International	Multinational	Global	Transnational
Configuration of assets and capabilities	Sources of core competencies centralized, others decentralized	Decentralized and nationally sufficient	Centralized and globally scaled	Dispersed interdependent, and specialized
Role of overseas operations	Adapting and leveraging partner company competencies	Sensing and exploiting local opportunities	Implementing parent company strategies	Differentiated contributions by national units to integrate worldwide operations
Development and diffusion of knowledge	Knowledge developed at the center and transferred to overseas units	Knowledge developed and retained within each unit	Knowledge developed and retained at the center	Knowledge developed jointly and shared worldwide.

Source: *Bartlett & Ghoshal, 2002, pp: 75*

As strategies evolve from international, global, and multinational to transnational, companies need to adjust their internal organizational design to a more flexible and efficient one that enhances learning, knowledge sharing and adaptability to an external complex environment (Child & McGrath, 2001; Feneuille, 1990). Therefore, companies' organizational structures respectively evolve from a functional and divisional structure, to a matrix structure and network model (Bartlett & Ghoshal, 2002; Dicken, 2011). A global network model is becoming the common choice of TNCs (Bartlett & Ghoshal, 2002), and no wonder we see the traditional mode of vertical integration is being substituted by vertical disaggregation and different forms of networks among globally distributed business units.

After studying 33 MNCs' global R&D organizations, Gassmann and von Zedtwitz (1999) identified five evolutionary types of R&D according to the dispersion of R&D activities and the degree of cooperation between individual R&D units (See Table 3). R&D is now being transformed into a polycentric R&D with multiple R&D centers or hubs, and is further evolved into an integrated network of R&D model with a more flexible coordination (Gassmann & Von Zedtwitz, 1999). The main features of an integrated network R&D organization are: highly globalized R&D activities; global mandate of R&D centers with different competencies; interdependencies and synergy between R&D subsidiaries; complex information flows (Gassmann & Von Zedtwitz, 1999). Similarly, based on strength of interconnections between central and periphery R&D sites, Medcof (2003) proposes a "structural cells model" towards globally dispersed R&D units. There are star, cluster, satellite and network cells (See Table 4).

Table 3: International R&D organization.

Type of R&D Organization	Organizational Structure	Behavioral Orientation
Ethnocentric centralized R&D	Centralized R&D	National inward orientation
Geocentric centralized R&D	Centralized R&D	International Cooperation
Polycentric decentralized R&D	Highly dispersed R&D, weak center	Competition among independent R&D units
R&D hub model	Dispersed R&D strong center	Supportive role of foreign R&D units
Integrated R&D network	Highly dispersed R&D, several competence centers	Synergetic integration of international R&D units

Source: *Gassmann & von Zedtwitz, 1999, pp: 235.*

Table 4: Structural cells.

Structural cells	Features
Star	Strong centre/periphery interconnections; Weak periphery/periphery interconnections
Cluster	Weak centre/periphery interconnections; Weak periphery/periphery interconnections
Satellite	Weak centre/periphery interconnections; Strong periphery/periphery interconnections
Network	Strong centre/periphery interconnections; Strong periphery/periphery interconnections

Source: *Medcof, 2003.*

As we can see from the above discussions, "global network model" (Bartlett & Ghoshal, 2002), "integrated R&D network" (Gassmann and von Zedtwits, 1999), and "network cells" (Medcof, 2003) are in line with each other.

More than reshaping companies' internal organizations, globalization is a strong force that helps to introduce collaboration among various types of organizations, since it opens a door for TNCs to identify and seek resources, in particular knowledge resources for innovation on a global scale (Rycroft & Kash, 2004; Zander, 2002). Due to increasing uncertainties, costs and risks of the innovation or R&D related tasks, it is almost impossible for a firm to do everything by itself. Furthermore, since critical and specialized knowledge resources required for innovation may not lie within the boundaries of a particular firm, firms need to utilize external knowledge resources by cooperating with external partners. Close relationships with other companies or organizations are potentially useful external R&D resources which can be used in various ways to achieve internal innovation purposes (Freeman, 1991; Håkansson & Laage-Hellman, 1984). Based on this logic, the transnational solution is no longer the privilege of big companies. Small and medium-sized companies can also be transnational through establishing innovation networks with global partners.

In general, the collaborative relationships among firms or other institutions, and TNC's globally distributed R&D sites aiming at innovation can be referred to as innovation networks or network organization for innovation. To some extent, innovation networks are co-evolving with the globalization trend (Rycroft & Kash, 2004). Transnational technological partnerships and other forms of innovation networks bring more globalized markets and institutions into being; while on the other hand, the globalization trend encourages more collaborative innovation due to increasing uncertainties and dispersal of valuable knowledge resources. In the next section, the relationships between the concept of network organization and innovation theories will be briefly reviewed.

The theoretical underpinning of network organization for innovation

In summary, this section has shown that the network organization theory draws on many different theories, and thus different authors with different theoretical backgrounds have put different perspectives into the concept of network organization. Thus, to some extent, the theory of network organization is an interdisciplinary theory.

Transactions cost theory and coordination cost

Firstly let us consider the concept of network organization as derived from the economic views, i.e. transaction cost theory (Coase, 1937; Williamson, 1991) and coordination cost concept (Jones & Hill, 1988; Rawley, 2010). Initially, transaction cost theory successfully explained that organizations emerged to reduce transaction costs, and this in turn supported the trend of vertical integration from the 1930s to 1970s. From the 1980s, a "turbulent time" came and many U.S. companies were forced to rethink their competitiveness and their existing inflexible organization structures. As a result, Williamson (1991) advances transaction cost theory by proposing "hybrid forms" as a middle form between market and hierarchy, which requires medium level transnational costs. As a result, transaction cost theory is still powerful to explain short-term network organization, but when it comes to long-term, the basic assumptions, i.e. bounded rationality and opportunism, is challenged. As complement to transaction cost, "coordination cost" is used to cope with the interdependencies of organizations, i.e. pooled, sequential, reciprocal, and team interdependencies (Van de Ven, Delbecq, & Koenig, 1976). The more uncertainty and complexity in an innovation project, and the richer the information links between value activities, the more powerful coordination mechanisms are needed, and thus, the higher the coordination cost.

Social capital

From the sociological view, one essential theory to understand network organization is social capital. People may discover that some do better than others and the explanation according to human capital is that those who do better are more intelligent, more attractive, more articulate and more skilled. Yet, another explanation is that they are better connected than others. This is the basic proposition of social capital. This capital is embedded within networks of mutual acquaintance and recognition and can be defined as "the sum of the actual and potential resources embedded within, available through, and derived from the network of relationships possessed by an individual or social unit" (Nahapiet & Ghoshal, 1998). Structural, relational, and cognitive are three dimensions of social capital. Firstly, the location of an actor in a social structure of interactions provides advantages for the actor. Structural holes are the source of value added, and actors across structural holes will generate predominant advantages (Burt, 2000). Secondly, the relational dimension indicates that trust and trustworthiness are rooted in relationships. Thus, actors that are regarded as trustworthy are more likely to gain others' support. The third aspect is a cognitive dimension which refers to the shared paradigm that facilitates collective goals and legitimate behaviors. In conclusion, the emergence of network organizations facilitate the generation of social capital, and social capital requires a network organization to embed itself in.

Organizational theories

Organizational theories such as the resource-based view (RBV), knowledge-based view (KBV), resource dependency theory (RDT), institutional theory and theories on capabilities such as dynamic capabilities and orchestration capabilities are related to network organization.

The institutional theory focuses on the deeper aspects of social structure and provides a powerful explanation for both individual and organizational action (Dacin, Goodstein, & Scott, 2002; Scott & Davis, 2007). The basic idea of institutional theory is that organizations are shaped by political and legal frameworks, the rules governing market behavior and general belief systems. Here, institutions are "composed of cultural-cognitive, normative, and regulative elements that, together with associated activities and resources, provide stability and meaning to social life" (Scott and Davis, 2007, pp: 258). Institutions can be seen as regulative systems that are comprised of rules, laws and sanctions. Institutions can be normative systems providing a moral framework for the conduct of social life, and institutions can be seen as culture-cognitive systems that emphasize shared beliefs and logics of action. Moreover, many culture theories, such as Hofstede's and Trompenaar's national culture theories, as well as Louis' and Schein's corporate culture theories, can be considered as supporting theories of the culture-cognitive dimension of institutional theory. In terms of global R&D, a subsidiary of a

TNC may construct a local innovation network with the host country's partners, not only due to low cost, but perhaps also due to the host country's policy requirements, business systems, peer pressure, as well as culture and beliefs. Furthermore, the features of an innovation network, such as content, size, density, and hierarchy of a network, is influenced by the institutional environment. More importantly, national innovation systems (Lundvall, 2010) and Triple Helix (Etzkowitz and Leydesdorff, 2002) of host countries can be seen as part of the institutional environment, or even as we mentioned in previous sections, as the context of innovation networks.

Organizational and strategic management scholars are moving from firms' internal organizational design and management to an interorganizational level of analysis. One of the main arguments is that innovation tends to be limited in mechanistic forms of organization where high levels of hierarchical control, clearly defined roles and tasks, and centralized decision-making impede flexibility and creativity (Hatch & Cunliffe, 2006). Thus organizations respond to the high-velocity global business environment and rapid technological development by evolving from centrally-coordinated hierarchies into network organizations that are characterized by flexibility, flatness, dynamism, and vertical-disaggregation (Biemans, 1996; Miles & Snow, 1992). Network organization can be regarded as an example of organizational innovation, which not only refers to the minimization of firms' internal layers of hierarchies, but also suggests various newly-emerging quasi-organizations that consist of multiple organizations, such as outsourcing, strategic alliances, strategic technological partnerships, global value chains, virtual organization, etc. (Child, Faulkner, & Tallman, 2005a; Gereffi, Humphrey, & Sturgeon, 2005; Scott & Davis, 2007; Sydow & Windeler, 1998a).

In line with the organizational scholars that move from an intraorganizational to an interorganizational level of research, strategic management scholars also suggest that a firm's sustained competitive advantages not only comes from valuable, rare, inimitable and nonsubstitutable resources that an individual firm holds (Barney, 1991), but also from idiosyncratic long-term oriented strategic alliances and relational rents that are generated jointly with partners (Dyer & Singh, 1998; Lavie, 2006). In order to successfully establish innovation networks and maintain them, firms are required to cultivate some network-related capabilities, such as relational capabilities (Capaldo, 2007), orchestration capabilities (Dhanarag & Parkhe, 2006; Ritala, Armila, & Blomqvist, 2009), and partner-specific absorptive capacities (Dyer & Singh, 1998).

International business and marketing

Since the 1970s, the IMP (industrial marketing and purchasing) scholars have been trying to search for a new approach of business research, i.e. the interaction approach which takes the relationship as its unit of analysis rather than the individual transaction. Within an interaction approach, it is not what happens within companies but what happens between them that constitutes the nature of business (Håkansson et al., 2009). Furthermore, it is through interaction that the benefits of these resources and activities flow between and into the companies in the network. More recently, they have begun to move from dyadic relationships to business networks, to n Activity-Resource-Actor (ARA) model, which indicates that the outcomes of the interaction process can be described in terms of three layers of networks between counterparts: activity links, resource ties and actor bonds. Managing international business then is a matter of establishing, developing and maintaining a firm's positions in international business networks (Johanson & Vahlne, 2003).

Innovation theories

Schumpeter's definition of innovation covers five aspects: 1. introduction of a new good or an improved quality of product; 2. the introduction of a new way of producing; 3. opening new markets; 4. finding new supply resources; 5. designing a new industry organization (Schumpeter, 1934). These five aspects of innovation can be summarized as: product innovation, process innovation, market innovation, input innovation and organizational innovation (Drejer, 2004). Similarly, (OECD, 2005) defines innovation as "the implementation of a new or significantly improved product (good or service), or process, a new marketing method, or a new organizational method in business practices, workplace organization or external relations". Though most research is focusing on product and process innovation, we should not ignore other forms of innovation such as organizational innovation through developing network relations with external partners. It is also worth noting that innovation is different from invention which is "the first occurrence of an idea for a new product or process" (Fagerberg, Mowery, & Nelson, 2006). Innovation must be something that has already come into reality and brings about changes. Thus, the process of innovation can be regarded as the commercial application of new or existing knowledge (Love & Roper, 2001), while a new idea is not an innovation or is just the early stage of an innovation.

Apart from the definition, scholars have noted a set of ongoing transitions in the innovation paradigm and concepts since the 1980s: from information to knowledge, from training and development to learning, from national to transnational, from technology push to market pull, from linear to evolutionary (Doz, 1996), from competitive to collaborative or "coopetition" (Bengtsson & Kock, 2000), from single innovative hero to "networks of innovators" (Freeman, 1991), from core competence to relational competitiveness (Dyer & Singh, 1998), and corresponding organizational change from vertical integration and hierarchy to network organizations (Miles & Snow, 1992; Rothwell, 1994).

Imai and Baba (1989) define a network organization as a basic institutional arrangement to cope with systemic innovation, and there has been a substantial amount of research showing the positive relationships between network organization and firms' innovation performances (Hagedoorn, 2002; Nieto & Rodríguez, 2011; Powell, Koput, & Smith-Doerr, 1996). The two key elements of a network are nodes (or actors) and ties (or relationships). Networks and network organizations comprehend the following concepts, as taken from the existing literature: inter-firm or multi-firm alliances or communities, strategic alliances or partnerships, strategy networks (Jarillo, 1988), interorganizational networks, dynamic networks (Miles & Snow, 1992), value networks, joint ventures, consortia, clusters, etc. However, it is hard to track the theoretical origins of the concepts of innovation networks and network organization, since they are inter-disciplinary concepts that appear in different theoretical domains, i.e. innovation theories, economic theories, organizational theories, sociology, marketing and international business theories.

Innovation theories such as national systems of innovation, triple helix, open innovation, user innovation, and innovation diffusion are all taking "networks" into account. In the national systems of innovation theory (NIS), interactive learning is a key assumption (Lundvall, 2010, pp: 1). Inter-firm interaction and industrial networks are descriptions of sub-systems of national innovation systems (Gelsing, 2010). The triple helix theory in essence is the network that comprises university, industry and government (Etzkowitz, 2002), and the synergetic effects from such network is the key stimulator of innovation. Open innovation suggests that firms utilize external knowledge resources to facilitate innovation, and different networks are shaping open innovation, i.e. in an interorganizational context, knowledge networks, value networks, etc. (Chesbrough, 2003; Chesbrough, Vanhaverbeke, & West, 2006). User innovation theory emphasizes the bottom-up innovation potential of users and declares the coming of democratized innovation (Von Hippel, 2005). Innovation diffusion theory suggests that innovation is communicated and diffused by different social networks and channels (Rogers, 1995).

What is a network organization: a debate

As shown in the previous discussions, network organization is a concept that exists in different theoretical disciplines. Yet, the definition of network organization is still ambiguous and even debatable.

First of all, the emerging "network" concept triggered discussions on the differences between networks and traditional market and hierarchies. Though some economists regard a network as an intermediate form that lies between market and hierarchy (Imai & Baba, 1989; Thorelli, 1986; Williamson, 1991), more and more scholars are regarding network as a distinct organizational form and organizing mechanism with its own rationales (Powell & Grodal, 2005; Powell, 1990). Moreover, some scholars are trying to break firms' existing boundaries and integrating firms' intraorganizational networks and networks with external partners. International business environments and global markets are then regarded as network organizations and context that firms are embedded in (Achrol, 1997; Ford & Håkansson, 2006; Johanson & Vahlne, 2003). Under such a network perspective/paradigm, a TNC's intraorganizational networks of globally distributed business units are seen as "interorganizational networks" (Ghoshal & Bartlett, 1990), and this network is embedded in a global business and market with massive networks of knowledge flows, physical resources and interfirm relationships. As a result, we can say that TNCs are "networks within networks" (Dicken, 2011).

When it comes to companies' internal organizational design, some scholars regard network organization as a new organizational form compared with traditional functional form or divisional form. In order to be an innovator or a prospector in the corresponding industry, a firm's organizations are evolving from hierarchy or matrix organization to network organization (Child et al., 2005; Child, 2005; Miles & Snow, 1992; Podolny & Page, 1998; Powell, Koput, & Smith-Doerr, 1996). In particular, TNCs that expand their technological capabilities globally and face fast-changing market environments in different countries can barely maintain a hierarchical and centrally-coordinated organization. Thus, an "integrated network model" is being increasingly adopted by TNCs (Bartlett, 1986; Bartlett & Ghoshal, 2002).

Yet, even among the scholars regarding network organization as a new design to cope with global innovation strategy, there are different understandings on what is a network organization. Some scholars regard that a key feature of a network organization is adopting market mechanism in order to substitute hierarchical structures (Baker, 1993; Miles & Snow, 1992)while some others suggest that the key characteristics of a network organization should be the interdependency, trustful relationships and collaboration between globally dispersed business units (Boutellier et al., 2008; Child, 2005; Child, Faulkner, & Tallman, 2005b).

Moreover, some scholars think that organizations naturally consist of different networks such as hierarchical networks and employee networks. Thus from their point of view, the so-called "network organization" is nothing new other than "bureaucracy-lite" (Hales, 2002), since hierarchy continues to "perform a number of seemingly indispensable functions" (Child, 2005, pp: 59). Moreover, some scholars think that an organization by nature consists of social networks and economic networks, therefore a hierarchical organization is a "hierarchical network form" (Borgatti & Foster, 2003; Burt, 2000).

118

Besides the debate over an organization or a firm's boundary, more and more scholars tend to regard interorganizational networks or interfirm networks as network organizations since different organizations share a common goal and even the same coordination system that is accepted by all members, which is in line with some basic principles of an organization. In line with this, strategic alliances, technological partnerships, value networks, joint ventures are various forms of network organizations. In addition, some scholars view the market as networks or network organization, for example, an industrial market can be seen as an interfirm (N. M. Reddy & Rao, 1990), and an industrial market is constructed by networks of actors, resources and activities (Håkansson, et al., 2009). Here, network organization is more a perspective or paradigm of the business world (Achrol, 1997; Borgatti & Foster, 2003), rather than just a specific structure or organizational form. Under such a network perspective, an organization is a social entity consisting of various forms of networks rather than a production or economic function (Podolny & Page, 1998; Podolny, 2001).

Therefore, it's no wonder that "the studies of network organizations have generated diverse, varied, inconsistent and contradictory findings" (Borgatti & Foster, 2003; Powell et al., 1996; Sydow & Windeler, 1998b). Different definitions of network organization make us feel confused and we cannot help but wonder: "what is a network organization?" As a result, in the next section, I will propose a three-level framework to clarify the understanding of network organization for innovation.

A Three-level Framework
A framework

Based on the above discussions, a three-level framework for understanding network organization for innovation is then proposed (See Figur 1).

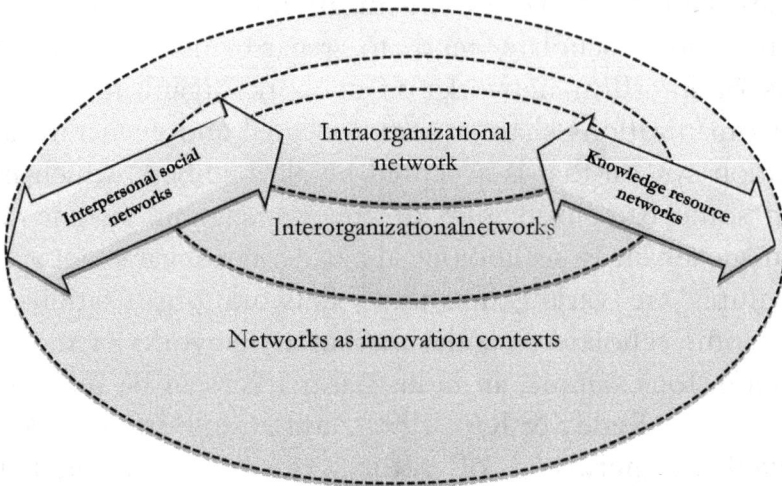

Figure 1: A framework showing different levels of network organizations.

The "three-layer onion" classifies different levels of network organizations according to the boundary of the organization and their scope. Intraorganizational network organization refers mainly to a firm or an organization's internal organizational design and networks between business units. Meanwhile, interorganizational networks refer to alliance or partnerships between different firms sharing the same innovation objective. However, it may not be true to say that interorganizational networks are "bigger" than intraorganizational network organizations in terms of number of actors, ties, or depth of collaboration as shown in the figure. For example, in the case of a transnational corporation that has hundreds of business units scattered across different countries, its intraorganizational network is obviously "bigger" than a technological partnership between one of its business units and an external partner.

As a result, Table 1 is an analytical abstract rather than a replication of the real business world. A network of actors as the context for innovation is a macro network perspective moving us towards a wider understanding of network organizations. Moreover, as we can see from the dotted lines, the boundaries between different layers are open rather than closed, indicating the intensive interactions between individuals, knowledge and informational flows, activities, and organizations.

Individual knowledge/information and human resources are basic constructs of innovation networks, so interpersonal social networks and networks of knowledge resources penetrate different layers of networks. Researches have shown that the connectedness and strength of virtual idea networks are positively related to the quality of the innovation ideas created(Björk & Magnusson, 2009); and the strength and connectedness of idea networks will influence the success of radical innovation process (Hage & Hollingsworth, 2000).

Many research studies have examined how social networks influence idea generation and innovation performances and how they evolve over time (Obstfeld, 2005). In particular, within a TNC, employees' social networks exist both within and outside of the firm's boundary and will influence the knowledge generation as well as innovation performance. (Rodan & Galunic, 2004) use a sample of 106 middle managers in a European telecommunications company and find that their interpersonal social networks as well as access to heterogeneous knowledge are critical for their individual managerial and innovation performance. Fichter (2009) defines an innovation community as an informal network of individuals, often from more than one organization and team, participating in a project aimed at promoting a specific innovation on one level or across several levels of an innovation system. The close and informal cooperation across organizational and functional boundaries between innovation promoters plays a key role in open innovation (Fichter, 2009). This research also confirms that interpersonal networks link different levels of networks together.

Intraorganizational networks

Generally speaking, there are two different perspectives as to what constitutes the internal network organization.

First of all, regarding TNCs as an organization with networks of business units, assets, and knowledge resources has become the mainstream perspective with regard to multinationals or transnationals (Cantwell & Janne, 1999). This can actually be regarded as a "network perspective" that tends to conceptualize organizations as networks of actors, resources and activities (Borgatti & Foster, 2003; Ghoshal & Bartlett, 1990; Håkansson, et al. 2009). Thus, a traditional organization with hierarchical layers can also be conceptualized as hierarchical networks of business units and knowledge flows.

From such a network perspective, a TNC aiming to implement innovation strategy can be seen as a network of specialized interdependent business units with the capacity to assimilate, generate and integrate knowledge on a global scale (Collinson & Wang, 2012; Frost & Zhou, 2005). Within such a network of knowledge flows, globally distributed subsidiaries can be knowledge receivers, disseminators, contributors and creators, thus making their roles more complex than ever (Asmussen, Pedersen, & Dhanaraj, 2007; Asmussen, Pedersen, & Dhanaraj, 2009). This actually requires a flattening of the traditional structure of layers and an increase in autonomy and interdependency of the subsidiaries, which is in line with the second view of intraorganizational network organization that will be discussed below.

Secondly, as opposed to a network perspective, some authors regard network organizations as a specific and new organizational design that evolves from a "centrally coordinated, multi-level hierarchy and matrix" (Miles & Snow, 1992), and incorporates itself into the transnational strategy (Bartlett & Ghoshal, 2002) and prospector's strategy (Miles & Snow, 1986). Such a network organization is less hierarchical and more loosely coupled, and power is distributed to different business units since no single unit can have all the knowledge, especially regarding innovation (Andersson, Forsgren, & Holm, 2007). Due to specialization of resources and different competences, business units are interdependent with each other and empowered to have a higher degree of autonomy.

The main features of a network organization show the change from in-house to outsourcing, from administrative to market mechanism-based, from passive to proactive, and from static to evolutionary. The conceptualization of how TNC's internal R&D organization evolves from centralized R&D headquarters, to a polycentric organization with multiple hubs, and then to an integrated network model (Gassmann & von Zedtwitz, 1999; Medcof, 2004).

Besides, many scholars point out that a network organization should adopt market mechanism to facilitate resource allocation and decision making among business units or subsidiaries (Boutellier et al., 2008; Foss, 2003; Miles & Snow, 1986). Foss (2003) shows how a firm radically changes its internal organization into a spaghetti organization, i.e. "an internal hybrid", by infusing market mechanism into hierarchies, and then changes back into a matrix organization due to problems such as lack of incentives, which also shows that it is very difficult to put such an organization into practice and sustain it unless potential problems can be solved.

Miles and Snow (1992) suggest that there are three types of network organizations: stable network, internal network and dynamic network. A stable network organization has a core firm that links upstream and downstream to a limited number of selected partners; an internal network form adopts market mechanism (buying and selling) between its business units; and a dynamic network form consists of multiple actors such as designers, suppliers, producers and distributors instead of one firm holding all functions and assets internally. Moreover, they propose that stable, internal and dynamic network organizations evolve respectively from functional organization, divisional organization and matrix organization. As a result, though network organization can be regarded as a specific organizational form, it may also include external partners and not be restricted within a firms' boundary. Thus, we can move the discussion outside of the boundary and to the interorganizational network level.

Interorganizational network organization

When we move out of a firm's legal boundary, network organization can be understood on a second level, i.e. interorganizational networks. Similar to intraorganizational network organization, there are also two perspectives on interorganizational network organizational for innovation.

The first view focuses on a firm's ego network organization, meaning that a network is a mode of organization that is purposefully designed and used by managers or entrepreneurs to implement their strategies and position their firms in a stronger competitive position within the industry (Jarillo, 1988). From this perspective a network organization is a set of selected preferable innovators, the relationships between different partners are trustful, interdependent and nonhierarchical (Freeman, 1991; Hatch & Cunliffe, 2006), and the networks can be either stable or dynamic (Miles and Snow, 1992). Therefore, purposefully designed strategic alliances or strategic networks, outsourcing, joint ventures, virtual corporation, and value chains are different forms of network organizations (Child et al., 2005a; Gereffi et al., 2005; Tidd & Bessant, 2009; Child et al., 2005; Gereffi, Hatch & Cunliffe, 2006; Humphrey, & Sturgeon, 2005; Tidd & Bessant, 2009). Hagedoorn (1990) gives a classification of six modes of inter-firm cooperation based on organizational interdependence, i.e. joint ventures, joint R&D agreements, technology exchange agreements such as cross-licensing, direct investment and cross-

124

holding, customer-supplier relations, and one-directional agreement such as licensing. Also, value chains can be seen as networks; there can be hierarchy, captive, relational and modular networks based on different levels of authority and specialization (Dicken, 2011; Gereffi et al., 2005). Snow et al. (2011) show how firms have moved from a single organization to a community-based organizational design consisting of multiple firms to implement the strategy of innovation through a single case study on "Blade.org". Such a multifirm network organization provides a clear institutional mechanism to support knowledge sharing and creation between member firms. Any member firm within this community can find willing partners to form temporary collaborative innovation networks (Snow, Fjeldstad, Lettl, &Miles, 2011). Thus, a firm can maintain its independent businesses while collaborating with other firms on R&D simultaneously.

On the other hand, when we move out of a firm's ego network organization, we may find that interorganizational network organizations also take the form of agglomerations of SMEs, regional clusters, incubators or science parks, and even inter-regional clusters. Through networking, SMEs can form agglomerations to integrate their capabilities and act efficiently to compete with competitors such as vertically integrated firms (Bianchi & Bellini, 1991). Sá & Lee, (2012) define a technology-based incubator as "an organization that provides services for new start-up and early-stage companies with a technological focus, and assists their survival and growth", and they show how an incubator encourages the formation of interorganizational networks and interplay between firms to facilitate their technological needs through a single case study on a Canadian technology-based incubator.

Besides incubators, regional clusters often consist of reciprocal ties between geographically co-located organizations such as firms, research institutes, intermediaries and governmental institutions, and the intensive knowledge interaction between organizations located in the cluster and the formation of collaborative research projects has significant impact on the innovation performance of the cluster and regional innovation systems (Whittington, Owen-Smith, & Powell, 2009). Baptista & Swann (1998) ask whether firms located in strong industrial clusters or regions are more likely to innovate than firms outside these regions, and their empirical research yielded a positive answer. Moreover, since interorganizational ties serve as channels of knowledge dissemination and interaction, geographically dispersed firms and clusters from different regions are actually connected and such an interregional network structure will facilitate innovation generation and diffusion at the system level (Gibbons, 2004), which leads us to the third level that will be discussed below.

Overlapping networks as innovation contexts

Until now, we have shown intra-and interorganizational network organizations, and one may question what there is outside of an interorganizational network organization. One answer could be "market", and from this perspective, outside of a network organization, there is a dangerous jungle full of competitors and all relationships are based on transaction. However, on the one hand, the role of network actors inside a network organization may change, i.e. one partner could have previously been a competitor; while on the other hand, different network organizations, though there may be boundaries and geographical disparities, are not unreachable to each other according to Milgram's "six degrees of separation" proposition.

Due to the existence of social networks and information networks, we are always able to reach another network by establishing some form of relationship. For example, an R&D unit can act as an intermediary between TNC's internal global R&D network and the local R&D network in host country, so the intra- and inter-organizational networks are overlapping, which is also in line with the thinking of a TNC as "a network within networks" (Dicken, 2011, pp: 121). Therefore, different network organizations, whether they be intra- or interorganizational, are linked to each other and overlapping. That is to say, compared to a neoclassical market consisting of independent suppliers and customers, these overlapping networks constructed by a web of relationships is the essence of the international business environment (Johanson & Vahlne, 2003; Johanson & Vahlne, 2009). No wonder Achrol (1997) proposes that the market can be divided into four types of networks: internal market network, vertical market network, inter-market network and opportunity network.

Based on the above discussions, we have moved to a new level of regarding overlapping networks as innovation contexts that firms embed themselves in, rather than a neoclassical market (Johanson and Vahlne, 2003, 2009). Thus, a regional cluster is connected with other clusters, and the interregional networks of clusters act as the context of an innovation system. These overlapping networks serve as an innovation environment or context that provides valuable innovation resources to be explored and utilized (Gulati, 1999), and in such a scenario, external firms are no longer enemies but potential partners. Managing a business then, is a matter of establishing, developing and maintaining the firm's position in international business networks (Forsgren & Johanson, 1992; Håkansson & Ford, 2002).

Network organization definition in broad and narrow senses

Regarding the examples shown above, some of them are "networks", and some are "network organizations", so when can we call a network an organization? Borgatti and Foster (2003) regard this as linguistic chaos, i.e. some scholars think all firms should transform from separated organizations to network organizations, while others think organizations are already combinations of network relationships. Within the literature on network organizations, there are also different perspectives: some think that all actors are interactively connected by cooperative and interdependent relationships and with a joint decision-making process can be seen as a network organization (Gassmann and von Zedtwitz, 1999; Jarillo, 1988; Malnight, 1996; Medcof, 2004); some regard a network organization as an organization with an internal market (e.g. Miles and Snow, 1986; Baker, 1993), while others may consider strategic alliances, virtual organizations, value chains, etc. as a network organization (Child, 2005; Gereffi, 2005; Hatch & Cunliffe, 2006).

A network can be simply defined as a combination of nodes and ties (Scott and Davis, 2007, p: 278). Nodes can be actors such as people, groups, organizations, or other entities such as ideas or resources. Ties can be physical linkages to contractual or personal relationships. An organization is a social structure created by individuals to support the collaborative pursuit of specified goals (Scott and Davis, 2007, pp: 11). It requires defining objectives, control and coordination by rules or incentives, resource allocation, selection of participants, etc. Thus, network organization is one type of "network" with the characteristics of an "organization", i.e. a social combination of actors and relationships with the aim of achieving certain goals and guided by certain rules. Podolny and Page (1998) define a network form of organization as "any collection of actors ($N \geq 2$) that pursue repeated enduring exchange relations with one another and, at the same time, lack a legitimate organizational authority to arbitrate and resolve disputes that may arise during the exchange." Network organization is an integration of strategy, structure and managerial process (Miles and Snow, 1992). It is incorporated into a prospector's strategy, adopts a loose and decentralized structure and discards hierarchical control by involving orchestration and coordination. Thus we can hardly call a social network between friends or a virtual knowledge network a network organization, though they can be integrated into different levels of networks (See Table 1).

As a result, we can summarize here that, in a broad sense, value chain, virtual organization, hollow network, and strategic alliances are all network organizations pursuing the goal of innovation. In a narrow sense, a network organization is one type of a firm's organizational design with characteristics such as flexibility, decentralized inclusive decision making, and cooperative ties. However, what about clusters, incubators and even interregional clusters that consist of interorganizational innovation networks? Are these networks network organizations? A few scholars classify market or clusters as organizations (Reddy & Rao, 1990). These networks aiming at promoting systematic innovation are parts of an innovation system and are coordinated by both the invisible hand of the market and the visible hand of governmental directions. Thus, they can be regarded as quasi-network organizations integrating both cooperation and competition between firms, relying much on self-organizing due to a lack of hub organizations and being much more complex than ever.

Conclusion

This chapter proposes that network organization for innovation can be understood on three levels, i.e. intraorganizational, interorganizational network organizations and networks as innovation contexts. In a narrow sense, a network organization refers to a new internal organizational design to promote innovation strategy through the following: encouraging more interaction between business units and knowledge sharing, introducing market mechanism to optimize internal resource allocation, and reducing hierarchies. In the broad sense, interorganizational innovation networks such as strategic technological partnerships, joint ventures, value networks and technological outsourcing and licensing can be seen as network organization as well. These interorganizational network organizations which are coordinated or jointly coordinated by hub organizations, rely on trustful relationships between partnering firms, encourage the pooling of knowledge resources, and ensure mutual benefits. Moreover, when we adopt a network perspective which is both a way of thinking and a research method that enables us to analyze organizations and business contexts by identifying nodes and ties, the market and the business environment can be conceptualized into networks that provide contexts for innovation. Thus, a national or regional innovation system and even the market itself can be seen as a quasi-network organization that relies heavily on self-organizing, culture, governmental policies, market mechanism, etc.

In conclusion, a network organization is an interdisciplinary concept and a popular research topic especially when regarding innovation. Hopefully, this chapter has clarified some chaos and ambiguities in this research area.

References

Achrol, R. S. (1997). Changes in the theory of interorganizational relations in marketing: Toward a network paradigm. *Academy of Marketing Science Journal, 25*(1), 56-71.

Andersson, U., Forsgren, M., & Holm, U. (2007). Balancing subsidiary influence in the federative MNC: A business network view. *Journal of International Business Studies, 38*(5), 802-818.

Asmussen, C. G., Pedersen, T., & Dhanaraj, C. (2007). Evolution of subsidiary competences: Extending the diamond network model. *Journal of International Business Studies,*

Asmussen, C. G., Pedersen, T., & Dhanaraj, C. (2009). Host-country environment and subsidiary competence: Extending the diamond network model. *Journal of International Business Studies, 40*(1), 42-57.

Baker, W. E. (1993). *The network organization in theory and practice.* Boston: Harvard Business School Press.

Baptista, R., & Swann, P. (1998). Do firms in clusters innovate more? *Research Policy, 27*(5), 525-540.

Barney, J. (1991). Firm resources and sustained competitive advantage. *Journal of Management, 17*(1), 99.

Bartlett, C. A. (1986). Building and managing the transnational: The new organizational challenge. *Competition in global industries* (pp. 367-401). Boston: Harvard Business School Press.

Bartlett, C. A., & Ghoshal, S. (2002). *Managing across borders: The transnational solution*. Boston, Massachusetts: Harvard Business Press.

Bengtsson, M., & Kock, S. (2000). " Coopetition" in business networks—to cooperate and compete simultaneously. *Industrial Marketing Management, 29*(5), 411-426.

Bianchi, P., & Bellini, N. (1991). Public policies for local networks of innovators. *Research Policy, 20*(5), 487-497.

Biemans, W. G. (1996). Organizational networks: Toward a cross-fertilization between practice and theory. *Journal of Business Research, 35*(1), 29-39.

Birkinshaw, J. M., & Morrison, A. J. (1995). Configurations of strategy and structure in subsidiaries of multinational corporations. *Journal of International Business Studies, 26*(4), 729-753.

Björk, J., & Magnusson, M. (2009). Where do good innovation ideas come from? exploring the influence of network connectivity on innovation idea quality. *Journal of Product Innovation Management, 26*(6), 662-670.

Borgatti, S. P., & Foster, P. C. (2003). The network paradigm in organizational research: A review and typology. *Journal of Management, 29*(6), 991-1013.

Boutellier, R., Gassmann, O., & Von Zedtwitz, M. (2008). *Managing global innovation: Uncovering the secrets of future competitiveness* Springer Verlag.

Burt, R. S. (2000). The network structure of social capital. *Research in Organizational Behavior, 22*, 345-423.

Cantwell, J., & Janne, O. (1999). Technological globalisation and innovative centres: The role of corporate technological leadership and locational hierarchy1. *Research Policy, 28*(2-3), 119-144.

Capaldo, A. (2007). Network structure and innovation: The leveraging of a dual network as a distinctive relational capability. *Strategic Management Journal, 28*(6), 585-608.

Chesbrough, H. W. (2003). *Open innovation: The new imperative for creating and profiting from technology* Harvard Business Press.

Chesbrough, H. W., Vanhaverbeke, W., & West, J. (2006). *Open innovation: Researching a new paradigm* Oxford University Press, USA.

Chiesa, V. (1996). Managing the internationalization of R&D activities. *Engineering Management, IEEE Transactions On, 43*(1), 7-23.

Child, J., Faulkner, D., & Tallman, S. (2005a). *Cooperative strategy: Managing alliances, networks, and joint ventures.* New York: Oxford University Press.

Child, J., & McGrath, R. G. (2001). Organizations unfettered: Organizational form in an information-intensive economy. *The Academy of Management Journal, 44*(6), 1135-1148.

Child, J. (2005). *Organization: Contemporary principles and practice* Blackwell Oxford.

Child, J., Faulkner, D., & Tallman, S. (2005b). *Strategies of cooperation: Managing alliances, networks, and joint ventures* Oxford University Press, USA.

Coase, R. H. (1937). The nature of the firm. *Economica, 4*(16), 386-405.

Collinson, S. C., & Wang, R. (2012). The evolution of innovation capability in multinational enterprise subsidiaries: Dual network embeddedness and the divergence of subsidiary specialisation in taiwan. *Research Policy, 41*, 1501-1518.

Dacin, M. T., Goodstein, J., & Scott, W. R. (2002). Institutional theory and institutional change: Introduction to the special research forum. *The Academy of Management Journal, 45*(1), 43-56.

de Meyer, A., & Mizushima, A. (1989). Global R&D management. *R&D Management, 19*(2), 135-146.

Dhanarag, C., & Parkhe, A. (2006). Orchestrating innovation networks. *Academy of Management Review, 31*(3), 659-669.

Dicken, P. (2011). *Global shift: Mapping the changing contours of the world economy.* London: Sage.

Doz, Y. L. (1996). The evolution of cooperation in strategic alliances: Initial conditions or learning processes? *Strategic Management Journal, 17*(S1), 55-83.

Drejer, I. (2004). Identifying innovation in surveys of services: A schumpeterian perspective. *Research Policy, 33*(3), 551-562.

Dyer, J. H., & Singh, H. (1998). The relational view: Cooperative strategy and sources of interorganizational competitive advantage. *The Academy of Management Review, 23*(4), 660-679.

Etzkowitz, H. (2002). Incubation of incubators: Innovation as a triple helix of university-industry-government networks. *Science and Public Policy, 29*(2), 115-128.

Fagerberg, J., Mowery, D. C., & Nelson, R. R. (Eds.). (2006). *The oxford handbook of innovation.* Oxford: Oxford university press.

Feneuille, S. (1990). A network organization to meet the challenges of complexity. *European Management Journal, 8*(3), 296-301.

Fichter, K. (2009). Innovation communities: The role of networks of promotors in open innovation. *R&D Management, 39*(4), 357-371.

Ford, D., & Håkansson, H. (2006). IMP–some things achieved: Much more to do. *European Journal of Marketing, 40*(3/4), 248-258.

Forsgren, M., & Johanson, J. (1992). *Managing networks in international business.* Amsterdam: Gordon and Breach.

Foss, N. J. (2003). Selective intervention and internal hybrids: Interpreting and learning from the rise and decline of the oticon spaghetti organization. *Organization Science, 14*(3), 331-349.

Freeman, C. (1991). Networks of innovators: A synthesis of research issues. *Research Policy, 20*(5), 499-514.

Freidman, T. (2006). *The world is flat.* London: Penguin.

Frost, T. S., & Zhou, C. (2005). R&D co-practice and 'reverse'knowledge integration in multinational firms. *Journal of International Business Studies, 36*(6), 676-687.

Gassmann, O., & Von Zedtwitz, M. (1999). New concepts and trends in international R&D organization. *Research Policy, 28*(2), 231-250.

Gereffi, G., Humphrey, J., & Sturgeon, T. (2005). The governance of global value chains. *Review of International Political Economy, 12*(1), 78-104.

Ghoshal, S., & Bartlett, C. A. (1990). The multinational corporation as an interorganizational network. *Academy of Management Review, 15*(4), 603-625.

Gibbons, D. E. (2004). Network structure and innovation ambiguity effects on diffusion in dynamic organizational fields. *Academy of Management Journal, 47*(6), 938-951.

Granstrand, O., Håkanson, L., & Sjölander, S. (1993). Internationalization of R&D—a survey of some recent research. *Research Policy, 22*(5), 413-430.

Hage, J., & Hollingsworth, J. R. (2000). A strategy for the analysis of idea innovation networks and institutions. *Organization Studies, 21*(5), 971-1004.

Hagedoorn, J. (2002). Inter-firm R&D partnerships: An overview of major trends and patterns since 1960. *Research Policy, 31*(4), 477-492.

Håkansson, H., & Ford, D. (2002). How should companies interact in business networks? *Journal of Business Research, 55*(2), 133-139.

Håkansson, H., Ford, D., Gadde, L. E., Snehota, I., & Waluszewski, A. (2009). *Business in networks.* West Sussex: Wiley.

Håkansson, H., & Laage-Hellman, J. (1984). Developing a network R&D strategy. *Journal of Product Innovation Management, 1*(4), 224-237.

Håkansson, H., & Snehota, I. (1989). No business is an island: The network concept of business strategy. *Scandinavian Journal of Management, 5*(3), 187-200.

Hales, C. (2002). 'Bureaucracy-lite'and continuities in managerial work. *British Journal of Management, 13*(1), 51-66.

Hatch, M. J., & Cunliffe, A. (2006). *Organization theory: Modern, symbolic & postmodern perspectives.* Oxford: Oxford University Press.

Imai, K., & Baba, Y. (1989). Systemic innovation and cross-border networks. *International Seminar on the Contributions of Science and Technology to Economic Growth at OECD, Paris,*

Jarillo, J. C. (1988). On strategic networks. *Strategic Management Journal, 9*(1), 31-41.

Johanson, J., & Vahlne, J. E. (2003). Business relationship learning and commitment in the internationalization process. *Journal of International Entrepreneurship, 1*(1), 83-101.

Johanson, J., & Vahlne, J. E. (2009). The uppsala internationalization process model revisited: From liability of foreignness to liability of outsidership. *Journal of International Business Studies, 40*(9), 1411-1431.

Jones, G. R., & Hill, C. W. L. (1988). Transaction cost analysis of strategy-structure choice. *Strategic Management Journal, 9*(2), 159-172.

Kuemmerle, W. (1997). Building effective R&D capabilities abroad. *Harvard Business Review, 75*, 61-72.

Kuemmerle, W. (1999). The drivers of foreign direct investment into research and development: An empirical investigation. *Journal of International Business Studies,* , 1-24.

Lavie, D. (2006). The competitive advantage of interconnected firms: An extension of resource-based view. *Academy of Management Review, 31*(3), 638-658.

Love, J. H., & Roper, S. (2001). Location and network effects on innovation success: Evidence for UK, german and irish manufacturing plants. *Research Policy, 30*(4), 643-661.

Medcof, J. W. (1997). A taxonomy of internationally dispersed technology units and its application to management issues. *R&D Management, 27*(4), 301-318.

Miles, R. E., & Snow, C. C. (1986). Organizations: New concepts for new forms. *California,*

Miles, R. E., & Snow, C. C. (1992). Causes of failure in network organizations. *California Management Review, 34*(4), 53-57.

Nahapiet, J., & Ghoshal, S. (1998). Social capital, intellectual capital, and the organizational advantage. *The Academy of Management Review, 23*(2), 242-266.

Nieto, M. J., & Rodríguez, A. (2011). Offshoring of R&D: Looking abroad to improve innovation performance. *Journal of International Business Studies, 42*(3), 345-361.

Nobel, R., & Birkinshaw, J. (1998). Innovation in multinational corporations: Control and communication patterns in international R&D operations. *Strategic Management Journal, 19*(5), 479-496.

Obstfeld, D. (2005). Social networks, the tertius iungens orientation, and involvement in innovation. *Administrative Science Quarterly, 50*(1), 100-130.

OECD. (2005). *Oslo manual: Guidelines for collecting and interpreting innovation data* OECD publishing.

Papaconstantinou, G. (1995). Globalisation, technology and employment: Characteristics and trends. *STI Review, 15*, 177.

Papanastassiou, M., & Pearce, R. (2009). *The strategic development of multinationals: Subsidiaries and innovation.* Hampshire: Palgrave Macmillan.

Phene, A., & Almeida, P. (2008). Innovation in multinational subsidiaries: The role of knowledge assimilation and subsidiary capabilities. *Journal of International Business Studies, 39*(5), 901-919.

Podolny, J. M. (2001). Networks as the pipes and prisms of the market. *American Journal of Sociology,* , 33-60.

Podolny, J. M., & Page, K. L. (1998). Network forms of organization. *Annual Review of Sociology, 24,* 57-76.

Powell, W. W., & Grodal, S. (2005). Networks of innovators. *The oxford handbook of innovation* (pp. 56-85). Oxford: Oxford University Press.

Powell, W. W., Koput, K. W., & Smith-Doerr, L. (1996). Interorganizational collaboration and the locus of innovation: Networks of learning in biotechnology. *Administrative Science Quarterly, 41*(1), 116-145.

Powell, W. W. (1990). Neither market nor hierarchy: Network forms of organization. *Research in Organizational Behavior, 12,* 295-336.

Rawley, E. (2010). Diversification, coordination costs, and organizational rigidity: Evidence from microdata. *Strategic Management Journal, 31*(8), 873-891.

Reddy, N. M., & Rao, M. V. (1990). The industrial market as an interfirm organization. *Journal of Management Studies, 27*(1), 43-59.

Reddy, P. (2011). *Global innovation in emerging economies* Taylor & Francis.

Ritala, P., Armila, L., & Blomqvist, K. (2009). Innovation orchestration capability—Defining the organizational and individual level determinants. *International Journal of Innovation Management, 13*(4), 569-591.

Rodan, S., & Galunic, C. (2004). More than network structure: How knowledge heterogeneity influences managerial performance and innovativeness. *Strategic Management Journal, 25*(6), 541-562.

Rogers, E. M. (1995). *Diffusion of innovations* Simon and Schuster.

Ronstadt, R. (1977). Research and development abroad by US multinationals.

Rothwell, R. (1994). Towards the fifth-generation innovation process. *International Marketing Review, 11*(1), 7-31.

Rycroft, R. W., & Kash, D. E. (2004). Self-organizing innovation networks: Implications for globalization. *Technovation, 24*(3), 187-197.

Sá, C., & Lee, H. (2012). Science, business, and innovation: Understanding networks in technology-based incubators. *R&D Management, 42*(3), 243-253.

Schumpeter, J. A. (1934). *The theory of economic development: An inquiry into profits, capital, credit, interest, and the business cycle.* Cambridge, MA.: Harvard University Press.

Scott, W. R., & Davis, G. F. (2007). *Organizations and organizing: Rational, natural, and open systems perspectives.* New Jersey: Pearson Prentice Hall.

Snow, C., Fjeldstad, Y., Lettl, C., & Miles, R. (2011). Organizing continuous product development and commercialization: The collaborative community of firms model. *The Journal of Product Innovation Management, 28*(1), 3.

Snow, C. C., Miles, R. E., & Coleman, H. J.,Jr. (1992). Managing 21st century network organizations. *Organizational Dynamics, 20*(3), 5.

Sydow, J., & Windeler, A. (1998a). Organizing and evaluating interfirm networks: A structurationist perspective on network processes and effectiveness. *Organization Science, 9*(3), 265-284.

Sydow, J., & Windeler, A. (1998b). Organizing and evaluating interfirm networks: A structurationist perspective on network processes and effectiveness. *Organization Science, 9*(3), 265-284.

Thorelli, H. B. (1986). Networks: Between markets and hierarchies. *Strategic Management Journal, 7*(1), 37-51.

Tidd, J., & Bessant, J. (2009). *Managing innovation: Integrating technological, market and organizational change.
* John Wiley &Sons Ltd.

Van de Ven, A. H., Delbecq, A. L., & Koenig, R. (1976). Determinants of coordination modes within organizations. *American Sociological Review, 41*(2), 322-338.

Von Hippel, E. (2005). *Democratizing innovation.* Cambridge, Massachussats: MIT Press.

Von Zedtwitz, M. (2004). Managing foreign R&D laboratories in china. *R&D Management, 34*(4), 439-452.

von Zedtwitz, M., & Gassmann, O. (2002). Market versus technology drive in R&D internationalization: Four different patterns of managing research and development. *Research Policy, 31*(4), 569-588.

Whittington, K. B., Owen-Smith, J., & Powell, W. W. (2009). Networks, propinquity, and innovation in knowledge-intensive industries. *Administrative Science Quarterly, 54*(1), 90-122.

Williamson, O. E. (1991). Comparative economic organization: The analysis of discrete structural alternatives. *Administrative Science Quarterly, 36*(2), 269-296.

Zander, I. (1999). How do you mean by 'global'? an empirical investigation of innovation networks in the multinational corporation. *Research Policy, 28*(2-3), 195-213.

Zander, I. (2002). The formation of international innovation networks in the multinational corporation: An evolutionary perspective. *Industrial and Corporate Change, 11*(2), 327.

CHAPTER SIX

Motivations, Valuation, Performance Assessment in Cross-border Mergers and Acquisitions: Theory and Field Evidence

Daojuan Wang and Hamid Moini

Abstract

This chapter focuses on three topics in cross-border mergers and acquisitions (CBM&As) field: motivations for CBM&As, valuation techniques and CBM&A performance (assessment and the determinants). By taking an overview of what have been found so far in academic field and investigating the practitioners' CBM&A practice, performance, and opinions using an online survey, we aim to improve and integrate understanding of these topics, as well as identify the research gaps. Based on survey evidence, we obtained some unexpected findings, and a couple of conclusions have been drawn in the end. Meanwhile, several future research directions have been provided.

Introduction

Numerous waves of mergers and acquisitions have led to substantial industrial restructuring in different parts of the world (DePamphilis, 2012, p.18). Since the beginning of the 1990s, an increasing share of M&As has taken the form of cross-border M&As (CBM&As) (Bertrand & Betschinger, 2012). The volume of global M&A transactions climbed to $2740 billion in 2011 (The Economic Times, Dec. 30, 2011). Paralleling with their popularity and practical importance, in both monetary and strategic terms, M&As have increasingly become a focus of study across different disciplines since the 1960s. However, a majority of research findings show that the performance of M&A deals has not significantly improved over these decades (Brouthers *et al.*, 1998; Bruner, 2002; King et al., 2004; Cartwright, 2005; Martynova & Renneboog, 2008). The growth in M&A activity, the volume of capital involved, and the pervasiveness of M&A stand in sharp contrast to their high rate of failure. This situation was usually described as "success paradox" (Cording et al., 2002). The researchers continue to be bewildered by the unpredictable nature of M&As, concluding their studies statements such as that "a huge portion of variance remains unexplained" (Stahl &Voigt, 2004). According to Meglio & Risberg (2010) "one has not learnt very much about how the M&A process unfolds over time, how to measure M&A performance, and what makes an acquisition succeed". Moreover, "the importance attached to factors motivating M&As changes over time" (Mukherjee et al., 2004) and the situation may be different in different countries. Besides, previous research on M&As is largely confined to the USA, UK, and the large continental European countries (Martynova & Renneboog, 2011), while Danish M&As have been rarely researched. Furthermore, cross-border M&As largely remain under explored compared to domestic M&As (Bertrand & Bestschinger, 2012). The reason may be that cross-border transactions in higher volumes only began in the 5th merger wave (1993 - 2000). Therefore, faced with these knowledge gaps and the coexistence of M&A' "popularity" and its "success paradox", we aim to investigate the following questions:

(1) What are the firms' primary motivations for conducting CBM&As?

(2) How is the target firm priced?

(3) How is the performance of CBM&As defined and assessed in academic field and by practitioners? Is the "success paradox" a general phenomenon around the world? In other words, how do the Danish acquirers perform?

Apparently, no single factor seems to be the cause of bad performance of CBM&As. Undoubtedly, the initial motivations for conducting CBM&As will guide the whole implementation process (e.g., target selection, valuation and integration), and then to a large extent influence the outcomes. "If M&As involve no or only a few technological components, they are expected to have little or no influence on the innovation routines of the acquiring firms" (Cloodt et al., 2006, p.643). Particularly, if M&As are conducted for the benefit of managers (i.e., agency problems) or out of irrational considerations (e.g., imitation, hubris), the acquiring firms' performance is likely to be negative. Besides, even if the initial motives are pure and reasonable, if the acquirers overpay for the targets, they are likely to be unable to achieve positive gains. It is also said that the failure of M&As to meet expectations, to a great extent, depends on how the failure is defined (DePamphilis, 2012, pp.44). Some scholars suggested that M&A performance should be assessed according to the original motives (Brouthers et al. 1998; Angwin, 2007; Das & Kapil, 2012). Meanwhile, a group of other researchers spend efforts seeking for the impacting factors to M&A performance (e.g., Moeller et al., 2004; Faccio et al., 2006). This study then aims to improve and integrate understanding of these widely discussed M&A topics, and identify the gaps where more research is needed by taking an overview of the research findings from academic field and investigating the practitioners' practices and opinions using an online survey. As mentioned before, this chapter will focus on CBM&A activities in Denmark, which have rarely been investigated and have quite distinct features. According to the statistics in Zephyr Database most of the Danish acquirers are small and privately owned. Therefore, our primary research method is questionnaire survey. CFOs are chosen as the respondents because they possess sufficient knowledge about the acquisition to complete our survey. Especially, they have the detailed information relating to valuation techniques, performance measures, and value creation. The investigation period (1/1/2000-1/1/2010) has covered the sixth merger wave (i.e., 2003-2007, see DePamphilis, 2012, P.19).

The reminder of this chapter is structured as follows: Section2 presents an extensive literature review on these three topics, which is our basis for designing an online questionnaire. Section 3 is a description of research design. Section 4 shows data from the questionnaire and analysis. The last section (i.e. section 5) concludes and offers some future research directions. This study is partially exploratory in nature, but we have some prior expectations to the answers from the CFOs, which will be presented in the next section.

Literature Review

Motivations for mergers and acquisitions

A great number of scholars have proposed and developed various theories and hypotheses for explaining M&A motivations (e.g., Ansoff, 1965; Gort, 1969; Roll, 1986). Hence, grouping the motivations for M&A transactions into various categories is often helpful. Based on an extensive literature review, this chapter has sorted out 22 theories of the motivations for M&As and we first classified them into two branches (see Table 1): In the first branch, M&As are undertaken pre-actively to fulfill decision-makers' objectives, and under the second branch M&As are reactively driven by shocks/disturbances in external environment. The first branch is further subdivided into two groups: one group is based on the hypothesis that decision-makers are rational, while another group based their inferences on bounded rational hypothesis. Furthermore, grounded on the rational hypothesis, one strand of scholars argued that M&A activities were conducted for the firms' benefits, whereas another strand of scholars contended that M&As were designed for the managers' interests (i.e., agency problems). In line with this logic, the following parts will present them in more detail.

Table 1: Summary of Theories/Hypotheses of M&A Motives

Criteria for classifying M&A motivations			Theory/hypothesis about M&A motivations	Suggested references
1. For realizing decision-makers' objectives (Proactive)	1.1 Rational hypothesis	Firm-serving motivations	(1) Monopoly theory (market power)	Stigler, 1950; Scherer & Ross, 1990
			(2) The market for corporate control (disciplinary)	Manne (1965); Jensen and Ruback (1983)
			(3) Tobin's Q theory	Tobin,1969; DePamphilis,2012,
			(4) Mis-valuation hypothesis	Loughran and Vijh, 1997; Shleifer &Vishny, 2003
			(5) Resource-based view (RBV)	Barney, 1986
			(6) Resource dependence theory (RDT)	Pfeffer & Salancik, 1978; Finklestein,1997
			(7) Organizational learning theory	Amburgey & Means, 1992; Haleblian & Kim, 2006
			(8) Real-option-based acquisition	Sudarsanam, 2010, p.77, p.141
			(9) Synergy theory	Ansoff ,1965; Williamson,1998
		Manager-self Serving motivations (Agency problems or managerialism)	(10) Empire-building hypothesis	Mueller, 1969
			(11) Defensive tactics (Excessive managerial risk aversion)	Amihud & Lev, 1981
			(12) Agency cost of free cash flow	Jensen, 1986, 1988
			(13) Managerial entrenchment	Shleifer and Vishny, 1989
	1.2 Bounded rational hypothesis		(14) Process theory	Duhaime & Schwenk, 1985
			(15) Hubris hypothesis (over-confident)	Roll,1986
			(16) Herding hypothesis (Imitation)	Scharfstein&Stein,1990; Graham ,1999
			(17) Escalating confirmation bias	Bogan & Just, 2008
			(18) Envy-based motivation	Goel & Thakor, 2010
2. For adapting to shocks from external environment (Reactive)	2.1 Rival-driven		(19) Preemption theory	Fridolfsson & Stennek, 2005;Molnar, 2007
	2.2 Country-level shocks		(20) Disturbance Theory	Gort ,1969
			(21) Population ecology theory	Hannan & freeman,1989
	2.3 Industry-level shocks		(22) Industry-level Shocks (e.g., technological innovations, supply shocks, deregulation)	Mitchell & Mulherin, 1996

Firm-serving motivations

Monopoly theory was once described as the main motive for the first big merger wave in America (1887-1904) (Stigler, 1950; Scherer & Ross, 1990). It states that the companies will utilize M&As to improve their market share and the entry barriers for other companies, and thus they can make profits by fixing prices autonomously. However, due to regulatory changes, this is not as important these days as before. Undoubtedly, within regulatory border, companies still keep pursuing market power to increase their negotiation position with the suppliers and customers (Bhattacharyya & Nain, 2009). Acquisition can also work as a disciplinary tool in "the market for corporate control" that is initially conceptualized by Manne (1965), and this hypothesis is then empirically supported by Jensen and Ruback (1983). It argues that the acquiring firm will take over the firms that have failed to make the most efficient use of their resources and capabilities, and then put them into more profitable use. Hostile takeovers are usually viewed as disciplinary, targeting companies where managers had failed to achieve shareholder objectives (Cosh and Guest, 2001).

According to Tobin's Q theory (Tobin, 1969), if the Q ratio of the market value of a firm to the replacement cost of its assets is greater than one –signifying more efficient use of assets, the firm should increase its capital stock in the form of both domestic investment and investment abroad (i.e., M&A or "green field") as investing is profitable. On the other hand, it suggests that firms can obtain the assets by acquiring a company with a market value less than the replacement cost of the assets (DePamphilis, 2012, pp.11). Consistent with the logic of "high-Q firm buy low low-Q firm" strategy of Q-theory, market mis-valuation theory explains M&A phenomena based on the hypothesis of inefficient capital market(Steiner, 1975; Shleifer & Vishny, 2003). According to this theory, the overvalued acquirers, who have more valuable information about the targets over the stock market, will take this chance to buy the relatively undervalued companies, and their overvalued shares are usually used for payment.

Other researchers explain the firms' M&A activities from a resource perspective, i.e., resource-based view (RBV, see Barney, 1986) and resource dependence theory (RDT, see Pfeffer & Salancik, 1978). RBV offers an internal perspective of how organizations specify resource needs and use M&A as an

144

instrument to obtain missing resources and/or enhance existing resources to maintain or improve their competitive advantages. Especially, the strategic resources with valuable, rareness, inimitability, and non-substitutability (VRIN) attributes, which are the reasons for sustained competitive advantage (Barney, 1991). "As some resources are not easy to trade on the market, the most effective way to get control over them is to acquire the whole company" (Colombo et al., 2007:203). RDT is the study of how the external resources of organizations affect the behavior of the organization. M&A is thus one of the options that a firm uses to reduce its environmental interdependence and uncertainties (Finklestein, 1997). Research on organizational learning theory (see Amburgey & Means, 1992; Haleblian & Kim, 2006) suggests that routines stemming from experience guide organizational behavior. It is thus used to account for serial M&A activities. Acquisition experience, it has been s found, positively enhances the acquirers' inclination to adopt a subsequent acquisition (Peng and Fang, 2010). Following the real option logic described in Sudarsanam's (2010:77 & 141), an acquisition can also be used as stepping stones for further investment opportunities, which contains an element of exploration.

Synergy theory has been the dominant theory in M&A research field and is the popular reason cited as the motive for doing M&As (Seth et al., 2000). Ansoff (1965) is the first researcher who related the synergy theory to M&A motives, which was later, expanded by Williamson (1998). This theory is based on the hypothesis that two companies combined can produce more benefits than two companies working independently. Standardization of synergies and revealing their sources are the central themes of several studies (see Ansoff, 1965; Chaterjee, 1986; Trautwein, 1990; Goold & Campnell, 1998). Based on these studies, we classify synergy sources into six categories in our questionnaire (see Table 3).

Confronted with the negative empirical evidence that M&As often destroy the bidding shareholders' wealth, the hypotheses of agency problems and bounded rationality were raised for explaining these value-destroying M&A activities.

Manager-self-serving motivations (Agency problems or Managerialism)

Agency problems or managerialism hypothesis asserts that managers make acquisitions for their own interests but at the expense of the firms' shareholders, for example, empire-building theory proposed by Mueller (1969), excessive managerial risk aversion presented by Amihud and Lev (1981), the agency cost of free cash flow stated by Jensen (1986, 1988), and managerial entrenchment proposed by Shleifer and Vishny (1989). Managers with empire-building tendency may have excessive taste for running larger firms, as opposed to simply profitable ones (Stein, 2003), so that they can get their personal benefits. Managers with excessive managerial risk aversion will seek to diversify their undiversifiable "employment risk" (i.e., risk of losing job, professional reputation, etc.) through conglomerate mergers and acquisitions (Amihud and Lev, 1981).According to the free cash flow hypothesis (Jensen, 1988), it is stated that managers who are endowed with free cash flow will invest it in negative net present value (NPV) projects rather than pay it out to shareholders. Managerial entrenchment proposition (Shleifer and Vishny, 1989) argue that managers can entrench themselves by making manager-specific investments to make it costly for the shareholders to replace them.

Overall, some empirical results positively support these hypotheses (e.g., Hadlock et al., 1999; Wright et al. 2002; Ismail, 2011). But the proposition of agency problems is challenged when considering the constraints of "the market for corporate control" (Manne, 1965), "manager market" (DePamphilis, 2012:11), "ownership structure" and "financial structure" (Caprio et al., 2011).

Bounded rational motivations

Under the hypothesis of bounded rationality, process theory (Duhaime & Schwenk, 1985; Jemison & Sitlin, 1986), hubris theory (Roll, 1986), herding theory (imitation) (Scharfstein & Stein, 1990), and escalating confirmation bias (Bogan & Just, 2008) were developed to explain M&A behavior. According to process theory, M&As are not the result of managers' rational decisions but rather that of an existing process influenced by the managers' limited information processing capability and their former experience, organizational routines and political power. Liu and Taffler (2009) find that overconfident CEOs are more likely to conduct M&As than economically rational CEOs. Herding behavior is used to explain M&A "wave" phenomenon. Graham (1999) states that managers with low ability will herd and managers with a high reputation will also herd to protect their reputation. More recently, Bogan and Just (2008) demonstrate the existence of confirmation bias in M&A decision-making process.

Reactive M&A motivations

Moreover, M&As may be conducted reactively due to external pressure, for instance, firms may merge to preempt their partner merging with a rival even if it may reduce their profits (i.e. Preemption Theory, see Jensen, 1989; Fridolfsson & Stennek, 2005), or they may conduct M&As out of institutional pressure (government/regulators/financial institutions) or drives from competitor, supplier, or customer's actions (Angwin, 2007).

Over the last century, there are two recurring phenomena: 1) mergers occur in waves; and 2) within a wave, mergers strongly cluster by industry (Gort, 1969; Mitchell & Muhlerin, 1996; Harford, 2003). Gort (1969) therefore proposed disturbance theory to explain this as discrepancies in expectations held by current shareholders and non-shareholders lead to a large number of shares changing hands. Specifically, when economic turbulence occurs, the insiders of the firms (potential targets) will turn pessimistic about their future, whereas the outsiders (the potential acquirers) turn out to be more optimistic, and then M&As will take place. The result is merger wave. Similarly, according to Hannan and freeman's (1989) population ecologytheory, merger is looked at as a natural selection and adaptation process according to regulatory and technological changes. Mitchell and Mulherin (1996) refer to this phenomenon as industry-level shocks (e.g. technological innovations, supply shocks, deregulation) and state that the industries react to these shocks by restructuring, often via mergers. Herding behavior is also used to explain this "wave" phenomenon. Graham (1999) stated that managers with low ability would herd and managers with a high reputation would also herd to protect their reputation. Recently, Goel and Thakor (2010) proposed and demonstrated that envy-based emotion was also a reason for generating the merger waves.

The above theories can be applied to explain both domestic and cross-border M&A activities. Compared with domestic M&As (DM&As), CBM&As offer a chance for the firms to search for new resources, capabilities, markets, and opportunities across different geographic locations. These studies and theories serve as part of theoretic basis for developing the questionnaire, whereas theories about agency problems are not included. It is not only because of the constraints mentioned earlier, such as "the market for corporate control", will reduce these problems, but also because most of Danish acquirers are private (around 70%), which tend to have less agency problems.

Valuation techniques

Overpayment for the acquisition is described as one of the reasons for M&A failures (Gadiesh et al., 2001; Hitt et al., 2001). According to Damodaran (2007), valuation methods fall into four groups: 1) discounted cash flow model (DCF); 2) market-multiple analysis model; 3) real option model; and 4) asset-oriented model. Each method has its applicability and limitation. For some particular industries and companies (such as cyclical companies, non-listed companies and the companies in trouble), some valuation methods will lose their usability. So there is no perfect method, and the challenge is to apply it correctly. Financial theory tells us that the value of any asset is equal to the present value of its future cash flows. Therefore, theoretically, DCF model is the most mature and logical valuation method. In DCF model, "the company is viewed as a cash flow generator and the company's value is obtained by calculating these flows' present value using a suitable discount rate" (Fernandez, 2007). Evidence shows that DCF takes predominant position in M&A valuation (Lie, E. & Lie, H. J., 2002; Mukherjee et al. 2004).

Using DCF model is not as easy as it seems, as different cash flows need different matched discount rates, and the cash flows need to be well adjusted according to the real situation. Admittedly, determining the discount rate is one of the most important tasks, as the risk and historic volatilities need to be taken into account. The basic difference between valuation for DM&As and CBM&As is that the latter involves converting cash flows from one currency to another and adjusting the discount rate for risks not generally found when the acquiring and target firms are within the same country.

Alternatively, the market multiple analyses are often used in financial markets, which were thought easy but in fact need almost the same adjustment job, where the goal is to get rid of the influence of capital structure and non-operating issues. Based on his experience as a business consultant, Fernandez (2007) has identified almost 100 common errors in valuations, among which there were 32 errors for setting up the discount rate, 13 errors for calculating the expected cash flows, and 6 errors when using multiples.

An investigation of the U.S. acquirers conducted by Mukherjee et al. (2004) finds that most of the firms use their own cost of capital for discounting equity cash flow from the targets in M&As. However, as we investigate the firms' cross-border M&As, we expect that the foreign nature of the targets will draw the acquirers' attention to the risks that cannot be found in domestic targets, which should be adjusted in discount rate. Therefore, we expect that the target firm's cost of capital/equity will be used as the discount rate when the acquirers adopt DCF as the valuation approach.

Performance measures and the empirical findings

M&A performance assessment has long been a challenge facing the researchers. As Zollo and Singh (2004) said, "there exists much heterogeneity both on the definition of the performance of M&As and on its measurement". Zollo and Meier (2008) have identified 12 metrics and three performance assessment levels (i.e., task, transaction, and firm level). Generally, on firm level, M&A performance measures can be summarized as five types: 1) stock-market-based measure (event study), 2) accounting-based measures, 3) subjective perception (i.e., top executives or expert informants' assessment), 4) innovation performance measure, and 5) divestiture. These measures have different underlying assumptions as well as pros and cons. In the following part, we will give a short summary and discussion of these five widely adopted performance measures and the relevant empirical findings.

Event study (see MacKinley, 1997; Binder, 1998) checks the change of the stock price surrounding the merger announcement (or completion date) and calculates the cumulative abnormal returns (CARs) in a couple of days (short-term event study) or several years (long-term event study). In short-term event study, the central underlying assumption is that the investors are capable of accurately predicting the combined firm's future cash flows, and it assumes that this event cannot be predicted before the event date. But the long-term event study (see Loughran & Vijh, 1997; Fama, 1998; Lyon et al., 1999) is designed on the consideration that stock price cannot immediately capture this event effects as some uncertainties can be eliminated during the M&A process. Event study, especially the short-term event study, dominates the research field of M&A performance with the attractive features, such as objective public assessment, and direct measurement of changes in stock price caused by acquisition. However, it is challenged by the facts that the stringent underlying assumptions are difficult to meet and what it assesses is the predicted outcomes. Besides, it overlooks the private acquirers' M&A performance. Since their logic for assessing the success or otherwise of a merger event is whether the M&A creates value for the shareholders, multiple motives for M&A are ignored. Furthermore, short-term event study cannot incorporate the important information of implementation (e.g., integration). The reliability of long-term event study has also been doubted as there is no convincing way to precisely measure long-term expected returns (Andrade et al., 2001), and the requirement of stability of the expected stock price is difficult to meet (Tuch & O'sullivan 2007). Generally, empirical findings, using short-term event study, show that the target shareholders make substantial gains, while the acquirer shareholders just break even or gain negative returns (Goergen & Reneboog, 2004; Tuch & O'Sullivan, 2007; Papadakis & Thanos, 2010). Stock market performance assessed though long-run event study highly depends on the estimation method used to predict the benchmark returns (Martynova & Renneboog, 2008).

Accounting-based performance measures are used to check the realized returns from M&A in long-term perspective (e.g., Zollo & Singh, 2004; Thanos et al., 2011). Return on equity (ROE), return on assets (ROA), market share, sales growth, operating cash flow are usually adopted as the metrics while ROA is the most popular one (Zollo & Singh, 2004). But Barber and Lyon (1996) state that in measuring the performance of firms after significant events such as takeovers, using operating cash flows is deemed more appropriate, as earnings can be easily manipulated.If mergers truly create value for shareholders, the gains should eventually show up in the firms' cash flows. Accounting-based approach has the advantages of being objective and checking the realized value from M&As, but suffering the potential manipulation of accounting data, limitation to different accounting rules, and incorporation of effects from other events (e.g., investment decisions). Since it is used to assess the M&A performance on the whole firm level and not a specific assessment of a particular acquisition's effect, the result will be invalid especially when the target size is much smaller than the acquirer's size. Broadly speaking, results about post-merger performances measured by accounting-based approaches are ambiguous (Campa & Hernando, 2004; Tuch & O'Sullivan, 2007; Martynova & Renneboog, 2008; Thanos and Papadakis, 2011), as studies vary in terms of definitions of operating performance, deflator choice (e.g., book value of assets/sales), performance benchmarks, samples, and time lags.

Surveying the top executives' or expert informants' perception of M&A results has the advantage of taking various M&A objectives into consideration, by using the private information, and reducing the outside noise (Capron, 1999; Hayward, 2002; Brock, 2005). Most importantly, it can be applied to all types of acquisitions. But it inevitably suffers from the shortcomings of decayed memory and potential self-justification bias. Besides, the expert informants may have limited information about the deal (Cannella & Hambrick, 1993). Hence, multiple informants are used to improve the reliability of their findings (Datta, 1991; Cannella & Hambrick, 1993). High correlation between performance assessed by executives and industry analysts in Datta' (1991) study indicate that the questionnaire responses are valid measures of performance (see also Schoenberg, 2006). Pakadakis and Thanos (2010) also report a positive relationship between accounting based measures and managers' subjective assessments. An earlier study conducted by Dess (1984) demonstrates that the top management executives' perception of how well their firms have performed is consistent with how firm actually performed vis-à-vis ROA and sales growth. Brouthers et al. (1998) suggest that since there have not been alternative performance measures other than stock-based measures, a better indicator of performance would be the achievement or non-achievement of the predetermined objectives of the merger. Overall, based on the top executives' assessment, more than 50 percent of them believed they had achieved their initial motivations or created value (Adolph et al. 2001; Bruner, 2002; Schoenberg, 2006).

Innovation performance is measured in terms of innovative inputs (e.g., R&D expenditures) or innovation outputs (e.g, patent intensity, innovation productivity). These indexes are usually applied to technology-based M&As (e.g., Puranam et al., 2007; Desyllas & Hughes, 2010). Generally, research on technology driven M&As report that it can be a way to improve the acquirer's innovation performance but contingent on a number of factors (see Ahuja & Katila, 2001; Phene et al., 2012).

The last relatively simple metric is divestment, which is to assess the outcomes of M&A by identifying whether an acquired firm has subsequently been divested based on the logic that merged companies deem to divest if the acquired firm's performance does not meet their expectations. However, divestment in some instances signals successful restructure and profitable sale (Kaplan & Weisbach, 1992) or appropriate resource reconfiguration in response to environmental change (Schoenberg, 2006). Kaplan and Weisbach (1992) found that 44 percent of the target companies acquired between 1971 and 1982 were divested by the end of 1989. However, only 44 percent of the acquirers who performed divestiture reported a loss on sale, and the divested units were found to be sold for more than they cost. Schoenberg's (2006) study indicates that 11 percent of acquisitions in the sample are subsequently divested within 6 years, rising to 30 percent after 9 years, and 56 percent after 13 years.

As can be seen above, different metrics shed light on different aspects of M&A performance, and the others can overcome one approach's drawbacks. Therefore, many studies use multiple measures, on the one hand, to improve the reliability of assessment and on the other hand to examine their relations. Healy et al. (1992) report significant and positive association between stock market's assessment and ex-post operating performance (see also Moeller et al., 2005). This is also demonstrated by Duso et al. (2010), who state that it is particularly true when using long event windows (25 or 50 days). In contrast, Ghosh (2001) fails to find the relationship between stock market's assessment and cash flow improvements. Later, Hayward (2002) uses both short-term event study and security analysts' assessment and reports that announcement returns are imperfect predictors of longer-term acquisition performance, which is confirmed by Schoenberg (2006). His findings show that ex-ante capital market reactions to an acquisition announcement exhibit little relation to corporate managers' ex-post assessment. Instead, there is a positive relationship between managers' and expert informants' subjective assessments. Zollo and Meier's (2008) study also reports that short-term event study is not linked to any of the other performance metrics. Similarly, Pakadakis and

Thanos (2010) finds that accounting-based measures are positively correlated to managers' subjective assessments while CARs are not correlated to both, drawing the conclusions that capital market is not efficient enough to predict the long-term success of an acquisition.

In summary, it seems that only short-term event study have some relatively consistent conclusions about M&A performance. However, it is still a puzzle whether ex-ante gains predicted by short-term event study are well correlated with ex-post realized gains evaluated by the other approaches. It strongly depends on the extent the assumptions of event study can be met. When it comes to the accounting methods, we face another problem of information accessibility and reliability. In some countries, the companies might not prepare their account rigorously in accordance with internationally accepted accounting principles. As mentioned earlier, M&A performance measures are suggested to be linked to the firms' initial motives, but it is difficult to perform it, especially, when the performance of a large number of firms is checked. Maybe the reliable way is to use multiple approaches,as acquisition performance by its nature is extremely complex and multifaceted, no individual way can grasp its different aspects (Zollo & Meier 2008).Since there is no perfect performance measure but the more suitable one, the rule of the thumb in selecting a measure is to make sure the theoretical logic behind the measures and questions under investigation are aligned and the time horizon need to be justified (Cording et al, 2010).

In addition to different performance measures that result in inconsistent findings of M&A performance, different assessment perspectives, sampling periods, sample sizes, contexts, observation time spans, benchmarks and statistical methodologies are also the reasons. Comparison among the empirical findings about M&A performance is hence difficult or even impossible. Besides, M&A activities are demonstrated to have conditional effect on post-acquisition performance. An array of conditions/variables on the country- (e.g., developed vs. developing countries, see Bertrand and Betschinger, 2012), industry- (e.g., high-tech vs. low-tech, see Cloodt et al., 2006), firm (e.g., public-listed vs private target, see Capron and Shen, 2007), and deal- level (e.g., method of payment, see Ghosh, 2001) have been proposed to have an impact on M&A performance. Especially, the impact of business relatedness, M&A experience, cultural difference, legal status (private- vs. public-listed) of the target, and method of payment have been widely discussed but with inconsistent findings. Therefore, in our questionnaire, we will seek for the practitioners' opinions on these potentially impacting factors.

Regarding the effect of business/industry relatedness, some scholars find that acquiring related firms can increase post-acquisition performance (Palich et al., 2000; Dos Santos et al., 2008), while some others do not (Seth, 1990; Kaplan & Weisbach, 1992). When checking technological performance of U.S.-based M&As, Valentini and Dawson (2010) find industry relatedness had an inverted U-shape relationship with it. Besides, a significant body of evidence documented that corporate diversification strategies destroy value (e.g., Maquiera et al., 1998; Doukas et al., 2002). However, Graham (2002) argues that diversification discount appears because the segments acquired were discounted before the acquisition, and diversification in itself does not destroy the value.

In terms of acquisition experience, some scholars find a positive relationship between experience and performance (e.g. Bertrand & Betschinger, 2012), while some scholars report a U-shaped relationship (Haleblian & Finkelstein, 1999; Zollo & Reuer, 2010). Others, however, state that the CARs of serial acquirers decline from deal to deal (e.g., Aktas et al., 2009). Rahahleh and Wei (2012) arrive at the same findings and report that it is more significant in civil-law countries than in common-law countries.

The effect of payment methods on the performance of M&As has also been investigated. Loughran and Vijh (1997) conclude that cash payment is qualified as an indicator of a good performance of the bidder, which is confirmed by a number of later researchers using the data from different countries (e.g., Ghosh, 2001; Goergen and Renneboog, 2004). Nonetheless, Powell and Stark (2005) indicate that payment method has an insignificant impact on operating performance of UK takeovers, while industrial relatedness has an impact. In Conn et al.,'s (2005) study, they find that non-cash payment plays a negative role in domestic public acquisition, but not in the acquisition of domestic private targets and that the method of payment has no significant influence in cross-border public acquisitions. Alexandridis et al. (2010) find that share-for-share offers are at least non-value-destroying for the shareholders in the rest of countries apart from the U.S. and UK.

With respect to the impact of the target firm' legal status, Bradley and Sundaram (2004) show that the two-year post-announcement returns in takeovers of a public target are not significant, but significantly negative when the target is private. On the contrary, Conn et al. (2005) find that acquisitions of private targets outperform acquisitions of public targets (domestic and cross-border) over both announcement and three-year post-merger period. They explain the results as arising from the fact that private targets have less bid competition and hubris is less likely in private bids. Faccio et al. (2006) also report higher acquirer ARs for private versus public targets, which is held over time and across western European countries. Similarly, Draper and Paudyal (2006) state that acquiring a private company is an attractive option for maximizing shareholder wealth. Bradley and Sundaram (2006) conclude that acquirer's size and the method of payment are not important determinants of market reaction to an acquisition announcement, but the target organization's form dominates everything else. And they find a negative

157

announcement effect for public-target acquisitions, and a positive effect for non-public-target acquisitions. However, Capron and Shen (2007) argue that acquirer returns from their target choice (private/public) were not universal but would depend on their attributes and integration.

On cultural differences,Weber (2012: 288-289) summarizes the existing empirical findings about their impact by observing that "many studies during the last two decades have provided corroborative evidence that cultural differences have a negative impact on M&A performance. On the other, several recent studies point to the fact that cross-cultural differences can have both negative and positive effects on M&A performance."

By conducting a meta-analysis of the existing empirical findings about these determinants, King et al. (2004:188) conclude that the widely studied variables, i.e., conglomerate acquisitions, related acquisitions, method of payment, and prior acquisition experience, do not impact post-acquisition performance. They, therefore suggest that, "future M&A researchers would be well advised to use variables from existing M&A research as a foundation to build new models of post-acquisition performance".

Prior expectations

This chapter is partially exploratory in nature, but we still have the following priori expectations on the above topics.

Regarding our first objective of investigating the reasons for performing CBM&As, because of the international nature of CBM&As compared with DM&As, and its speed advantage compared with "organic growth" and "greenfield investment", we expect "geographical expansion" and "rapid growth" to be the main reasons for the acquirers to conduct CBM&As. Besides, as synergy theory is dominant in M&A research field and is the most cited reason for doing M&As, we, hence, anticipate that most of CBM&As will be synergy related. Besides, we want to go a step further and check which resource the synergy mainly comes from.

Since DCF is the most popularly used method of valuation, we expect that the acquired firm's cost of capital/equity will be adopted as the discount rate.

Regarding the impacting factors to M&A performance, as discussed above, we are interested on the effect of the widely studied and controversial factors, such as "M&A experience", "business/industry relatedness", "legal status", and "cultural difference". And we expect that "M&A experience" and "industrial relatedness" can be helpful in achieving better CBM&A performance.

Concerning M&A experience, it would be fair to say that prior empirical work on its effect on acquisition performance has been inconclusive. However, prior acquisition experience may build facilitating identification and integration process of the target firms (King et al., 2004). "The success of Banc One, Cisco Systems and General Electric do suggest that acquisition experience impacts focal acquisition performance at least partly through building expertise at post-acquisition management" (Puranam & Srikanth, 2007). Therefore, we aim to investigate the Danish firms' attitude toward their M&A experience, and we expect that their prior experience can help them do better in future CBM&As.

With respect to business relatedness effect, the researchers also report quite different findings. But we expect that related business can help them do better. Singh and Montgomery (1987) argue that all three forms of synergy (operational, financial and administrative) are theoretically available in related acquisitions, but only financial synergies and administrative efficiencies are available in unrelated acquisitions, related acquisitions will create more value than unrelated ones. Especially when performing CBM&As, "the sensitivity of post–acquisition management is likely to increase when it is cross-border in scope, with the acquirer and acquired firm coming from different countries, bearing different management philosophies and practices as a result" (Child, 2001:17). The challenges, such as "liability of foreignness", "double-layered acculturation" and "more asymmetric information" tend to block the realization of administrative synergy and operational synergy. Related acquisition, under this circumstance, is supposed to buffer these negative impacts instead of bringing more uncertainties, which unrelated one may do. Moreover, related acquisitions can enable the acquiring firm's pre-existing resources to be productively leveraged and redeployed in new businesses where those resources are more likely to be valued and relevant (King et al., 2004).

Research Design

Survey instrument and non-response bias

The research reported in this study was carried out through an online survey of 131 Danish firms.Each company in the sample was sent an e-mail, identifying a Danish university as the sponsor, requesting their participation in the study.

This study is inspired by Mukherjee et al's (2004) research, so we would like to express our thanks here. As they stated, "surveys of managers do not replace the other general approaches to examine M&A behavior, but they complement them and yield additional insights." Moreover, as reported by Baker and Mukherjee (2007:3) "investment decisions and practices", are the top finance issues that would benefit the most from survey-based research according to the editors' opinion from 7 top journals in finance field. Besides, it is suggested to use survey research to learn what people actually do and why they do it and then compare the results with theoretical conclusions. And such an approach is said to help bridge the gap between theory and practice, which is quite consistent with our research logic. Most importantly, there is nowhere else to get the detailed information, such as the motivations for doing acquisition, valuation methods, performance assessment, etc. In the meantime, we aim to collect their perceptions and opinions on some research findings from academic field. Therefore, a survey data collection was deemed most appropriate.

Admittedly, survey method has its strengths and weaknesses. The strengths can be: 1) it can produce data unavailable from other sources; 2) survey responses can suggest new avenues for future research; 3) direct responses from decision makers add value; and 4) sometimes there is no other way to answer a research question. However, survey questionnaires have some weaknesses such as non-response bias, self-report bias, and limited knowledge to response to a question. In this study, to make sure the respondents know the information about these questions, we selected the firms in which the CFOs have been working in the firm for at least 5 years. For reducing potential self-report bias, we assured the anonymity and confidentiality of their answers, and also stressed that there was no right or wrong answers. We checked the possible non-response bias by comparing the dimensions of average size (total asset), industrial affiliations (use acquirers' primary UK SIC code) and legal status between the responding firms and the population. Our t-test shows (see Table 2) that they are similar on these aspects. By checking the legal status of respondents and non-respondents, the public listed firms account for 28 percent of the respondents, and 30 percent among non-respondents. Therefore, non-response bias is not a problem in our study.

Table 2: Non-response bias analysis

	Identity	N	Mean	Std. Deviation	t	Sig. (2-tailed)
Total assets	Respondents	30	835582.75	1853558.96	-0.991	0.324
	Non-respondents	91	2502775.05	9131260.20	-1.642	0.103
Industry type (Primary UK SIC code)	Respondents	30	3964.33	2250.94	-1.243	0.216
	Non-respondents	91	4597.01	2469.38	-1.303	0.198

Based on a comprehensive literature review, we developed the original questions and adopted several questions from Mukherjee et al.'s (2004) study. While their research concentrates on the U.S. M&As during 1992-2000, this study focuses on the Danish CBM&As during 2000-2010. Initially the survey instrument was pre-tested with six companies. We changed the wordings on some questions to improve their clarity, and deleted some questions at the same time. The survey was conducted during April, 2012. We first sent the questionnaire to 131 Danish acquirers and reminded them twice later by using a reminder email in two weeks.

The survey is designed in 6 sections: Section 1 provides a general overview of the participating firms' CBM&A activities. Section 2 identifies the firms' primary motivations for conducting CBM&As. Section 3 attempts to gain insights about valuation techniques used by the acquirers. Section 4 checks how the responding firms assess their CBM&A performance and their perception of the results. Section 5 examines their attitudes and opinions towards the investigated impacting factors such as M&A experience and business relatedness. And finally, section 6 gathers the responding firms' views on some statements about M&As. Most of the questions are closed, and a number of open questions are designed to get additional or unexpected information.

Sample

As allowed for a minimum assimilation period of 2 years, the sample was restricted only to those acquisitions, which were completed before January 2010. Initially, we obtained the information on 750 CBM&A deals completed by 346 Danish firms during the period of 1/1/2000 to 1/1/2010 from Zephyr Database. Furthermore, we only considered firms in which CFOs have been working for the company for more than 5 years, and as some CFOs could not be identified, the sample size thus shrank to 131 firms. These 131 firms formed the bases of our investigation. We contacted the CFOs in these firms through e-mails and requested their participation and received 35 replies with 3 partially completed, which were later dropped. So our final sample consists of 32 usable replies.

Survey Findings and Discussion

The survey findings are presented in five parts: 1) general information about the Danish firms' CBM&A activities; 2) motives for CBM&As; 3) valuation techniques; 4) performance assessment practice and the results; and 5) other views on CBM&As.

General information about the Danish firms' CBM&As

During the last 10 years while 37 percent of Danish firms conducted 1-3 CBM&As, 31 percent of them conducted more than 10 CBM&As. And the acquired firms were generally private (30 out of 32). This was probably because most of the acquirers were private firms (72 percent). Sixty two percent of the firms acquired targets companies with less than €50 million in total asset (See Table 3).When we further checked the respondents' information, we found that their average latest total assets is only €11 million, so it makes sense that their targets are not as big as those targeted by the U.S. firms. The payment methods they used were mainly internal cash or cash combied with debt, which was probably due to their private ownership.

Table 3: General Information about the Danish firms' CBM&As

Times of CBM&As conducted during last 10 years (1/1/2000-1/1/2010) (Single choice)	n	%
1-3	12	37.5
4-7	9	28.1
8-10	1	3.1
Above 10	10	31.3
Total	32	100
The size of prefered target companies (asset) (Single choice)	n	%
Less than € 50 million	20	64.5
€ 50 million - € 150 million	7	22.6
€ 151 million - € 1 million	3	9.7
Over € 1 billion	1	3.2
Total	31	100
Legal status of their target companies (Single choice)	n	%
Most of them are privately-held firms	30	93.8
Most of them are publicly-held firms	1	3.1
Half and half	1	3.1
Total	32	100
Payment methods frequentlly used (Single choice)	n	%
Internal cash	13	50
Internal cash and debt	9	34.6
Internal cash and stock	4	15.4
Stock	0	0
Total	26	100

Motives for CBM&As

Based on the theories/hypotheses proposed in the existing literature, we developed 19 motives for conducting CBM&As including an "other" option. According to their choices (see Table 4), which were consistent with our expectation, "geographical expansion" and "achieving more rapid growth" were chosen by most of the respondents, followed by the choice of "gaining economies of scale/scope", "the expansion or improvement of the product mix", and "acquiring technical knowledge and expertise". It is clear that Danish firms performed CBM&As mainly out of strategic and economic considerations rather than being triggered by external environment shocks (e.g., government's incentives, pressure of being taken over, or to prevent a possible acquisition) and direct financial motives (e.g., use of excess free cash, obtain tax advantages). However, sometimes the psychology of imitation is a force driving CBM&A action as one respondent chose "following CBM&A trend" as the reason. Generally, as one respondent put it *"there is always a multiple reasons for an acquisition – differing from case to case"*.

According to their ranking, "geographical expansion" and "achieving more rapid growth" were ranked as the most important reasons for engaging in CBM&As by most of the respondents. As discussed before, CBM&As are usually described as an entry mode into foreign market. As stated by Child (2001, p.9) "globalization is the key feature of the new competitive landscape within which the M&A frenzy is taking place". "Geographical expansion" is thus well-deserved for its top position. The second popular reason of "achieving more rapid growth" signfies that, under the new competitive landscape, speed advantage have been given much importance by Danish firms.

Table 4: The Respondents' Choices and Ranking about Their Motives for CBM&As

Motives (multiple choice)	Number of respondent (Multiple choice)	Ranking of CBM&A Motives						
		Times of being No. 1	Times of being No. 2	Times of being No. 3	Times of being No. 4	Times of being No. 5	Times of being No. 6	Times of being No. 7
a) Expand geographically	29	14	5	4	1	0	0	0
b) Achieve more rapid growth	24	13	4	4	0	0	0	0
c) Gain economies of scale/scope	19	4	6	6	1	0	0	0
d) Expand or improve the product mix	18	5	4	3	5	1	0	0
e) Acquire technical knowledge and expertise	13	6	2	2	0	0	0	0
f) Gain better control over supply of sources and/ or retail outlets	6	2	2	0	1	1	0	0
g) Spread risk through diversification	5	2	0	0	1	0	0	0
h) Acquire a company below its replacement cost	4	0	0	0	0	0	2	0
i) Obtain managerial talent	3	0	0	0	0	0	1	1
j) Enhance the power and prestige of the firm	2	0	0	1	1	0	0	0
k) Use excess free cash	2	0	0	0	0	1	0	0
l) Follow the CBM&A trend	1	0	0	0	0	1	0	0
m) Obtain tax advantages	1	0	0	0	0	0	0	0
n) Adapt to the changes/disturbance of external environment (e.g. deregulation)	1	0	0	0	0	0	0	0
o) Make use of the government incentives	1	0	0	0	0	0	0	0
p) Counter cyclical of seasonal sales	0	0	0	0	0	0	0	0
q) Replace poor management	0	0	0	0	0	0	0	0
r) Prevent a possible takeover made by other companies	0	0	0	0	0	0	0	0
s) Defend against being taken over	0	0	0	0	0	0	0	0
t) Others (Please fill in.):	0	0	0	0	0	0	0	0

As mentioned earlier, synergy is, either directly or indirectly, one of the primary motives for CBM&As. Seventy five percent respondents reported that their companies have been involved in synergy-related CBM&As. According to their replies, synergy effect mainly come from operating synergy (e.g.,economies of scale/scope, increased joined sales and market power), and financial synergy (e.g., lower tansaction costs, tax reduction) contributed very little, which was confirmed again by the respondents' choices and rankings on the motivations for CBM&As (e.g, tax advantage is only cited once). These findings are similar to Mukherjee et al.'s (2004), Fields, et al.'s (2007), and Devos, et al.'s (2009) research results. Mukherjee et al. (2004), for example, reported that that 89.9 percent of the respondetns chose operational synergy as the main synergy resource. Fields et al. (2007) found that the postitive stock market returns to the bidder are principally attributed to the investors' perceptions of potential economies of scale and scope. Devos et al.' (2009) study shows that over 80 percent of positive synergies are from operating efficiencies, while tax savings contribute only 1.64 percent in additional value, suggesting that tax consideration is not a major source of merger gains. However, "synergy evaluation and realization" are still described by most of the respondents as the challenge in CBM&As.

In terms of M&A style, horizontal M&A is the popular one over the others (see Table 5), which means they tend to acquire the companies with identical products operating in the same or different markets. Besides, all of the respondents either "strongly agreed" or "agreed" that an acquisition in a related industry was worth more than an acquisition in a non-related industry, which was consitent with our expectaion. However, they have no consistent opinion about whether diversification was a justifiable motivation for M&As, citing some respondents' words here *"there is no simple answer to this question, which depends on many factors"* and *"if you want to go into a new segment rapidly, you may need it"*.

Table 5 Merger Type and Synergy Sources

Merger type(multiple choice)	n	%
Horizontal merger (Mergers between firms with identical products operating in the same or different markets)	23	51.1
Vertical merger(Mergers happened in which a buyer-seller relationship exists or could exist between the two firms)	10	22.2
Concentric merger (Mergers between firms with highly similar production or distributional technologies)	9	20
Conglomerate merger products (The acquiring firms that have no buyer-seller relationship, no technical and distributional relationship, and do not deal with identical products).	3	6.7
Total	45	100
Synergy sources (multiple choice)	n	%
Operating synergy (resulting from economies of scale/scope)	20	31.74
Increase joint sales (access to new geographic markets; cross-sell the complementary products)	15	3.81
Increased market power (lower degree of competition)	14	22.22
Share intangible resources (Know-how; Brand)	7	11.11
Managerial efficiency (acquirer's management is more efficient)	5	7.93
Financial synergy (lower transaction costs; tax reduction; more coverage by analysts)security	2	3.17
Differential efficiency (acquiring firm's management is more efficient)	0	0
Other sources (Please fill in)	0	0
Total	63	99.98

Valuation practice

DCF and market-multiple valuation analysis are the dominant methods used by Danish firms, while DCF can be the most popular valuation method for pricing both publicly- and privately-held target firms (see Table 6). However, a majority (71 percent) of Danish firms used their own weighted average cost of capital (WACC) as the discount rate in valuing target firms, which is consistent with Mukherjee's (2004) findings. Then there will be a mismatch between cash flows and discount rate, especially for cross-border M&As. No matter what kind of cash flows are calculated (Dividends, FCFE or FCFF), the target countries' systematic risk (e.g., macroeconomic fluctuations, political risk, etc.) need to be considered when determining discount rate, as it should be matched with the cash flows produced by the foreign acquired firms. This inappropriate definition of discount rate can be a reason of over-pricing the target firms.

Table 6: Valuation Techniques Used for Target Firms

Valuation of publicly-held target firm	n	%
Discounted cash flow model plus market multiple analysis	16	53
Discounted cash flow model only	10	33
Market multiple analysis only	2	7
Market multiple analysis plus others	2	7
Others	0	0
Total	30	100
Valuation of closely-held target firm	**n**	**%**
Discounted cash flow model plus multiple analysis	14	44
Discounted cash flow model only	9	28
Market multiple analysis only	7	22
Others (e.g., negotiated price, evaluate the specific project)	2	6
Total	32	100
Discount rate used to value a target firm	**n**	**%**
The acquirer's weighted average cost of capital	22	69
The target's weighted average cost of capital	7	22
The acquirer's cost of equity capital	3	9
The target's cost of equity capital	0	0
Others	0	0
Total	32	100

Overpayment has been identified as one reason for merger failure, which is again confirmed by our study. Eighty seven percent of our respondents indicate that they have experienced overpricing, and the primary reason is their overconfidence about the potential benefits from CBM&As (see Table 7). This finding is further confirmed by their replies to an open-end question, for which "avoiding synergy trap, evaluating synergies correctly, and realization of synergy" are described as the thorniest issues when performing CBM&As. Besides, asymmetric information, inappropriate valuation methods used, and competition from other buyers are also stated as reasons for driving up the price.

Table 7: Overpricing experience and the reasons

Evidence about overpricing the targets	n	%
Never	3	13
Rarely	12	50
Sometimes	7	29
Very often	2	8
Always	0	0
Total	24	100%
Reasons for overpricing the targets	**n**	**%**
Overoptimistic about the potential benefits	25	76
Asymmetric information about the target companies	4	15
Inappropriate valuation methods	1	3
Others(i.e., underestimating risks and competition from other buyers)	2	6
Total	32	100

Performance assessment of CBM&As

As discussed before, there is no agreement on the best way to measure acquisition success, but the more suitable approach. Many scholars suggest linking performance measures with the acquirers' initial motives. Since this study is not focused on one specific acquisition case but on the company's general CBM&A activities, we thus use the index of overall goal attainment to measure their general CBM&A performance (see Kiessling &

Harvey, 2008). Meanwhile, we have another intention to check how the practitioners measure the outcomes of their CBM&As, and seek for their views about "whether and how CBM&As help their companies create value".

To our surprise, almost half of the acquirers (15 out of 32) had no performance measures to assess their CBM&A outcomes and some of the companies did not set up any index for monitoring the performance during and after M&As, some of them just did it occasionally (see Table 8). If there is no performance assessment metrics, how can the synergy realization or value creation be tracked, how do they know whether their initial objectives have been achieved or not? Or maybe there is no clear objective or plan for doing the acquisitions. Undoubtedly, such somewhat imprudent attitude and operations are likely to be the reasons for disappointing M&A outcomes. However, all of these questions may only be answered by an in-depth research design, for example, case studies.

For those respondents who had performance measures, we used open-end questions to identify which measures they used in their evaluation. Most respondents linked the performance measures to their original objectives or business plan, the methods they used, for example, *"follow up the budget for the target"*, *"follow up initial DCF-valuation logic"*, *"track the assumptions of the benefits"*, *"track the integration milestones by monthly financial key performance indicators"*, *"compare the financial targets to initial business plan"*, and *"follow up earn-out threshold to be achieved in year 1-4"*. Financial indicators are mainly used, by them for assessing CBM&A performance such as profitability, sales/revenue, EBIT, and cost cutting. In addition, whatever their motives, 83 percent of respondents expected to achieve their motivations within 3 years. Therefore, accounting measures are thought to be the proper way for assessing CBM&A outcomes, and 3 years after CBM&As is enough for most of the acquirers to reap the benefits, and is thus suitable time horizon for the external researchers to assess the performance.

Concerning the performance of Danish international acquirers, only two companies stated the outcomes of CBM&A fully met their initial expectations, and around half of the companies only achieved their objectives by 60 percent or less. The reasons may be cultural difference, overvaluaion, overoptimism, and imprudent operation, based on the evidence such as, "cultural difference" and "synergy prediction" were described by the respondents as the tough issues in CBM&A; most of them have experienced overpricing the targets; they were overoptimistic about the anticipated benefits; half of them had no performance assessment indicators for their CBM&A activities. Further research is needed to investigate the reasons for these unsatisfied results. Nevertheless, compared with alternative growth strategies (e.g., strategic alliance and Greenfield investment), around 70 percent of the companies thought the risk adjusted return from CBM&As was higher. This finding contradicts the negative depiction about CBM&As in prior research from the other angle. It tells that at least returns from CBM&As are larger than the opportunity cost of other growth strategies. Moreover, 99 percent of our respondents stated that CBM&As can help their companies create value, and value creation from CBM&As was said to come from: 1) offering better geographical position to the market; 2) technology driven advantages; 3) market shares increase; 4) economies of scale; 5) new products/business, sourcing and logistic optimizing; and 6) speed advantage and global footprint. Some of the respondents even said: *"without M&A there is a risk of the value to decline", "in our line of business, we can only create value by doing CBM&As", and "our customers are global, we need to be global to serve our customers and get economies of scale to optimize sourcing and logistics which is the key factors in our industry."* According to their replies, we can see "value" created by CBM&As in their views is not just immediate financial improvement but also the gained strategic resource for future development or the only way for survival. Therefore, combining accounting-based measures with the managers' assessment can better check the multifaceted outcomes of CBM&As, covering both economic and strategic benefits.

Table 8: Performance AssessmentPractice and the Results

Please indicate if your company has some performance evaluation measures to assess the outcomes of your cross-border M&A activities.	n	%
Yes	17	53.13
No	15	46.88
Total	32	100
Please indicate how many years your company expects to wait before realizing the initial objectives for performing cross-border M&As.	n	%
1 year	2	6.67
2 years	12	40
3 years	11	36.67
4 years	3	10
5 years+	2	6.67
Total	30	100.01
Does your company set some indices related to the preliminary objectives of conducting cross-border M&As in advance for monitoring them during and after mergers?	n	%
Never	4	12.5
Rarely	3	9.4
Sometimes	12	37.5
Very often	4	12.5
Always	9	28.1
Total	32	100
Compared to the other alternative growth paths (e.g. strategic alliance and Greenfield investment), the risk adjusted return of cross-border M&As is _____?	n	%
Significantly lower	2	7.41
Slightly lower	1	3.7
Almost the same	5	18.52
Slightly higher	13	48.15
Significantly higher	6	22.22
Total	27	100

This study also investigated the Danish firms' attitude toward their CBM&A experience/knowledge (see Table 9). Sixty seven percent of the firms have specific team/section responsible for CBM&As. In addition, 56 percent of the respondents stated that they stored the experience and knowledge of CBM&As. However,

173

88 percent of the respondents replied that they had no training programs for relevant staff to gain knowledge about CBM&As. Based on these findings, it seems there are still a number of firms which did not pay much attention to CBM&A experience and knowledge, even for the firms which had conducted more than 10 CBM&As during 1/1/2000-1/1/2010.

However, consistent with our expectation, 74 percent of the respondents stated that previous experience of CBM&As could help them do better in later activities. Further, we examined the relation between respondents' perceptions of the CBM&A results with the number of times they conducted CBM&As. Among the group, which conducted 1-3 CBM&As, 72 percent of the acquirers performed unsatisfactorily (they only achieved their expectation by 60 percent or less), while only 25 percent performed unsatisfactorily in the group which have done CBM&As more than 4 times. We may owe this difference to the help of CBM&A experience. Nonetheless, we have to admit that CBM&A experience sometimes exerts harmful effects as was stated by five respondents. Further research is needed on when and how M&A experience is harmful, and how M&A experience can be better used.

Moreover, we used open-end questions to investigate the trickiest issues faced by the practitioners in their CBM&A activities. The keywords in their replies were "cultural difference". These results are consistent with what Cartwright & Schoenberg (2006:8) stated in their study where they declared that "poor culture-fit or lack of cultural compatibility have become much cited, if rather poorly defined, reasons for M&A failure". High levels of cultural distance can prevent the success of the M&As integration (e.g., Brouthers & Brouthers, 2000). However, a fair amount of culture clash is said to be desirable to prompt positive debate about what's best for the organization and to avoid group think (DiGeorgio, 2003). Hence, cultural difference has both potentially negative and potentially positive effects, and its final impact will be mediated by managerial efforts, such as "whether they perceived and evaluate cultural differences early enough during the evaluation stage to avoid buying a company too difficult to integrate? Are cultural differences accounted for during the integration process to avoid major pitfalls and misunderstandings?"(Teerikangas & Very, 2006:39). More research is needed on the acquirer's implementation and a process perspective will be helpful for investigating these issues.

Table 9: Attitudes towards Experience and Knowledge of CBM&As

Does your company store the experience and knowledge of CBM&A?	n	%
Yes	18	56.25
No	14	43.75
Total	32	100
Does your company have specific team or section responsible for M&As?	n	%
Yes	16	66.67
No	8	33.33
Total	24	100
Does your company have some training program for relevant staff to learn the knowledge about CBM&A?	n	%
Yes	4	12.5
No	28	87.5
Total	32	100
Please indicate if you previous experience with CBM&A have helped you firm do better in later CBM&As.	n	%
Harmed significantly	0	0
Harmed moderately	5	16.13
Neither helped nor harmed	3	9.67
Helped moderately	16	51.61
Helped significantly	7	22.58
Total	31	99.99

Table 10: Level of Agreement or Disagreement with Statements involving CBM&As

Q#	Questions Statement	n	Strongly agree +2	Agree +1	No opinion 0	Disagree -1	Strongly disagree -2	Mean	t-value
32	A hostile takeover often results in higher payment to the acquired company than a friendly merger.	31	10	71	19	0	0	0.90	9.333***
33	An acquisition in a related industry is worth more than an acquisition in a non-related industry.	30	33	60	3	0	3	1.20	8.163***
34	An all-cash offer is more effective in a hostile merger than in a friendly merger.	30	3	37	40	20	0	0.23	1.563*
31	Returns from cross-border M&As are often more positive when the targets are private or subsidiary rather than public.	30	3	23	60	13	0	0.16	1.306
6	Please indicate if you agree that diversification is a justifiable motivation for CBM&As?	32	19	25	22	28	6	0.27	1.216
36	A higher premium is justified for the targets, when the economies of the targets' countries have a much lower correlation with the economy of Denmark.	30	0	17	38	41	3	-0.31	-2.073**
35	Most of the gains from CBM&As usually accrue to shareholders of the acquired firm.	30	3	23	37	37	0	-0.07	-0.421
30	Cash (or cash mixed with stock) payment requires a higher premium in CBM&As than a straight stock-exchange transaction.	30	3%	33%	23%	33%	7%	-0.07	-0.348

*, **, *** *Indicates statistical significance at the 0.1, 0.05, and 0.01 level respectively.*

Other views on CBM&As

Table 10 is used to display the respondents' opinions about the existing research findings (from strongly agree to strongly disagree

176

labeled on a five-point scale). Generally, these statements are agreed by the respondents except for Questions 30, 35, and 36. Three of the statements (Questions 32, 33, and 34) show a positive mean value statistically (using one-sample t-test) different from zero (no opinion). For Question 36, the negative mean level is statistically different from zero at 0.05 level. Similar to Mukherjee et al.'; (2004) study on the USA acquirers, our study reports same findings to Questions 32, 33, and 34. But for Question 35, our investigation shows almost the opposite result. Besides, Question 30 was disagreed on a significant level in their study, but is not significant in our research. On the contrary, Question 36 is more strongly supported by the respondents.

For Question 32, 81 percent of the respondents agree that "a hostile takeover often results in higher payment to the acquired company than a friendly merger", which is consistent with some other findings (e.g., Chen & Cornu, 2002). And cash is usually used in hostile takeovers (see also Q34).

Consistent with our anticipation, 93 percent of the respondents support the statement of Question 33 - "an acquisition in a related industry is worth more than an acquisition in a non-related industry".However, there is no consistent opinion about whether diversification is a justified reason for conducting CBM&As in this study (see Question 6).

For Question 35, the statement, "most of the gains from M&As usually accrue to shareholders of the acquired firm" was agreed to by a majority of the respondents in Mukherjee et al.'s (2004) study, but was slightly disagreed by our respondents. Lastly, most of the respondents do not agree that "a higher premium is justified for the targets, when the economies of the targets' countries have a much lower correlation with the economy of Denmark" (Question 36).

Conclusions and Future Research

An Online survey was conducted among CFOs from 131 Danish firms in order to obtain information on their motives for conducting CBM&As, valuation practice, and M&A performance (assessment and empirical findings). In addition, we collected their views about some inconclusive statements in M&A research field. Some conclusions have been drawn from their responses and several research directions are provided.

Five primary motives for conducting CBM&As have been identified, which are: 1) geographic expansion; 2) achieving more rapid growth; 3) the expansion or improvement of the product mix; 4) gaining economies of scale/scope; and 5) acquiring technical knowledge/expertise. Based on their replies, it is clear that CBM&As are conducted out of strategic consideration (e.g, geographic expansion, gaining good position to the market) and seeking for economic benefits (e.g., economies of scale/scope), rather than being triggered by external environmental stimulus (e.g., technologic or regulatory shocks, government's incentives) and financial reasons (e.g., tax advandage and lower cost of capital). However, the irrational factors like overconfidence and imitation play a role in decision making. Although "geographic expansion" and "achieving more rapid growth" have been ranked by a number of the respondents as the most important reasons for doing CBM&As, the other respondents have quite different primary motivations. Therefore, as Ranft and Lord (2002) stress, research on acquisitions will be refined by distinguishing the specific motivations for an acquisition and the type of resources being acquired.

Furthermore, most of CBM&As conducted by Danish firms are synergy related and horizontal acquisition is the prefered type. Operational synergy is described as the major synergy source while "financial synergy" and "managerial efficiency" contribute little. However,"prediction and realization of synergy" are still described as the biggest chanllenges in CBM&As. In Ficery et al.'s (2007) study, they also mentioned that most of the acquiring executives fail to identify, value, and capture the synergy, and they pointed out six most common mistakes that acquiring executives tend to make, such as "defining synergies too narrowly or broadly" and "missing the window of opportunity". In an earlier study conducted by Goold and Campbell (1998), they indicated four managerial biases that make synergy seem more attractive and more easily achievable than it truly is. For instance, the executives may have synergy bias to overestimate the benefits and underestimate the costs of synergy. Information asymmetry between the acquirer and the target can also be the reason for difficulty of synergy prediciton. Therefore, more research efforts are needed in these aspects, such as how can the synergy effects be well predicted? What are the efficient strategies and required resources/capabilities for synergy realization? And what are the barriers to synergy relization?

DCF is the dominant valuation method used by Danish firms, but there is a mismatch of cash flow and discount rate, where they use the cash flow produced by the target firms but use their own WACC as the discount rate. Especially, in CBM&As, the target firm is located in another country, and the problem of mismatch will be exacerbated. This unexpected mismatch can be a reason for overvaluation and then lead to overpayment. Besides, over-optimism has been identified as another main factor causing overpayment.

Related to "value creation" in CBM&As, this investigation reports some positive evidence contradicted with negative depiction in prior research, where 99 percent of the respondents stated that CBM&As could help their companies create value. And the "value" created by CBM&As in the practitioners' view not just point to immediate financial improvement but also mean strategic foundation gained for future development. CBM&As not only can help to enhance the firms' value, but also can protect the firms' value from loss, or even sometimes is the only way for the firm to survive. Furthermore, risk-adjusted returns from CBM&As are thought to be higher than the alternative internationalization strategies (e.g., strategic alliance, Greenfield investment). This may also help to answer the general and ongoing question: "why do so many M&A still take place when most are doomed to fail?".

Regarding performance assessment, to our surprise, almost half of the respondents had no metrics to assess the outcomes of CBM&As. We hence doubt the quality of the whole implementation process. These seemingly imprudent no-plan operations tend to be the recipes producing disappointing results regardless of the widely discussed contextual factors (e.g., cultural difference). Therefore, more in-depth investigation on the whole CBM&A implementation process rather than on separated stages or just contextual factors may significantly contribute to finding the antecedents of CBM&A performance. For those respondents who had performance measures, the measures have been linked to their original objectives or business plan, and financial indicators are mainly used. In the academic field, there is still no agreement on the best way but the more suitable method, depending on the research question. Probably, combining the other objective measures (e.g., accounting-performance) with the managers' assessment can better check the realized multifaceted benefits from CBM&As, and offset the disadvantages of different measures at the same time. And three years after CBM&As is considered enough time for the acquirers to begin to reap the benefits, and is thus suitable time horizon for the external researchers to assess the performance. Efforts are still needed to refine the metrics and it is still a puzzle whether short-term event study can predict long-term realized benefits.

Generally, the performance of Danish international acquirer is not good, only two respondents stated the outcomes of CBM&A fully met their initial expectations, and around half of the respondents only achieved their objectives by sixty percent or less. The reasons can be cultural difference, overpayment, over-optimism, the difficulty in synergy prediction as discussed earlier. Further research is welcome.

This study has also asked the practitioners' opinions on several widely discussed impacting factors (i.e., M&A experience, cultural difference, relatedness, and the targets' legal status) in M&A research field. M&A experience is found helpful, but can be harmful as was reported by several respondents. However, almost half of them did not pay attention to manage or accumulate CBM&A experience and knowledge. Then how can M&A experience/knowledge be helpful? For these reasons, more systematic studies are needed to investigate the practitioners' attitude and practice about CBM&A experience/knowledge and the learning mechanisms. This research can also help to answer the question, i.e., M&A has been been researched for more than 60 years, why is it that the accumulated knowledge cannot help improve the acquiring performance? About cultural difference, it is stated by almost all the respondents as the thorniest issue in their CBM&As. Therefore, it is necessary to investigate how the acquirers deal with cultural difference, and whether and how its negative effects can be overcome and its positive effect can be fully used. About relatedness effect, 93 percent of the respondents agree that an acquisition in a related industry is more worthy than the one in a non-related industry. When it comes to the legal status effect, there is no conclusive finding as 60 percent of them give no opinion about whether the acquirer can gain more benefits from private targets compared with public targets. There is therefore the need for additional research about this.

Limitation

This study has some potential limitations. This relatively small sample may not be strong enough to generalize our findings, but their replies are based on their CBM&A experience over nine years, covering hundreds of deals. And it happens that most of the companies have similar answers to some questions, several meaningful conclusions can still be drawn from their replies. Besides, the possibility of non-response bias is always the drawback of survey studies. But our t-test on the differences of industrial affiliates, size (total assets), and legal status between respondents and non-respondents remove the worry of non-response bias.

Another limitation is that although we tried to cover as many topics in this survey as possible, we limited our questionnaire to four pages to ensure we have a viable response rate. This page limit requirement led to elimination of certain questions. Besides, it is impossible to elicit the motives for conducting CBM&As such as agency problems by survey (see Angwin, 2007). However, our aim here is to investigate firms' pure motives for conducting CBM&As (i.e., CBM&As are conducted for the companies' benefits). Therefore, agency problems are of no interest to us. Besides, as mentioned before, agency problems can be constrained by "the market for corporate control", "manager market", "ownership structure" and "financial structure". Most importantly, in our case, 80 percent of Danish CBM&As were conducted by private firms during the period of 2000 to 2010 according to the records in Zephyr Database. Hence, the agency problems probably did not exist widely.

References

Ansoff, H. I. (1965). The Firm of the Future, *Harvard Business Review 43*(5), 62-178.

Andrade, G., Mitchell, M. L. and Stafford, E. (2001).New Evidence and Perspectives on Mergers. Journal of Economic Perspectives 15(2), 103-120.

Angwin, D. (2007). Motives archetypes in mergers and acquisitions (M&A): the implications of a configurational approach to performance, in Sydney, F. & Cooper, C. L. (Ed.). *Advances in Mergers and Acquisitions (Vol.6,* pp.77-105*)*, UK, Elsevier JAI Press.

Amihud, Y. and Lev, B. (1981). Risk Reduction as a Managerial Motive for Conglomerate Mergers, *Bell Journal of Economics 12*, 605-617.

Adolph, G., Buchanan, I., Hornery, J., Jackson, B., Jones, J., Kihlstedt, T., Neilson, G., and Quarls, H. (2001). Merger Integration: Delivering on the Promise. *Booz-Allen & Hamilton.*

Ahuja, G., & Katila, R. (2001). Technological acquisitions and the innovation performance of acquiring firms: a longitudinal study. *Strategic Management Journal 22*(3), 197-220.

Amburgey, T.L. and Miner, A.S. (1992). Strategic Momentum: The Effects of Repetitive, Positional, and Contextual Momentum on Merger Activity. *Strategic Management Journal13*(5), 335-348.

Alexandridis, G., Petmezas, D., and Travlos, N.G. (2010). Gains from Mergers and Acquisitions Around the World: New Evidence. *Financial Management (Winter)*, 1671-1695.

Aktas, N., Bodt, D. and Roll, R. (2009).Learning, hubris and corporate serial acquisitions.*Journal of Corporate Finance 15*(5), 543-561

Barney, J. B. (1986). Strategic Factor Markets: Expectations, Luck, and Business Strategy. *Management Science 32*, 1231-1241.

Barney, J. (1991). Firm resources and sustained competitive advantage. *Journal of management 17*(1), 99-120.

Bertrand, O. and Betschinger, M.-A. (2012). Performance of domestic and cross-border acquisitions: Empirical evidence from Russian acquirers. *JournalofComparativeEconomics* 40(3), 413–437.

Bhattacharyya, S. and Nain, A. (2009). Horizontal Acquisitions and Buying Power: A Product Market Analysis. *Journal of Financial Economics* 99(1), 97–115.

Bogan, V. L. and Just, D. R. (2008).What Drives Merger Decision Making Behavior? Don't Seek, Don't Find, and Don't Change Your Mind. *Journal of Economic Behavior and Organization 72*(3), 930-943.

Brouthers K.D., van Hastenburg P., van den Ven J.(1998). If Most Mergers Fail Why Are They so Popular? *Long Range Planning* 31(3), 347-353.

Brouthers, K. D., and Brouthers, L. E. (2001).Explaining the national cultural distance paradox.*Journal of International Business Studies* 32, 177-189.

Binder, J. J. (1998). The Event Study Methodology Since 1969, Review of Quantitative Finance and Accounting 11(2), 111–137.

Bruner, R. F (2002). Does M&A pay? A survey of evidence for the decision-maker.*Journal of Applied Finance* 12(1), 48-68.

Brock, D.M. (2005). Multinational acquisition integration: the role of national culture in creating synergies. *InternationalBusinessReview* 14(3), 269–288.

Bradley, M. and Sundaram, A. K. (2004). Do Acquisition Drive Performance or Does Performance Drive Acquisitions?.Working paper, Duke University.

Bradley, M. and Sundaram, A. K. (2006). Acquisitions and Performance: A Re-Assessment of the Evidence. Available at SSRN: http://ssrn.com/abstract=592761.

Baker, H. K., and Mukherjee, T. K. (2007). Survey research in finance: views from journal editors. *International Journal of Managerial Finance 3*(1), 11-25.

Cannella, A. A., and Hambrick, D. C. (1993). Effects of executive departures on the performance of acquired firms. *Strategic Management Journal* 14, 137-152.

Caprio L., Croci E., and Giudice A. D., (2011). Ownership structure, family control, and acquisition decisions, *Journal of Corporate Finance* 17(5), 1636–1657.

Capron, L. (1999).The long-term performance of horizontal acquisitions.*Strategic Management Journal* 20, 987-1018.

Capron L. and Shen J.-C. (2007). Acquisitions of Private vs. Public Firms: Private Information, Target Selection, and Acquirer Returns. Strategic Management Journal 28, 891–911.

Cartwright, S. (2005). Mergers and acquisitions: An update and appraisal, in G.P.Hodgkinson and J.K. Ford (eds.). *International Review of Industrial and Organizational Psychology* **20**, 1-38, John Wiley, Chichester.

Cartwright, S., & Schoenberg, R. (2006). Thirty years of mergers and acquisitions research: Recent advances and future opportunities. *British Journal of Management 17*(S1), S1-S5.

Child, J., Faulkner, D., and Pitkethly, R. (2001).*The Management of International Acquisitions.* Oxford, Oxford University Press.

Chatterjee, S. (1986). Types of Synergy and Economic Value: The Impact of Acquisitions on Merging and Rival Firms. *Strategic Management Journal* 7(2),119-139.

Cording, M., Christmann, P., & Bourgeois Iii, L. (2002). A focus on resources in M&A success: a literature review and research agenda to resolve two paradoxes. *Academy of Management.*

Cording, M., Christmann, P., and Weigelt, C. (2010).Measuring theoretically complex constructs: the case of acquisition performance.*Strategic Organization* 8(1), 11-41.

Conn, R.L. Cosh, A., Guest, P. M., and Hughes, A. (2005). The Impact on UK Acquirers of Domestic, Cross-border, Public and Private Acquisitions, *Journal of Business Finance &Accounting* 32 (5-6), 815–870.

Cosh, A.D. and Guest, P.M. (2001). The Long-Run Performance of Hostile and Friendly Takeovers: UK Evidence, Centre for Business Research Working Paper No. 215 (Cambridge University).

Chen, C., and Cornu, P. (2002). Managerial Performance, Bid Premiums, and the Characteristics of Takeover Targets. *Annals of Economics and Finance* 3(1), 67-84.

Campa, J. M. and Hernando, I. (2004). Shareholder Value Creation in European M&As. *European Financial Management* 10(1), 47-81.

Cloodt, M., Hagedoorn, J., & Kranenburg, H. V. (2006). Mergers and acquisitions: Their effect on the innovative performance of companies in high-tech industries. *Research Policy 35*(5), 642-654.

Colombo, G., Conca, V., Buongiorno, M., & Gnan, L. (2007).Integrating cross-border acquisitions: A process-oriented approach.*Long Range Planning*, 40(2), 202-222.

Datta, D.K. (1991). Organizational fit and acquisition performance: Effects of post-acquisition integration. *Strategic Management Journal* 12, 281-297.

Duso, T., Gugler, K., and Yurtoglu, B. (2010). Is the event study methodology useful for merger analysis? A comparison of stock market and accounting data, *International Review of Law and Economics* 30(2), 186-192.

Depamphilis D.M. (2012). Mergers, Acquisitions, and Other Restructuring Activities: an integrated approach to process, tools, cases, and solutions. USA, Academic press of Elsevier, 6th edition.

Dos Santos, M. B., Errunza, V. R., and Miller, D. P. (2008). Does corporate international diversification destroy value? Evidence from cross-border mergers and acquisitions.*Journal of Banking & Finance 32*(12), 2716-2724.

Doukas, J. A., Holmen, M., and Travlos, N. G. (2002).Diversification, Ownership and Control of Swedish Corporations.*European Financial Management* 8(3), 281-314.

Duhaime, I. M. and Schwenk, C. R. (1985).Conjectures on Cognitive Simplification in Acquisition and Divestment Decision Making.*Academy of Management Review* 10(2), 287-295.

Damodaran, A. (2007). Valuation Approaches and Metrics: A Survey of the Theory and Evidence. USA, Now Publishers Inc.

Das, A. and Kapil, S. (2012), Explaining M&A Performance: A Review of Empirical Research. *Journal of Strategy and Management* 5 (3), 1-41.

Desyllas, P., & Hughes, A. (2010). Do high technology acquirers become more innovative? *Research Policy 39*(8), 1105-1121.

Draper, P. and Paudyal, K. (2006). Acquisitions: Private versus Public, European Financial Management 12(1), 57-80.

Devos, E., Kadapakkam, P., and Krishnamurthy, S. (2009). How Do Mergers Create Value? A Comparison of Taxes, Market Power, and Efficiency Improvements as Explanations for Synergies.*Review of Financial Studies* 22(3), 1178-1211.

DiGeorgio, R. M. (2003). Making mergers and acquisitions work: what we know and don't know (Part II). *Journal of Change Management* 3(3), 259-274.

Ficery, K., Herd, T., & Pursche, B. (2007). Where has all the synergy gone? The M&A puzzle. *Journal of business strategy 28*(5), 29-35.

Fama, E. F. (1998). Market Efficiency, Long-term Returns, and Behavioral Finance.*Journal of Financial Economics* 49(3), 283-306.

Finkelstein, S. (1997). Inter-industry merger patterns and resource dependence: A replication and extension of Pfeffer (1972). *Strategic Management Journal* 18(10), 787-810.

Fernandez, P. (2007). Company Valuation Methods: the Most Common errors in Valuation. *Available at SSRN: http://ssrn.com/abstract=274973.*

Fishman, M.J. (1989). Preemptive Bidding and the Role of the Medium of Exchange in Acquisitions.*Journal of Finance* 44(1), 41-57.

Fridolfsson, S.-O.and Stennek, J. (2005). Why Mergers Reduce Profits and Raise Share Prices-A Theory of Preemptive Mergers. *Journal of the European Economic Association* 3(5), 1083-1104.

Faccio, M., McConnell, J.J., and Stolin, D., (2006).Returns to acquirers of listed and unlisted targets.*Journal of Financial and Quantitative Analysis* 41, 197-220.

Fields, L., Fraser, D. R., and Kolari, J. W. (2007). Bidder returns in bancassurance mergers: Is there evidence of synergy? *Journal of Banking* and *Finance* 31(12), 3646-3662.

Goergen, M. and Renneboog, L. (2004).Shareholder Wealth Effects of European Domestic and Cross-border Takeover Bids.*European Financial Management* 10(1), 9-45.

Gort, M. (1969).An Economic Disturbance Theory of Merger. *Mergers and Acquisitions* 83(4), 624-642.

Goold and Campnell (1998).Desperately Seeking Synergy, Harvard Business Review 76(5), 131-143.

Graham, J. (1999). Herding among investment nesletters: Theory and evidence.*Journal of Finance* 54, 237-268.

Graham J. R., Lemmon, M. L., and Wolf, J. G. (2002). Does Corporate Diversification Destroy Value? *The Journal of Finance* LVII (2), 695-720.

Goel, A. M. and Thakor, A. V. (2010). Do Envious CEOs Cause Merger Waves? *Review of Financial Studies* 23(2), 487-517.

Gadiesh, O., Ormiston, C., Rovit, S., and Critchlow, J. (2001).The Why and How of Merger Success.*European Business Journal* 13(4), 187-193.

Ghosh, A. (2001). Does operating performance really improve following corporate acquisitions? *Journal of Corporate Finance* 7, 151-178.

Goold, M., & Campbell, A. (1998).Desperately seeking synergy.*Harvard Business Review 76*(5), 131-143

Hannan, M. T., and Freeman, J. (1989).Organizational Ecology. Cambridge, Mass, Harvard University Press.

Harford, J. (2003). Efficient and Distortional Components to Industry Merger Waves, AFA 2004 San Diego Meetings.*Available at SSRN:*http://ssrn.com/abstract=388441.

Hadlock, C., Houston J., and Ryngaert M., 1999. The role of managerial incentives in bank acquisitions, *Journal of Banking & Finance*, 23(2-4): 221-249.

Hayward, M. L. A. (2002). When do firms learn from their acquisition experience? Evidence from 1990-1995. *Strategic Management Journal* 23, 21-39.

Hitt, M.A., Ireland, R.D., Camp, S.M., and Sexton, D.L. (2001). Strategic entrepreneurship: entrepreneurial strategies for creating wealth.*Strategy management* 22(Special Issue), 479-491.

Healy, P., Palepu, K., and Ruback, R. (1992). Does corporate performance improve after mergers? *Journal of Financial Economics* 31, 135-175.

Haleblian, J. and Finkelstein, S. (1999) The Influence of Organizational Acquisition Experience on Acquisition Performance. *Administrative Science Quarterly* 44(1), 29-56.

Haleblian, J., Kim, J., & Rajagopalan, N. (2006). The influence of acquisition experience and performance on acquisition behavior: Evidence from the U.S. commercial banking industry. *Academy of Management Journal 49*(2), 357-370.

Ismail, A. (2011). Does the Management's Forecast of Merger Synergies Explain the Premium Paid, the Method of Payment, and Merger Motives? *Financial Management*, 40(4), 879-910.

Jemison, D. B. and Sitkin, S. B. (1986). Corporate Acquisitions: A Process Perspective. *The Academy of Management Review* 11(1), 145-163.

Jensen, M. C. (1986). Agency costs of free cash flow, corporate finance, and takeovers. *American Economic Review* 76, 323-329.

Jensen, M. C.(1988). Takeovers: Their causes and consequences, *Journal of Economic Perspectives* 2(1), 21-48.

Jensen, M. and Ruback, R. (1983). The market for corporate control: The scientific evidence, *Journal of Financial Economics* 11(1-4), 5-50.

Kaplan, S. N., and Weisbach, M. S. (1992). The success of acquisitions: Evidence from divestitures. *Journal of Finance* 47, 107-138.

King, D., Dalton, D., Daily, C. and Covin, J. (2004).Meta-analyses of post acquisition performance indications of unidentified moderators.*Strategic Management Journal* 25, 187-200.

Kiessling, T., & Harvey, M. (2008).Determining Top Managements"'Value": Pre/Post Acquisition.*Journal of Business and Management 14*(1), 5-24.

Lie, E. and Lie, H. J. (2002). Multiples Used to Estimate Corporate Value. *Financial Analysts Journal* 58(2), 44–54.

Liu, Y., Taffler R., and et al., 2009. CEO Value Destruction in M&A Deals and Beyond, *Long range planning*, 31, 347-353.

Lyon, J. D., Barber, B.M., and Tsai, C.-L.(1999). Improved Methods for Tests of Long-Run Abnormal Stock Returns.*Journal of Finance* 54(1), 165-201.

Loughran, T. and Vijh, A. M., (1997). Do Long-Term Shareholders Benefit From Corporate Acquisitions? *The Journal of Finance* 52(5), 1765-1790.

Manne, H. G. (1965). Mergers and the Market for Corporate Control.*Journal of Political Economy* 73, 110-120.

MacKinley, (1997).Event studies in economics and finance. *Journal of Economic Literature* 35(1), 13-39

Meglio, O. and Risberg, A., (2010). Mergers and acquisitions-Time for a methodological rejuvenation of the field?*Scandinavian Journal of Management* 26, 87-95.

Mueller, D. C. (1969) A theory of conglomerate mergers.*Quarterly Journal of Economics* 83, 643-659.

Mitchell, M. L., and Mulherin, J. H. (1996).The Impact of Industry Shocks on Takeover and Restructuring Activity.*Journal of Financial Economics*41, 193-229.

Moeller, S.B., Schlingemann, F.P., and Stulz, R.M. (2004).Firm size and the gains from acquisitions. Journal of Financial Economics 73, 201-228.

Moeller, S.B., and Schlingemann, F. P. (2005). Global diversification and bidder gains: A comparison between cross-border and domestic acquisitions. *Journal of Banking & Finance* 29, 533-564.

Mukherjee, T. K., Halil K., and Kent, B. H. (2004). Merger Motives and Target Valuation: A Survey of Evidence from CFOs. *Journal of Applied Finance* 14(2), 7-24.

Martynova, M. and Renneboog, L. (2008). A century of corporate takeovers: What have we learned and where do we stand? *Journal of Banking* and *Finance* 32(10), 2148-2177.

Martynova, M., and Renneboog, L. (2011). The performance of the European market for corporate control: Evidence from the fifth takeover wave. *European Financial Management 17*(2), 208-259.

Maquieira, C. P., Megginson, W. L., and Nail, L. (1998). Wealth creation versus wealth redistributions in pure stock-for-stock mergers.*Journal of Financial Economics 48*(1), 3-33.

Pfeffer, J. and Salancik, G. R. (1978). The External Control of Organizations: A Resource Dependence Perspective, New York, Harper & Row.

Puranam, P., and Srikanth, K. (2007). What they know vs. what they do: How acquirers leverage technology acquisitions. *Strategic Management Journal* 28, 805-825.

Papadakis, V. M., and Thanos, I. C. (2010).Measuring the performance of acquisitions: An empirical investigation using multiple criteria.*British journal of management 21*(4), 859-873.

Powell, R. G. and Stark, A. W. (2005). Does operating performance increase post-takeover for UK takeovers? A

Comparison of Performance Measures and Benchmarks, Journal of Corporate Finance 11(1-2), 293– 317.

Palich, L. E., Cardinal, L. B., and Miller, C. C. Curvilinearity in the diversification–performance linkage: an examination of over three decades of research. *Strategic management journal 21*(2), 155-174.

Phene, A., Tallman, S., and Almeida, P. (2012). When Do Acquisitions Facilitate Technological Exploration and Exploitation, *Journal of Management 38*(3), 753-783.

Peng, Y. S. and Fang, C. P. (2010). Acquisition Experience, Board Characteristics, and Acquisition Behavior.*Journal of Business Research* 63, 502-509.

Roll, R. (1986). The hubris hypothesis of corporate takeovers, *Journal of Business* 59(2), 197-216

Ranft, A. L., & Lord, M. D. (2002).Acquiring new technologies and capabilities: A grounded model of acquisition implementation. Organization Science, 13(4), 420-441.

Stigler, G. J. (1950). Monopoly and Oligopoly by Merger.*The American Economic Review* 40 (2), 23-34.

Steiner, P. (1975). *Mergers: Motives, Effects, Policies.* University of Michigan Press, Ann Arbor.

Scharfstein, D. S., and Stein, J. C. (1990). Herd behavior and investment, *American Economic Review* 80(3), 465-479.

Stein, J. C. (2003). Agency, information and corporate investment.*Handbook of the Economics of Finance1*, 111-165.

Sudarsanam, S. (2010).Creating Value from Mergers and Acquisitions: the Challenges 2nd ed. UK, Pearson Education Limited.

Scherer, F.M. and Ross, D. (1990).*Industrial Market Structure and Economic Performance.* Third Ed. Boston: Houghton Mifflin Co.

Seth, A. (1990). Value Creation in Acquisitions: A Reexamination of Performance Issues, *Strategic Management Journal* 11, 99-115.

Seth, A., Song, K. P., and Richardson, P. (2000).Synergy, Managerialism or Hubris? An Empirical Examination of

Motives for Foreign Acquisitions of U.S. *Journal of International Business Studies* 31(3), 387-405

Shleifer, A., and Vishny, R.W. (2003).Stock Market Driven Acquisitions.*Journal of Financial Economics* 70(3), 295-311.

Shleifer, A. and Vishny, R.W. (1989). Management Entrenchment: The Case of Manager-Specific Investments, *Journal of Financial Economics* 25, 123-139.

Stahl, G. and Voight, A. (2004).Meta-analyses of the performance implications of cultural differences in mergers and acquisitions.*Best Paper Proceedings of the Annual Meeting of the Academy of Management*, New Orleans, 11-15.

Schoenberg, R., (2006). Measuring the Performance of Corporate Acquisitions: An Empirical Comparison of Alternative Metrics.*British Journal of Management* 17(4), 361-370.

Singh, H. and Montgomery, C. (1987). Corporate Acquisition Strategies and Economic Performance, *Strategic Management Journal* 8(4), 377-386.

Tobin, J. (1969). A General Equilibrium Approach to Monetary Theory, Journal of Money, *Credit and Banking* 2(1), 15-29.

Trautwein, F. (1990).Merger Motives and Merger Prescriptions.*Strategic Management Journal* 11(4), 283-295.

The Economic Times (2011). Global M&A volume marginally down to USD 2.70trillion (Dec., 30) http://articles.economictimes.indiatimes.com/2011-12-30/news/30573006_1_global-m-a-volume-m-a-deals-worth-usd-dealogic.

Tuch, C. and O'Sullivan, N. (2007). The impact of acquisitions on firm performance: a review of the evidence. *International Journal of Management Reviews* 9, 141-170.

Thanos, I. C., and Papadakis, V. M. (2011). The Use of Accounting-Based Measures in Measuring M&A Performance: A Review of Five Decades of Research, in Sydney, F. & Cooper, C. L. (Ed.). *Advances in Mergers and Acquisitions (Vol.10, pp.103-120)*, UK, Elsevier JAI Press.

193

Teerikangas, S., & Very, P. (2006). The culture–performance relationship in M&A: From yes/no to how. *British Journal of Management* 17(S1), S31-S48.

Valentini, G., & Dawson, A. (2010). Understanding of The Effects of M&A on Technological Performance, In Sydney, F. & Cooper, C. L. (Ed.).*Advances in Mergers and Acquisitions* (Vol. 9, pp. 177-197), UK, Elsevier JAI Press.

Williamson, O. E. (1998). The Institutions of Governance.*American Economic Review* 88(2), 75-79.

Weber, Y. and Shlomo, Y. T. (2012), Mergers and acquisitions process: the use of corporate culture analysis, Cross Cultural Management: An International Journal 19(3), 288-303.

Wright P., Kroll M., and Elenkov D., 2002. Acquisition Returns, Increase in Firm Size, and Chief Executive Officer Compensation The Moderating Role of Monitoring. *Academy of Management Journal,* 45(3): 599-608.

Zollo, M., and Singh, H. (2004). Deliberate learning in corporate acquisitions: Post-acquisition strategies and integration capability in U.S. bank mergers. *Strategic Management Journal* 25, 1233-1256.

Zollo, M. and Meier, D. (2008). What is M&A performance? *Academy of Management Perspectives* 22, 55-77.

Zollo, M., and Reuer, J. J. (2010).Experience spillovers across corporate development activities.*Organization Science 21,* 1195–1212.

CHAPTER SEVEN

The Competitiveness of Nations and Firms in a Global Context - Implications for Poverty Alleviation in Developing Countries

John Kuada

Abstract

This chapter focuses attention on the human side of national and firm-level competitiveness in a dynamic global business environment. It introduces the concept of *human capability development* into the business economics literature, arguing that competitiveness depends on the overall capability of people, not only in a technical sense of having required work competencies and applying them efficiently but also on work attitude and behaviours that produce inter-human trust and collaboration. The human capability development construct is defined in terms of the following four sets of factors - (1) the *cultural and civil societal characteristics*, (2) the overall *institutional capabilities* of the nation, (3) *leadership and governance capabilities*, and (4) the *global orientation* of individuals, organisations and the society as a whole (as well as the integration of firms and institutions within the global family). It argues that competitiveness can only be sustained if an appropriate balance is maintained between these factors which can be of a conflicting nature.

Introduction

Private enterprise-driven economic growth has proven to be a relatively more viable model of development than other approaches to economic development that human societies have experimented with during the last 100 years. Empirical evidence suggests that as the number of enterprises grows the number of job opportunities for people (especially the youth) increases and the overall wealth of nations increase as well. This strengthens individuals' capacity to care for themselves and their families. Furthermore, as these enterprises grow, they provide a larger source of tax revenues necessary for anti-poverty and welfare policies of governments. This awareness has encouraged most developing countries to adopt policies and initiatives that seek to enhance their competitiveness as nations and those of their firms. Hitherto, these policies and initiatives have been based on neoclassical liberal economic theories that are generally anchored on structuralism as a paradigm. Particularly influential in this regard are the works of competitiveness theorists with macroeconomics and business management persuasions, including Michael Porter, Alan Rugman, Joseph D'Cruz, Alain Verbeke, John Dunning as well as the network theorists such as Jan Johanson and Lars-Gunnar Mattsson, to mention a few.

One central conclusion from this strand of research is that the competitive potentials of firms and nations may depend partly on the configuration of resources that they possess, and partly on their linkages with institutions, firms and markets that internationally will determine the extent to which these resources can be effectively deployed. International linkages also provide access to specialized resources that are unavailable in particular nations.

Although contributions to this stream of research have provided remarkable insights into the mechanisms and processes of firms' competitiveness within a dynamic international business context, studies in economic sociology suggest that they do not adequately address the challenges that face developing countries in their drive to reduce poverty. Thus, there are still gaps in our current knowledge about enterprise development and poverty reduction initiatives in developing economies. In 1985 Mark Granovetter made an impassioned plea to economists and sociologists to theorize economic action in ways that acknowledge its strong linkages to social structure. An economy, he argued, is structurally embedded in social networks that affect its functioning. Thus, a fruitful analysis of economic actions "requires us to avoid the atomization implicit in the theoretical extremes of under- and oversocialized conceptions. Actors do not behave or decide as atoms outside a social context, nor do they adhere slavishly to a script written for them by the particular intersection of social categories that they happen to occupy. Their attempts at purposive action are instead embedded in concrete, ongoing [social] systems..." (See Granovetter, 1985:487) He re-introduced the concept of "embeddedness" into the economic sociology literature in order to capture the social contextuality of economic activities and as a critique to the Williamsonian perspectives on economic transactions (Williamson, 1975 and 1985). To him, relational constituents such as social and emotional attachments, information flows and general inter-personal processes contribute immensely to explaining the growth potentials of economic systems and entrepreneurial activities in different societies.

In addition to the concerns expressed by economic sociologists, social-psychologists also criticise the neoclassical economic theorists as well as business economists for avoiding an explicit articulation of the role of the individual in the governance of economic relationships. They argue that organizations collaborate through people. Thus, without explicitly factoring the individual into the models of business relationships, scholars and policy makers tend to have an incomplete basis for understanding what drives the outcomes (positive or negative) of enterprises.

My aim in this chapter is to build on these dissenting perspectives from economic sociologists and social-psychologists in order to augument existing internationalization and national competitivenss theories that guide economic policies in developing countries. The premise of the arguments in this chapter is that a good deal of competitive advantage resides in human beings more than in the structures and systems that have been at the centre stage of contemporary theories. My focus is therefore on the human side of economics with an emphasis on how actions that individuals undertake and the socio-cultural context within which they act impact the competitiveness of nations and firms. Building on this understanding, I will introduce the concept of *human capability development* as a national instrument for building dynamic and sustainable competitive advantages for nations and firms within the global context.

The chapter continues with this brief introduction by presenting and reflecting on the central theories and models of national competitiveness and internationalization of firms. It then introduces perspectives from economic sociology and social psychology. These discussions then form the bedrock for the human capability development model that I present. The chapter ends with a section discussing the policy, strategy and research implications of the model presented.

Macro Level Theories of International Competitiveness

Economists argue that each nation has a constellation of factors of production, which serve as necessary inputs for competing in any industry. Industrial economists classify these factors into two broad categories: *basic* and *advanced* factors of production. Basic factors are those factors that may be described as being passively inherited by nations, or whose creation requires relatively modest or unsophisticated private and social investment (Porter, 1990). They include natural resources, climate, location, unskilled and semiskilled labour, and finance capital. Advanced factors, are those which are created, upgraded, and tailored to the needs of specific industries. Their development demands large and often sustained investments in both human and physical capital. There is a general understanding among economists that the contribution of basic factors to competitiveness has declined sharply during the past half a century or more. This means that the rates at which advanced factors are created and upgraded determine the competitiveness of nations (Rugman and D'Cruz, 1993; Moon *et al.*,1995). Thus, factor-creating mechanisms in a nation are more important to *competitive advantage* than the nation's current factor pool.

198

Some economists argue that abundance of some basic resources may result in complacency and their unproductive usage in some nations. Innovations aimed at circumventing selective factor disadvantages may not only economise on factor utilisation but can also create new factor advantages if they trigger firms and nations to develop more sophisticated resources (Porter, 1990). This implies that basic resource disadvantages may turn out to be blessings for some nations if they are encouraged by these disadvantages to innovate.

Porter also draws distinction between *generalised* and *specialised* factors. The generalized factors are those that can be deployed in a wide range of industries. Physical and social infrastructural investments are clear examples of generalized factors. The specialized factors involve specific categories of skilled personnel, infrastructure with specific properties, knowledge bases in particular fields and other factors with relevance to a limited range of businesses and/or organizations. They usually require more focused, and often riskier, private and social investment.

Many researchers have adopted Porter's conceptualization of competitiveness to study economic growth strategies of specific nations and regions of the world. While some of these scholars have seen the model as a bridge between strategic management and international economics (Grant,1991), others consider it inadequate in capturing the complexity and dynamics of globalized economies. For example, Krugman (1990) has been uncomfortable with Porter's notion that nations, like corporations, compete with each other. Similarly, Rugman and his colleagues criticised Porter for limiting his model to a single country. They therefore suggested an extension of the model by introducing *the Double-Diamond model*(Rugman and D'Cruz, 1993). The central thesis of the Double-Diamond model is that countries do not depend entirely on their own factor conditions to remain competitive; they may be linked to the diamond of another country to tap into some specific resources or take advantage of demand conditions in those countries to maximise the value of their specialized resources. Building on this understanding, some scholars argue that it is more appropriate to see national compettitiveness in terms of "multiple linked diamonds', rather than specific national diamonds, analysed in isolation (see Cartwright, 1993 for New Zealand and Hodgetts,1993 for Mexico).These perspectives have encouraged Moon *et al.* (1995) to introduce *the Generalized Double-Diamond (GDD)model.* In addition to emphasising the multiple linkages of national diamond models, the generalized model explicitly incorporates Transnational Firms into the diamond models. It is also useful to see the configurations of the various national diamonds in a dynamic global context; they change over time, and this changes the competitive profiles of individual nations over time.

Firm Level Theories of International Competitiveness

The second broad strand of theories of competitiveness is from the international business management research. This literature reflects two dominant streams of studies. One group of scholars have adopted the view that the domestic demand for nearly all goods and services in most developing economies is too small to allow them to reap scale advantages. Thus, entering foreign markets provides these firms and countries the opportunity to make optimal use of their productive resources. By competing on international markets, the firms are also compelled to remain up-to-date in production, sourcing, and marketing techniques. This stimulates innovation and enhances their overall competitiveness (Fafchamps *et al,* 2001). Second, due to the limited domestic demand for consumer goods, support industries that serve the producers of the consumer goods in these countries are virtually non-existent in most developing countries. Manufacturers of consumer goods must either produce their own inputs or import them from Western industrialised countries.

Several of the scholars endorsing the above perspective have focused attention on understanding the processes that relate to firms' initial entry into foreign markets, including their motives for internationalization, their choice of entry modes, as well as the strategies that they adopt to chart the path of their onward process of internationalization and to improve their performance (Bilkey and Tesar, 1977; Johanson and Vahlne, 1977, 2009; Cavusgil and Nevin, 1981; Leonidou and Katsikeas, 1996; Morschett, *et al.*, 2010; Leonidou and Katsikeas, 2010). These scholars have been inspired mainly by the theories of firm growth and of innovation-diffusion processes, treating internationalization as an innovation that is based on the acquisition of new market knowledge. To them, the internationalization process of firms is path-dependent, - i.e. it proceeds in stages and at a tempo that the innovation and learning process of firms allows. Firms acquire knowledge experientially, i.e. through reflections on individuals' actions as well as through their collective actions. They, therefore, initiate their internationalization processes by entering countries with little psychological distance where the perceived market unfamiliarity is lowest and therefore require minimum new knowledge to operate in. They then move incrementally into more distant countries, using experiences gained in each cycle of international operational events as knowledge base for subsequent market entry decisions. This explanation of the internationalization process of firms is referred to as the *stages process of internationalization* and focus on what Kuada and Sørensen (2000) have labelled as *downstream internationalization.*

Other firm-level researchers have focused their attention on the strategic decisions of firms to obtain parts or all of their inputs (including technology, knowledge and human resources) from foreign sources. This is usually done through a hybrid of cross-border linkages aimed at facilitating joint task performance, input deliveries, as well as upgrading their technological and managerial capacities. Some of the firms involved in these cross-border linkages may sell their products only on the domestic markets and consider the linkages as prerequisites for their competitiveness at home. This approach is denoted as *upstream internationalisation* in the literature (Welch and Luostarinen, 1993; Kuada and Sørensen, 1999).

Some strands of the upstream internationalization research have leaned on the resource based perspective of the firm to argue that where the resources required by a firm to generate its value-adding activities are of a general character, easily identifiable or substitutable, the firm may depend on the market to acquire them and may use them in-house to perform the value-added activities that form the core of its business. But if they are of intangible nature (e.g. tacit knowledge and firm capabilities) the attributes of such resources would render them nearly impossible to buy directly. Therefore, the firm enters into collaborative arrangements with other firms to jointly create and share with the required resources. Thus, most contributions to this stream of research draw on theoretical traditions such as the resource-based perspective on firms (Barney, 1991 and 2001), competence-based perspectives (Prahalad and Hamel, 1990) and knowledge-based perspective (Inkpen and Crossan, 1995; Gulati, 1998). These scholars argue that collaborations enable partners to access the embedded knowledge of co-partners and/or facilitate new knowledge generation (Inkpen and Crossan, 1995).

These observations have motivated Mathews (2006) to argue that some developing country firms can reduce their resource disadvantages through linking, leveraging and learning from firms in other countries (i.e. cross-border interfirm collaborations). Thus, to him internationalization of firms is a dynamic process in which firms are positioned in webs of relationships. The wisdom in upstream internationalization has also informed discussions in the international supply chain management literature where the focus has been on the management of relations with suppliers in foreign countries and the coordination of an integrated network of business processes.

This understanding has informed another dominant strand of research into firm-level competitiveness – i.e. the network perspective of internationalization of firms. To network scholars business exchanges are not characterised by actions of sellers and reactions of buyers. Transactions are rather defined by interactions of active participants in the exchange relationship (Ford *et al.*, 1998). Through *networking* firms obtain access to important complementary assets, markets and technologies without incurring organisational or locational costs (which are typical of internal growth strategies), and free themselves from the limits of local (and internal) competence (See Turnbull and Cunningham, 1981; Ford, 1990; Axelsson and Easton, 1992; Ford *et al.*, 1998). Networks are found to be both relatively stable (because relationships take time and effort) but at the same time dynamic since actors may be on the lookout for more rewarding relationships. Relational bonds are identified to have technical, planning, knowledge, socioeconomic and legal components. In the words of Johanson and Mattsson (1987: 36) network relationships "are constantly being established, maintained, developed, and broken in order to give satisfactory, short-term economic returns and to create positions in the network that will assure the long-term survival and development of the firm".

Interactions with other network participants provide each participant with an opportunity to revise and redefine its needs and, in this way, find new possibilities within the network. This is referred to in the literature as the *interactive effect*. Thus, position is an important concept in the network theory. The position a firm occupies at any given point in time is the outcome of own resources and previous activities combined with changes in external conditions and the firm's resources. Current position again determines the possibilities of resource sharing with others within the network as well as the importance of future positions that the network participants may occupy.

In sum, the neoclassical economic perspective of competitiveness focuses attention on non-human dimensions of exchanges where businesses are seen as key actors (organizations) in leveraging resources to produce and deliver values. Human beings are treated as abstract role players in the exchange relationships.

Sociological and Psychological Perspectives on Competitiveness

Institutional Considerations

In contrast to the economistic perspectives outlined above, economic sociologists focus attention on how and why particular patterns of economic organization ' become established, reproduced, and changed in specific socio-historical circumstances. To them, economic activities are more meaningfully understood as being socially constructed. As such, economic actors' perceptions and beliefs constitute the guiding principles of their behaviour within an economic context. Similarly, the institutional economists argue that the effectiveness of the different modes of capitalist business systems is shaped, to a large extent, by the institutional contexts within which they operate. Thus, a good starting point in understanding the success or failure of economic activities is to analyse the institutional context within which people who make economic decisions are embedded.

Institutional literature shares the structuralist perspectives of neoclassical economists by defining institutions both as structures and mechanisms that reproduce and convey norms, rules, conventions, and habits that govern and shape economic and political life (see North *et al*, 2009). Others see them as arrangements that define networks of relationships within societies (e.g. markets, states, corporate hierarchies, administrative units communities (see Hollingsworth and Roger, 1991).But they hold the view that economic actors must be guided by societal values and norms for them to create values that are socially rewarding. Thus, institutional mechanisms are seen as repositories of value sets that help to contain the socially undesirable consequences of unguarded market systems, levelling the playing field for all stakeholders. Strong institutional capabilities therefore help expand the circle of opportunity and promote an inclusive developmental and welfare-oriented economic growth processes.

The Role of Individuals

The contribution of social psychologists to the international competitiveness debate lies partly in their insistence that firms and institutions are managed by individuals. This is particularly true in international collaborative relationships between firms and nations where uncertainties emanating from geographical divide and risk of opportunism may render decision makers hesitant to make commitments that are vital for success. People "on the spot" make key decisions, communicate with others, negotiate deals and supervise specific aspects of contracted collaborations. In the process theyare able to register errors of interpretation of ideas and thoughts conveyed by their negotiation partners and rectify them quickly enough to avoid misunderstandings that may sow the seed of mistrust between firms (Campbell, 1997). Thus, when individuals within firms understand and appreciate each other's viewpoints, they are able to arrive at a working consensus and manage the relationship between their firms more effectively.

It has also been argued that people tend to make relationship-specific investments (e.g. emotional commitments) to relationships that mean much to them personally or to their career and social mobility. They see these emotional investments as pledges for collaboration. Furthermore, direct personal contacts of key individuals in foreign markets could be used to identify new opportunities, obtain business advice, and open doors in markets where the internationalizing firm may have no previous presence.

The concept of *personal bonding* (Williams *et al.*, 1998) has been introduced into the literature to characterise the individual's role in exchange relations. The emphasis here is on the capabilities that individuals possess in acting as translators of organizational knowledge and competencies and communicating it to other actors in a manner that enhances understanding and creativity within and between organizations, institutions and countries. This is in contrast to structural bonding that characterises inter-organisational and inter-institutional relationships discussed by network scholars, sociologists and political scientists. Personal bonding defines the personal and social relationships that individuals in one firm have with their counterparts in another firm. These bonds contribute immensely to the stability and predictability of the relationships.

Human Capability Development and International Competitiveness

The sociological and psychological perspectives outlined above justify positioning the individual at the centre stage of international enterprise development and management in general. For an individual to succeed in playing an inter-organizational bridging role that helps leverage resources and improve the competitiveness of firms and nations, they need a set of capabilities. I therefore submit that *human capability development* process is at the foundation of sustainable socioeconomic development of any nation. It provides the vital input for creativity, innovation and enterprise development.

I have chosen the term "development" in the human capability development construct purposefully. It connotes change over time and space within individuals and also within the network of relationships that constitutes a society. It also connotes change that signals improvement. Thus, "capabilities" in this theoretical framework are not static. They are dynamic in a manner similar to what Teece and his colleagues describe as "dynamic capabilities" (see Teece *et al.*, 1997; Teece, 2007). This understanding of the term "development" also assumes that individuals take action to transform their capabilities and contribute to the transformation of their societies from one state to the other.

I suggest a classification of human capabilities in terms of three distinct but related categories: (1) *basic capabilities*, (2) *formal capabilities* and (3) *combined capabilities*. *Basic capabilities* in my conceptualization reflect the innate qualities of individuals that are essential for developing core competencies needed for co-existence in groups of other persons. It is also that inner drive that encourages people to challenge their circumstances, seek knowledge and take actions that move them forward in life. I therefore see human capability as unique to each person and rooted in each individual's history. It is therefore difficult to be imitated by others. As such these capabilities must be painstakingly built over time – i.e. they are products of individuals' upbringing and socialization processes that occur through complex interactions among myriads of cultural transmission mechanisms within a given society. *Formal* capabilities are those skills and knowledge acquired through formal (and some degree of informal) education and training. The *combined* capabilities are manifested in abilities that pull together the basic and formal capabilities. This also requires guidance and socialization processes (occasionally in the form of mentoring). The first two of these capabilities are necessary but not sufficient requirements for competitiveness of firms and nations (i.e. they cannot on their own bring people to a state of readiness to take actions necessary for organizational performance). It is the combination of the two that defines the quality of human capability development in a given society. But each provides latent (potential) conditions for efficient and effective enterprise management and economic progress (granting an enabling and supportive environment).

In addition to the three defining characteristics outlined above, human capabilities can also be analysed at different levels of aggregation – individual, group, organizational, societal and international. The collective human capabilities are reflected in the values and attitudes of the groups or organizations to which individuals belong and are therefore related to the concept of culture. Cultural values signalize the types of competencies that a society expects the majority of individuals in a given society to acquire. It also rewards the effective application of these competencies in value creation endeavours of people. This partly accounts for the differences in the resource mobilization potentials of societies.

The Contextual Constructs

The overall framework for human capability development is presented skematically in Figure 1. It shows that there are four main sets of "essential factor conditions" that shape the human capability development processes of individuals and societies. These are (1) the *cultural and civil societal characteristics*, (2) the overall *institutional capabilities* of the nation, (3) *leadership and governance capabilities*, and (4) the *global orientation* of individuals, organisations and the society as a whole (as well as the integration of firms and institutions within the global family). Stated differently, the interplay between these four factor conditions in a given country produces unique set of resources that enhance the country's capacity to manage enterprises in competitive business environments and to develop.

The term "civil society" in the first factor condition is used to depict and analyse self-organization of social relationships outside state (read government) control and can be likened to the "capability architect" – defining the values, norms and visions of individuals and capturing the aspirations of the society as a whole. It therefore constitutes the bedrock on which the other factor conditions rest.

Sociologists use the concept of "civility" to describe the sense of collective social obligation – i.e. the obligation of people to fulfil their individual needs without jeopardising the chances of others to fulfil theirs or the entire community to survive and progress. Where such civility is lacking, jungle rule tends to prevail, creating a de-constructive social structure. Thus, the social and cultural characteristics of a nation can harbour forces of innovation, collective efficiency, network resources and human drive that combine to shape firm-level economic action. Conversely, the social contexts can also be a source of constraining forces in the form of collective inefficiencies and disadvantages as well as inclinations to mediocre performance of firms and institutions.

The other three factor conditions serve as *transmission conduits* – i.e. vehicles for interpreting societal aspirations and rules of accepted behaviour and translating them into actionable opportunities. In this way, the institutional capabilities of the nation, its management/leadership and governance capabilities, and its global orientation jointly prescribe what can be done, proscribe what cannot be done, and promote the accepted courses of action. They therefore help shape individual and collective mindsets and motivate action. Said differently, the framework suggests that the four factor conditions are organically related to each other and jointly influence innovation and enterprise development and thereby economic growth.

Figure 1: Determinants of Human Capabilities Development and Economic Growth

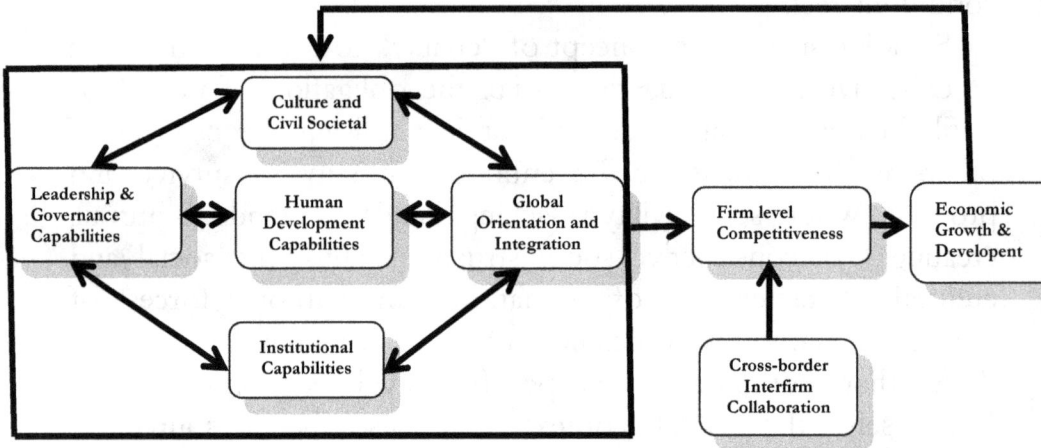

Institutions define the rules of the economic game and establish the structures that regulate the power relations among all stakeholders of an economy. They also facilitate and coordinate the exchange mechanisms among the actors. Thus, accountability, rule of law, political stability, bureaucratic capability, property rights protection and contract enforcement, are frequently listed as mutually reinforcing aspects of growth-enhancing institutions. Consequently, societies with weak institutional quality are normally faced with very high costs in market transactions (Rodrik, 1997). But the reverse can also be true – i.e. a higher level of development will generate the need for and lead to better institutions (Paldam and Gundlach, 2008).

The next factor condition is good leadership and governance in firms and societies. It is often said that good leaders are expected to "lift ordinary people to extraordinary heights" (Boal and Bryson, 1988: 11), motivate citizens to "perform above and beyond the call of duty" and to think innovatively. Thus, while enculturation mechanisms in societies guide individuals' action pathways, leaders serve as instruments that lead people to these pathways and encourage them to travel them and overcome the challenges along the journey.

Thus, leadership can be seen as the underlying energy in every collective endeavour, be it in groups, organizations, communities and/or nations. Organisational members are linked through these energy flows and it is this energy that brings the organisation into life for its members. In the same vein, Dahlberg (2004) argues that leaders with the right frame of mind and psychological dispositions can facilitate the flow of positive energy that improves their followers' ability to develop. Such leaders can encourage divergent and convergent thinking, attitudes of curiosity, risk-taking, tolerance for ambiguity and openness among followers. In other words, good leaders verbalize the collective convictions of the progressive segments of a population and translate them into actionable plans and strategies. As people join to implement their actions, they share the convictions underlying them and become "transmitters" of the conviction, thereby extending its geographic outreach. With sustainable efforts, increasing segments of the population embrace the conviction and encourage others to adopt it.

Global orientation of individuals, businesses, institutions and societies also contribute to capability development in several ways. Global orientation shapes peoples' mind-sets, encourages open mindedness and guides them in acquiring inter-cultural competence skills, thus contributing to the construction of a fellowship that enhances the overall capabilities of individuals and societies. It is now acknowledged that many of the pressing problems that the world faces today are beyond the solution of any single country or society. Cross-border collaborations, increasing commitment to civil society at the global level and greater citizen awareness of their role in public life, are therefore viable ways of sustainable co-existence.

Implications for Competitiveness in Developing Countries

Building on the above discussions and the premise that economic activities must be purposefully organized in social settings for them to produce their transformational impact, I submit that the degree of human capability development in nations can help explain the differential competitiveness of nations within a global economic context. The understanding that I wish to forward isthat the collective mindsets that emerge out of dialogues around shared experiences can propel economic and social development. This happens if the social resources are captured and galvanized by visionary and transformational leaders in households, organizations, communities and societies. But the reverse can also be true.This means poverty alleviation in developing countries will depend on how individuals who manage institutions and the civil society organizations are able to help improve the human capability development processes in societies – i.e. giving individuals the mental capacity to reflect on their situations and make decisions that take them out of poverty. This will help societies to collectively create environments that reinforce the capacity of individuals to chart pathways that lead them to the fulfillment of their hopes through the bolder pro-developmental mindset. But the interactions can also produce sets of values or mindsets that constrain economic and social development. It is therefore often argued that culture is the most important asset of any country, but it can also be its worst liability.

The absence of effective institutions is considered a key factor hampering competitiveness of most developing economies and their firms. Similarly, Acemoglu and Robinson (2012) classify institutions into two broad categories – inclusive or extractive institutions. They argue that inclusive economic institutions create the incentives and opportunities necessary to harness the energy, creativity and entrepreneurship in society. Such institutions also protect private property rights, enforce the principles of rule of law and maintain predictable enforcement of contracts. Extractive institutions do not. Thus, poor countries on average are dominated by extractive institutions while rich ones have inclusive ones.

Well-developed human capabilities will also enable individuals and their societies to leverage domestic and foreign resources to efficiently produce and market goods and services in demand at home and abroad. This will depend significantly on the extent to which the dominant cultural characteristics are growth enhancing rather than creating social liabilities (as opposed to social capital) for key economic actors. It will also depend very much on leadership and governance capabilities available at all levels of organized activities – economic or otherwise.

Furthermore, there is evidence indicating that clusters of civil society entities – including academics, interest groups, and parliamentarians who share a common understanding of the role of enterprises in the development of nations – can help shape the competitive trajectories of developing nations. These interest groups are now establishing formalized pressure groups such as *Network of Civil Society Organisations on Competition* (NCSOC) in some countries. In countries where they have taken roots, these groups are bringing the voices of these new social actors into the policy debate. They also serve to re-focus the debate on the modalities by which enterprises can help alleviate poverty and how existing policies, institutions as well as cultural norms and values promote or constrain enterprise competitiveness (Scholte, 1999).

Summary and Conclusion

The main message from the discussions in this chapter is that national and firm-level competitiveness depends on the overall capability of people, not only in a technical sense of having

213

required work competencies and applying them efficiently but also on work attitude and behaviours that produce inter-human trust and collaboration. Thus, country differences in competitiveness can be explained partly by attributes of the civil society and the human development capabilities of their citizens. Human capability development in turn depends on the interplay of four sets of factors - (1) the *cultural and civil societal characteristics*, (2) the overall *institutional capabilities* of the nation, (3) *leadership and governance capabilities*, and (4) the *global orientation* of individuals, organisations and the society as a whole (as well as the integration of firms and institutions within the global family).Competitiveness can only be sustained if an appropriate balance is maintained between these factors which can be of a conflicting nature.

An inclusive civil society, high institutional quality and leadership are critical in energizing individuals and a society and get them properly oriented towards their developmental objectives. I have also argued that internationalization also provides firms with the opportunity to fulfil the twin objectives of resource leveraging and market growth. Strong international competitiveness also creates the resources that enable material improvements in living standards and resources for investments that promote both individual wellbeing and further national competitiveness.

References

Acemoglu, Daron and James Robinson (2012): *Why Nations Fail*, CrownBusiness

Arndt S. and H. Kierzkowski (2001), *Fragmentation: New Production Patterns in the World Economy*, Oxford: Oxford University Press

Axelsson, B and Easton, G. (Eds) (1992) *Industrial Networks – A New View of Reality* London: Routledge.

Barney, J. B. (1991) "Firm Resources and Sustained Competitive Advantage.*Journal of Management*, 17, pp.99-120.

Barney, J.B. (2001), "Resource-based theories of competitive advantage: A Ten-year Retrospective on Resource-based View" *Journal of Management* 27 pp: 643-650

Bilkey, W. J., and Tesar, G.(1977), "The Export Behavior of Smaller-Sized Wisconsin Manufacturing Firms".*Journal of International Business Studies*, 8, pp.93-98.

Boal, K.B., and Bryson, J.M. (1988).Charismatic leadership.In Hunt J.G., Baliga B.R., Dachler H.P., and Schriesheim C.A. (Eds.) *A Phenomenological and structural approach*.Emerging leadership vista. Lexington, New York. (pp. 11-28).

Borys, B. and Jemison D.B. (1989), "Hybrid Arrangements as Strategic Alliances: Theoretical Issues in Organizational Combinations" *Academy of Management Journal* 14 (2): 234-49

Burt, R. S. (1992), The Social Structure of Competition. (In) Nohria, N. and R. G. Eccles, eds.: *Networks and Organizations*. Harvard Business School Press: Boston.

Cambell, Alexandra (1997) "Buyer-supplier partnerships: flip sides of the same coin" *Journal of Business and Industrial Marketing* Vol.12 No. 6: 417-434

Cartwright, W. R. (1993). Multiple linked "diamonds" and the international competitiveness of export-dependent industries: The New Zealand experience. *Management International Review*, 33(2), 55.

Cavusgil, S. Tamer and John R. Nevin (1981), "Internal determinants of export marketing behaviour: an empirical investigation" *Journal of Marketing Research* Vol. XVIII

Cohen, Westley M., & Levinthal, Daniel A. (1990), "Absorptive Capacity: A New Perspective on Learning and Innovation", Administrative Science Quarterly, 35: 128-152

Dahlberg, Steven (2004) "Creativity by Choice, Not by Chance: Developing Imagination in the Intelligence Community" *Available at www.appliedimagination.org* Assessed on 9 January, 2014

Dunning, John H. (1988), "The eclectic paradigm of international production: a restatement and some possible extensions" *Journal of International Business Studies*, Spring, pp 1-31

Fafchamps, Marcel, Teal, Francis and Toye, John (2001), "Towards a Growth Strategy for Africa" Centre for the Study of African Economies ,University of Oxford REP/2001-06

Ford, D. (Ed.) (1990) *Understanding Business Markets: Interaction, relationship and networks* London Academic Press Limited

Ford, D., Gadde, L., Håkansson, H., Lundgren, A., Snehota, I., Turnbull, P. and Wilson, D. (1998) *Managing Business Relationships* Chichester: John Wiley and Sons

Gereffi, G. (1994), 'The organization of buyer-driven global commodity chains: how U.S. retailers shape overseas production networks', in G. Gereffi and M. Korzeniewicz (eds) *Commodity Chains and Global Capitalism*, Westport: Praeger, pp. 95--122.

Gereffi, G., Humphrey, J., & Sturgeon, T. (2005). The governance of global value chains. Review of international political economy, 12(1), 78-104.

Granovetter, M. S. (1985), "Economic Action and Social Structure: The Problem of Embeddedness", *American Journal of Sociology*, Vol. 91, No.3, pp. 481-510.

Grant, R.M. (1991). Porter's Competitive Advantage of Nations: An Assessment. *Strategic Management Journal*, 12(7), 535.

Gulati, Ranjay, (1998), Alliances and networks, *Strategic Management Journal*, vol. 19, p.293-317

Gupta, Sanjeev and Yang, Yongzheng (2006) "Ublocking Trade" *Finance and Development* Vol.43 No.4 pp.22-25

Heinelt, H (2010) *Governing Modern Societies Towards Participatory Governance*, Oxford, Oxford University Press.

Hodgetts, R. M. (1993). Porter's Diamond Framework In A Mexican Context. *Management International Review*, 33(2),41.

Hollingsworth, J. Rogers 1991."The Logic of Coordinating American Manufacturing Sectors."In John C. Campbell, J. Rogers Hollingsworth, and Leon Lindberg, eds. *Governance of the American Economy.*New York: Cambridge

Inkpen, Andrew C. & Mary M. Crossan (1995), "Believing is seeing: Joint ventures and organization learning," *The Journal of Management Studies*, 32(5): 595-618.

Johanson, J. and J.-E. Vahlne (1977), "The Internationalization Process of the Firm -- A Model of Knowledge Development and Increasing Foreign Market Commitments," *Journal of International Business Studies* 8 (1), 23-32.

Johanson, Jan and Mattsson, Lars-Gunnar (1987) "Inter-organisational relations in industrial systems: A network approach compared with the transaction-cost approach" *International Studies of Management and Organisation* Vol. 17 No. 1: 34-48

Katsikeas, Constantine S. and Robert E. Morgan (1994), "Differences in Perceptions of Exporting Problems Based on Firm Size and Export Market Experience" *European Journal of Marketing* Vol, 28 No. 5

Krugman, P.R. 1990. *Rethinking International Trade*. Cambridge, MA: MIT Press.

Kuada, John and Olav Jull Sørensen (1999), "Upstream and Downstream Processes of Internationalization: Some Ghanaian Evidence" *The Journal of Euromarketing* Vol 7 No. 4 pp: 7-41

Kuada, John and Olav Jull Sørensen (2000), *Internationalization of Companies from Developing Countries:* (NY. The Haworth Press Inc.)

Leonidou LC, Katsikea CS. (2010). "Integrative assessment of exporting research articles in business journals during the period 1960–2007". *Journal of Business Research* 1-9.

Leonidou, L. C. and C.S Katsikeas, (1996), "The Export Development Process: An Integrative Review of Empirical Models" *Journal of International Business Studies*, 27, pp.517-551.

217

Mathews, John A. (2006) "Catch-up Strategies and the Latecomer Effect in Industrial Development" *New Political Economy*, Vol. 11, No. 3, pp: 313-335

McDougall, P. P., Shane, S. and Oviatt, B.M. (1994)."Explaining the formation of international new ventures: The limits of theories from international business research." Journal of Business Venturing **9**(6): 469-487.

Moon, C., Rugman, A.M. & Verbeke, A. 1995. 'The generalized double diamond approach to international competitiveness', In Rugman, A., Van den Broeck, J. & Verbeke, A. (eds), *Research in Global Strategic Management: Volume V*. Beyond the Diamond. Greenwich, CT: JAI Press.

Morschett, D., H. Schramm-Klein and B. Swoboda (2010), 'Decades of research on market entry modes: What do we really know about external antecedents of entry mode choice?',*Journal of International Management*, **16** (1), 60-77

North, D.C., Wallis, J.J., and Weingast, B.R. (2009), Violence and Social Orders: A Conceptual Framework for Interpreting Recorded Human History. *Cambridge: Cambridge University Press*

Paldam, M., Gundlach, E., (2008). Two views on institutions and development: The Grand Transition vs. the primacy of institutions. *Kyklos* 61, 65-100

Porter, M.E. 1990. The Competitive Advantage of Nations. New York: Free Press, MacMillan

Prahalad, C., & Hamel, G. (1990), The Core Competence of the Corporation, Harvard Business Review, May-June: 79-91

Rodrik Dani (1997) "The 'Paradoxes' of the Succesful State" *European Economic Review* 41:411-442.

Rugman, A.M. & D'Cruz, J.R. 1993. 'The double diamond model of internationalcompetitiveness: the Canadian experience', *Management International Review*, 33(2):17–32.

Rugman, A.M. & Verbeke, A. 1993. 'The double diamond model of internationalcompetitiveness: the Canadian experience', *Management International Review*, SpecialIssue, 33: 17–39.

Scholte, J.A., (1999) 'Global Civil Society: Changing the World?' CSGR WP 31/99, Centre for the Study of Globalisation and

Regionalisation, University of Warwick
http://www.warwick.ac.uk/fac/soc/CSGR

Teece, D. J., Pisano, Gary and Shuen, Amy (1997) Dynamic Capabilities and Strategic Management *Strategic Management Journal*, Vol. 18, No. 7. pp. 509-533.

Teece, David J. (2007). "Explicating Dynamic Capabilities: The Nature and Microfoundations of (Sustainable) Enterprise Performance," *Strategic Management Journal*, 28(13): 1319-1350.

Turnbull, P.W. and Cunningham, M.T. (1981) *International Marketing and Purchasing* London: Macmillan

Turnbull, Peter W. (1987), "A challenge to the stages theory of the internationalization process" in P.J. Rosson and S.D. Reid (eds.) *Managing Export Entry and Expansion* (NY. Præger) pp: 21-40

Weiss, H. M., and Adler, S. (1984) "Personality and organizational behaviour" *Research in Organizational Behavior* 6:1-50.

Welch, Lawrence S. and Luostarinen, Reijo (1993), "Inward-outward connections in internationalization", *Journal of Internaitonal Marketing*, Vol. 1, no. 1, 44-56.

Wiedersheim-Paul, F., H.C. Olson and L.S. Welch (1978), "Pre-export and activity: the first step in internationalization" *Journal of International Business Studies* 9 (1) 47-58

Williams, Jerome D., Han, Sang-Lin, and Qualls, William J., (1998) "A conceptual model and study of cross-cultural business relationship" *Journal of Business Research* 42, 135-143

Williamson, O. E., (1975) *Markets and Hierarchies: Analysis and Antitrust Implications* (The Free Press)

Williamson, O. E., (1985) *The Economic Institution of Capitalism* (The Free Press)

CHAPTER EIGHT

Country-of-Origin effect on Brand Perception – A Systematic Review of the Literature between 1993 and 2013

Andreea Iacob

Abstract.

This chapter presents the results of a systematic review of 77 papers that have studied the links between COO and consumer brand perceptions from1993 to 2013. The review traces the development of the country-of-origin construct in order to provide scholars and practitioners with an analytical assessment of the existing research on this topic. By following the grounds of the systematic literature, this study seeks to establish a solid base for country-of-origin research review. The findings suggest that the existing knowledge of the impact of the COO effect on brand perception has some conflicting views. Further consumer behavioural studies need to be undertaken in the following areas: relationships between multiple countries of origin and brand perception; COO, CE and brand perception; COO and brand evaluation, and COO, purchase intention and brand perception.

1. Introduction

Past research has shown that preconceptions and attitudes towards people of a given country tend to influence consumers' evaluation of products coming from that country (Gurhan-Canli and Maheswaran, 2000; Wang and Yang, 2008). Thus, the country of origin of a product is an important piece of information in consumers' decision-making process. There has therefore been considerable academic interest in studying the effect of the country of origin on consumers' perception of product quality (Solomon *et al.,* 2010). A general conclusion from most of the previous empirical research is that products from industrialised countries generally enjoy positive country image both at home and abroad, while products from the emerging market economies suffer liabilities of negative country image (Usunier and Cestre, 2008).

There have also been studies of the link between the country of origin of products and consumers' brand perception. It has been suggested that brand name can affect quality perceptions in such a way that a well-known brand name can overcome negative country image of the country of manufacture (Haubl, 1996). Some studies have however suggested that multinational production and global branding tend to blur the COO issue. There has also been some empirical evidence suggesting that, for the most part, consumers do not know the correct country of origin of well-known brands (e.g. see Balabanis and Diamantopoulos, 2008; Samiee *et al.*, 2005).Thus, although there is a general acknowledgement among researchers that COO impacts consumer perceptions in various ways and can therefore influence market performance, there are serious disagreements within the accumulated research evidence about the nature and magnitude of the relationships. Despite the disagreements, academic interest in the topic thrived until the 1980s with a large number of published articles and books. This interest began to wane in the late 1980s with the globalisation of markets. Theodor Levitt stated in his article "Globalisation of Markets" that "the result is a new commercial reality - the emergence of global markets for standardised consumer products on a previously unimagined scale. [...] Gone are accustomed differences in national or regional preference" (Levitt, 1983:2). The impact of globalisation thus translated into the belief that COO effects are now nonexistent (Johansson and Nebenzahl, (1985). The argument here was that consumers have become used to interacting with products from different countries. Furthermore, consumers were not interested in, or did not know the correct country of origin of different brands (Samiee *et al.,* 2005; Usunier, 2006). This understanding led to the consideration that COO effects are not a major issue in international marketing anymore.

During the past decade however, there has been a revival of academic interest in the subject. Two developments, that have restructured the global market place, have enabled this revival. Firstly, the historic transfer of wealth from West to East and the rise of emerging markets have encouraged Western brands to bid aggressively for market shares in this part of the world (Van Gelder, 2003; Xie and Boggs, 2006). Secondly, firms from emerging markets are targeting Western countries. This suggests that research into how Western consumers perceive these companies and their brands is needed (Essoussi and Merunka, 2007). These two trends coupled with multi-country production activities have made consumers more confused about the origin of the products and brands. These arguments affected the consumers' need for guidelines in their decision making and the COO effect was found to play an important role in this regard (Pharr, 2005).

Several scholars have reviewed the accumulated evidence from past research and have published their results in 9 review articles. These include Samiee (1994) who studied purchase decision processes within the context of source-country influences; Peterson and Jolibert (1995) who conducted a meta-analysis of past COO studies concerning general perceptions about the quality of products made in different counties; Nebanzahl, *et al.*,(1997), Al-Sulaiti and Baker, (1998)who studied the effect of country of origin on consumer perceptions of products and services.; Verlegh and Steenkamp (1999) who examined the cognitive, affective, and normative aspects of the country of origin. A full overview of these review articles are provided in Table 1.

All these review papers may be criticised for adopting what Jesson *et al.,* (2011) describes as a traditional or narrative approach which is based on the preconceived notions of what is worth including in the list of papers to be reviewed (see Jorgensen *et al.*, 2006). This is in contrast to a systematic approach to literature review whereby the reviewer engages in a systematic, transparent means of gathering, synthesising and appraising the findings of studies on a particular topic (Jesson *et al.*, (2011:104). Systematic literature reviews are generally considered as fulfilling the scientific requirements for internal validity and the review process usually holds grounds against the possibility of being biased. Furthermore, Petticrew and Roberts (2008) note that a systematic review is of particular value when there is uncertainty about what the evidence on a particular topic shows. These observations have led some COO scholars to call for such a systematic review within the field as well (see Booth *et al.*, 2012). The present review contributes to filling this knowledge gap – i.e. the need for a systematic literature review in COO studies. It has been guided by the following questions:

1. Which countries and products have received COO researchers' attention between 1993 and 2013?
2. What methods of data collection and analysis have researchers adopted?
3. What empirical evidence is available on the relationship between COO and brand perception?
4. What are the main conclusions from these studies?
5. What research gaps have they identified that still need to be addressed?

The study has the additional objective of guiding my own investigations into the relationship between country-of-origin and brand perception in both developed and emerging markets. The period covered is from 1993 to early 2013. The reason is that this period is characterised by a rapid increase of different streams of country-of-origin research, which includes the reinvention of country-of-origin research in terms of brand origin and product-country image, and also an interest in researching the country of origin in relation to services

(Dinnie, 2004). Furthermore, the international marketplace was characterised in the early 1990s by structural changes due to the rise of emerging markets, and the growing impact of globalisation on the economic landscape, which have made the country-of-origin factor an interesting research area for practitioners and scholars alike (Pharr, 2005).

Table 1: Overview of past literature reviews on the COO phenomenon

Year	Authors	Title	No. of papers reviewed	Objectives	Main conclusions
1994	Samiee	Customer evaluation of products in a global market	N/A	The objective is to rationalise the purchase decision processes within the context of source-country influences by emphasising the role of age, income, education, familiarity with the country of origin and involvement in the purchase of specific products, in explaining differences in the perception of country of origin. Furthermore, it offers a conceptual framework for further development of the construct.	The findings indicated that COO influences the individuals' purchase decisions and that the higher the consumers' educational level, the more unfavourable their perception of products made in newly-industrialised countries is.
1995	Peterson and Jolibert	A meta-analysis of country-of-origin effects	187	Meta-analysis of past COO studies concerning general perceptions about the quality of products made in different counties.	The findings showed that COO has a strong influence on product evaluation, and that the effects are "only somewhat generalisable" and that "the phenomenon is still not well understood" (pp.894).
1997	Nebanzahl, Jaffe, Lampert and Shlomo,	Towards a theory of country image effect on product evaluation	N/A	This paper reviews existing constructs concerning the country image effect and proposes a model where the factors that influence the country image effect are drawn and hypotheses are formulated.	The model suggests that the image of the country of origin of the brand (OC) and the country whose name appear on the product made-in label (MC), affects product evaluations.
1998	Al-Sulaiti and Baker	Country-of-origin effects: a literature review	99	Literature review on the effect of country of origin on consumer perceptions of products and services.	Consumer perceptions differ significantly when it comes to product/service and country of origin, and the question of how much influence the country of origin has in product and service evaluations is still unanswered.
1999	Verlegh and Steenkamp	A review and meta-analysis of country-of-origin research	41	Literature review on the cognitive, affective, and normative aspects of country of origin, while assessing the effect of COO upon perceived quality, attitude, and purchase intentions.	The authors found that country of origin has a larger effect on perceived quality than on attitude toward the product or purchase intention, and that the COO effect is lower when the COO information is presented alongside other information cues like price and warranty information.

225

Table 1 Continues

2003	Dinnie	Country of origin: 1965-2004. A literature review	50	Literature review focusing on the conceptual development of the country-of-origin construct.	The author identified the main periods in the chronological development of country-of-origin research
2005	Pharr	Synthesising country-of-origin research from the last decade: Is the concept still salient in an era of global brands	50	Review of the impact of COO on product evaluation and other cues like price and brand.	The findings suggested that purchase intention was found to have a direct impact on brand perception, but not on COO. Furthermore, the effect of the brand on the consumer's perception has the same effect as the COO on brand and subsequently consumer perception.
2007	Bhaskaran and Sukumaran	Contextual and methodological issues in COO studies	96	The study investigates and identifies the reasons for contradictory conclusions in past studies of country-of-origin (COO) influences on buyers' beliefs and purchase intentions.	The findings showed that COO cannot be treated as a self-contained marketing strategy, without interacting with other influences on customer beliefs and buying intentions.
2012	Saran and Gupta	Country of origin vs. Consumer Perception: A Literature Review	18	Literature review on the relationship between COO and Brand Origin.	

Approach

According to Pettigrew and Roberts (2008), there are seven stages in a systematic literature review:

1. Clearly define the question that the review is setting out to answer
2. Determine the types of studies that need to be located in order to answer your question
3. Carry out a comprehensive literature search to locate those studies
4. Screen the results of that search (that is, sift through the retrieved studies, deciding which ones look as if they fully

meet the inclusion criteria, and thus need more detailed examination, and which do not)
5. Critically appraise the included studies
6. Synthesise the studies and asses heterogeneity among the study findings
7. Disseminate the findings of the review

These steps have been followed in the present review process. The process started with a systematic search of the ABI/Inform database, where terms "country of origin" and "brand" were used to identify the available published papers within the defined time range. The first hit showed a total of 22.079 journal articles. I then limited my search by including terms like: "country–of-origin effect", "brand perception", "consumer behaviour" as alternative search items in order to capture only the most relevant articles. At the same time, I widened my search from looking only into scholarly articles to also include working papers and conference papers and proceedings. Based on the above criteria 6396 articles were found from 99 journal publications, (searches conducted in August 2013) within 9 research domains according to the ABS journal ranking (ABS version 4, 2010): Marketing, Business Ethics and Governance, Sector Studies, International Business and Area Studies, Social Science, Economics, Business History, General Management, and finally Tourism and Hospitality Management.

The next step into the data search was to identify the top 20 journals within these areas. According to the ABS journal list (2010) all journals graded as four or three publish the most original and best executed research. As top journals in their field, these journals have the highest citation impact factors within their field. In order to extend the research and by applying the backward snowballing approach, journals which are graded 2 or 1, within the field of Marketing, are also taken into consideration. According to ABS (2010), two and one rated journals publish original research of an acceptable standard. In addition to the lower graded journals I also included a number of influential articles through the backward snowballing techniques, by identifying key articles and authors referenced in a number of selected papers. In total, 2163 articles were found that either mention the COO effect or actually discuss it.

The third step was to read all abstracts and keywords of the 2163 articles. The aim was to exclude those articles that were not specifically concerned with country-of-origin effect and brand perception. This process resulted in the selection of 127 articles. After reading the 127 articles, I found 77 of them to be particularly relevant in terms of the objectives of the review. They are from 18 different international journals with most of them from International Marketing Review, The European Journal of Marketing, Asia Pacific Journal of Marketing and Logistics, The Journal of Product and Brand Management, and The Journal of Consumer Marketing. The 77 articles were written by 163 authors, with Ahmed writing as many as 6 articles (5 of them with d'Astous) (see Table 2).

Table 2: Overview of identified articles

Research Area	Publication title	Number of identified articles
	1. International Marketing Review	16
	2. European Journal of Marketing	11
	3. The Journal of Product and Brand Management	8
	4. The Journal of Consumer Marketing	6
	5. Journal of Brand Management	2
	6. International Journal of Retail and Distribution Management	1
1. Marketing	7. Journal of International Consumer Marketing	5
	8. Psychology and Marketing	1
	9. Journal of Advertising	1
	10. Journal of Retailing	1
	11. Journal of Business and Industrial Marketing	1
	12. Asia Pacific Journal of Marketing and Logistics*	10
	13. Journal of East-West Business*	3
	14. The Journal of Business and Industrial Marketing*	2
	15. Australasian Marketing Journal*	2
2. Sector Studies	16. British Food Journal	1
3. International Business and Area Studies	17. Journal of International Business Studies	3
	18. International Journal of Business and Management*	2
Total number of articles reviewed		77

* Note: *Articles that scored a grade of 2 or lower but still found to be of interest for the literature review due to the backward snowballing approach.*

Findings

Countries, Product Focus and Methodological Considerations

All the articles were written on the basis of empirical investigations done in 28 countries. Sixty-six of them were based on survey data, 6 were based on interviews and 2 were based on experiments. The USA topped the list of countries in which data were collected with 15 articles; Australia came second with 8 articles; followed by China (7) and then Taiwan (6), India (5). Four articles were written on Japan, Canada, Thailand and Singapore, while 3 were written on Mexico and two each were written on the UK, Lebanon and Malaysia. The following countries had one article each: Austria, Belgium, Germany, France, Russia, Poland, Hungary, Slovenia, Greece, Kyrgystan, Tunisia, Burkina Faso, Ghana, Ivory Coast, Mali, Nigeria, Vietnam, Indonesia, Bangladesh and Iran. Thus, a disproportionate number of articles were written on developed countries with the emerging market economies (including Central and Eastern Europe) distinctly under-represented in the investigations.

Most of the studies focused attention on products (71 articles), predominantly cars (23 articles), clothing (15 articles), electronics (13 articles) and TVs (10 articles). Seven articles were written on computers and food products, while 7 were written on household products and electrical appliances as well as beverages (beer -5 articles and wine -1 article). For services (6 articles), emphasis was put on researching cruise lines, franchising firms, airline travel services, insurance and catering services, toy stores and educational systems.

Well-known brands such as Sony, BMW, and Whirlpool featured prominently among the products studied. However, some of the studies included less familiar brands such as Osborne Computers or Belarus tractors; and fictitious brand names, like Schneider beer and Fiesta chips. The reasoning behind using fictitious brands in direct comparison with well-known brand names is to study the links between consumers' perception of both global and potential new brands and their countries of origin.

Twenty-three of the papers reported studies with a student sample, seeing them as a younger generation of global consumers who have developed a diversity of perspectives and created a patchwork culture that is not indigenous to any one country due to their exposure to worldwide communications via the internet (Walker, 1996; Knight and Kim, 2007). The remaining 52 papers were based on samples of ordinary consumers. The sample sizes ranged from 112 (Kinra, 2006) to 1752 (Sharma, 2011), with response rates falling generally between 20 and 60 percent. Two of the studies had response rates under 10 % (Schaefer, 1997; Balestrini and Gamble, 2006).

Twenty-five of the studies used analysis of variance (ANOVA) as the main statistical tool, 17 used structural equation modeling (SEM), while 9 used a multivariate analysis of variance (MANOVA). Regression and correlations analysis was done for 13 articles. The remaining papers used other statistical tools such as independent and pairwise sample t-tests (5 articles), conjoint analysis (3 articles), chi-square testing and correspondence analysis (2 articles each). Although not all articles showed a clear analytical process, there are some examples of articles which presented clear methodology for their studies. Examples include ANOVA (Ahmed and d'Astous, 1996; Nebenzahl and Jaffe, 1996; Pecotich and Rosenthal, 2001; Pappu, Quester and Cooksey, 2006), SEM (Parameswaran and Pisharodi, 2002; Essoussi and Merunka, 2007; Wang and Yang, 2008; Diamantopoulus *et.al*, 2011), regression (Yagci, 2001) and MANOVA (Pappu, Quester and Cooksey, 2007).

Forty-nine articles specifically stated the scales that the authors have used in their studies. On the whole, two sets of country-based scales were used; one strand of research adopted conventional COO scales while another strand adopted multi-country scales – COD and COM. Consumer ethnocentrism has been tested using the CETSCALE developed by Shimp and

231

Sharma (1987). There were six brand-related scales covering brand image, awareness, equity, loyalty, and personality. There were also four product-related scales and 2 scales testing purchase behaviour and intentions. Table 3 provides a complete list of the scales and the articles in which they have been adopted.

Table 3: Scales used in the articles reviewed

Scale	Authors
COO image	Nagashima (1970), Parameswaran and Yaphank (1987), Darling and Wood (1990), Roth and Romeo (1992), Jaffe and Nebenzahl (1993), Martin and Errol (1993), Pisharodi and Parameswaran (1992 and 1997), Haubl (1996), Chen (2000), Laroche *et al.* (2005).
COD image/product fit and COM image/product fit	Keller and Aaker (1992).
COD and COM	Pisharodi and Parameswaran's (1992), Aaker (1996), Michell *et al.* (2001), Riel *et al.* (2005), Davis *et al.* (2008).
Consumer ethnocentrism	CETSCALE (Shimp and Sharma, 1987)
Brand image **Table 3 continued**	McGee and Spiro (1991), Heimbach (1991) (Nebenzahl and Jaffe (1991) and Gupta and Ratchford (1992), Lee and Bae (1999), Yoo *et al.* (2000).
Brand equity	Aaker (1991, 1996, 1997), Yoo *et al.* (2000), Yoo and Donthu (2001)
Brand loyalty	Yoo *et al.* (2000), Chaudhuri (1995), Aaker (1991).
Brand awareness	Yoo *et al.* (2000) Yoo and Donthum, 2001
Brand profitability performance	Jaworski and Kohli (1993), Lusch and Brown (1996), Moorman and Rust (1999)
Brand personality	(Aaker 1996)
Product evaluation	(Belk and Russ, 1993); Shimp *et al.* (1993), Lim *et al.* (1994), Steptoe *et al.* (1995), Yong (1996), Lee and Ganesh (1999), Gurhan-Canli and Maheswaran (2000) Cervin~o *et al.* (2005), Laroche *et al.*(2005),
Product quality	McGuire (1968), Aaker (1991), Dodds *et al.*, (1991), Keller and Aaker (1992), Chao (1993, 1998), Erevelles *et al.*(1999), Yoo *et al.*, (2000), Ahmed and d'Astous (2004), Ashill and Sinha (2004), Insch and McBride (2004).
Product knowledge	Brucks (1985), Lin and Zhen (2005).

Table 3 continues

Product involvement	Zaichkowsky (1994), Chin (2002).
Product-origin congruency	Josiassen *et al.* (2008).
Price perception	Kulwani and Chi (1992).
Purchase decision	Edell and Staelin (1983), Mackenzie (1986), (Dodds *et al.* (1991), McQuarrie and Muson (1992), Grewal, Gotlieb and Marmorstein (1998), Chin (2002), Janssens and de Pelsmacker (2005), Ettenson and Klein (2005), Teng and Laroche (2007).
Purchase intention **Table 3 Continued**	Dodds *et al.* (1991), Papadopoulos and Heslop (1993), Laroche *et al.*(2005).
Trust	Ganesan (1994), Doney and Cannon (1997).
Perceived favorability	Liu (2001)
Materialism	(Richins, 2004)
Animosity	Klein (2002), Ettenson and Klein (2005), Hoffman *et al.* (2011)
Value consciousness	Lichtenstein, Netemeyer and Burton (1990)
Risk perception	Aaker (1991), Yoo and Donthu (2001), Keller (2003).
Consumers' aspiration **Table 3 continued**	Yoo *et al.*(2000)
Need for cognition	Beatty and Kahle (1988), Dodds, Monroe, and Grewal (1991), Yoo, Donthu, and Lee (2000), Yoo and Donthu (2001)
Evaluation of cars	Brucks (1985), Scott and English (1989), Bayus (1991), Gupta and Ratchford (1992), Chaiken and Maheswaram (1994), Thanasuta *et al.* (2009)
Wine knowledge	Bruwer and Buller (2012)
Retailer-perceived brand equity (RPBE) on the customer-based perspective	
Marketing mix activities as antecedents of RPBE	
Retailer-perceived quality:	

Definitions of country of origin

In general terms, the country-of-origin cue was conceptualised by the researchers as a form of country stereotyping which consumers use when other roduct-specific information is not easily available. In such situations, consumers tend to use their image of people from a particular country as a reflection of the quality of the products made in that country (Haubl, 1996; Knight and Calantone, 1999; Demirbag *et al.*, 2010).

Most of the authors adopted the view that a country-of-origin effect can be related either to the economic stage of the focal country (macro) or products/brands produced in the country (micro). The macro country image is defined by Martin and Eroglu, (1993:193) as "the total of all descriptive, inferential and informational beliefs one has about a particular country". The micro dimension of COO has been related to the "made-in" notion (Nahashima, 1970), which usually denotes the "country of manufacture" where the final assembly of a product is completed (see Chao and Rajendran, 1993; Agbonifah and Elimimian,1999; Javalgi *et al.*, 2001; Darling and Puetz, 2002); Speece and Nguyen (2005); Pappu *et al.*, (2006); Balestrini and Gamble (2006); Ahmed and d'Astous (2007); Thanasuta *et al.* (2009); Chu *et al.* (2010). Others define the COO effect as any influence (positive or negative) that the country of manufacture might have on the consumers' choice behaviour (see: Samiee, 1994; Ahmed *et al.*, 2002; Hamin and Elliott, 2006).

An extension of the last definition was provided by Papadopoulus (1993) who introduced the notion of multiple countries of origin, the country of manufacture, assembly, design, and parts. The multiple COO concept was adopted by authors such as Samiee (1994), Insch and McBride (1998), Ahmed *et al.*(2002), Hamin and Elliott (2006), Essousi and Merunka (2007), Zolfgharian and Sun (2010).

The brand country origin is defined by Thakor and Kohli (1996) as the place, region, or country where the product or the brand is perceived to have originated from.This definition is premised on the view that the place where the product is produced may not be as important as the perceived birthplace that consumers affiliate the brand to (Hui and Zhou, 2003). Studies that adopted this definition include Ettenson (1993), Lim and O'Cass (2001); Jo *et al.*(2003), Hui and Zhou (2003), Paswan and Sharma (2004), Jin *et al.* (2006), Kwok *et al.*(2006) and Thanasuta *et al.* (2009).

Other scholars see the country of origin as the country in which firms locate their corporate headquarters - i.e. the firm's home country (Ahmed and d'Astous (1996), Kinra (2006), Karunaratna and Quester (2007). Table 4 provides a summary of the most commonly used definitions of the COO effect.

Table 4: COO Definitions used in the reviewed articles

Authors	COO definition	Adopted by the following studies
Nagashima (1970)	The COO is defined as "the picture, the representation, and the stereotype that businessmen and consumers attach to products from a specific country. This image is created by such variables as representative products, national characteristics, economic and political background, history and tradition".	Chao and Rajendran (1993), Agbonifah and Elimimian (1999), Javalgi *et al.* (2001), Darling and Puetz (2002), Speece and Nguyen (2005), Pappu *et al.*, (2006), Balestrini and Gamble (2006), Ahmed and d'Astous (2007), Thanasuta *et al.* (2009), Chu *et al.* (2010).
Thakor and Kohli (1996)	The "origin of the brand" is defined as the place, region, or country where the product or the brand is perceived to have originated from.	Ettenson (1993), Lim and O'Cass (2001); Jo *et al.*(2003), Hui and Zhou (2003), Paswan and Sharma (2004), Jin *et al.* (2006), Kwok *et al.*(2006) and Thanasuta *et al.* (2009).
Johansson *et al.* (1985)	The country of origin is that country where the corporate headquarters of the company marketing the product or brand is located (the company's home country).	Ahmed and d'Astous (1996), Kinra (2006), Karunaratna and Quester (2007).
Papadopoulos (1993)	A product's country of origin is defined as multiple COO- "the	Samiee (1994), Insch and McBride (1998), Ahmed *et*

Table 4 continues

	country of manufacture, assembly, design, or parts"	*al.*(2002), Hamin and Elliott (2006), Essousi and Merunka (2007), Zolfgharian and Sun (2010)
Haubl (1996)	THE COI reflects a consumers' general perceptions about the quality	Knight and Calantone (1999), Demirbag *et al.* (2010)
	of a product made in a particular country, and the nature of people from that country have on the consumers' choice processes or subsequent behaviour	

The Findings Reported in the Articles/ Main research topics

This analysis groups the 77 articles in terms of the focus of their investigations.

As shown in Table 5, 24 of the articles focused attention on COO and brand evaluation, 19 on COO, purchase intention and brand perception, 12 on multiple countries of origin and brand perception, 10 on COO and CE and brand perception, 7 on COO and quality assessment, and 5 on COO and brand equity. Fifty-nine of the studies showed that the country-of origin effect can either have a positive or a negative impact on consumer perception, depending on whether the country factor represents developed or developing countries. Fifteen of the studies found that COO has no impact on brand perception or product assessment.

236

Research topic	1993-1997 Y	N	1998-2002 Y	N	2003-2007 Y	N	2008-2013 Y	N	Total
COO and brand evaluation	3	2	1	1	7	1	7	2	24
COO and purchase intention	3	1	3		3		7	2	19
Multiple countries of origin	3				1	2	4	2	12
COO and CE	1			2	3		3	1	10
COO and quality assessment	1		3		2		1		7
COO and brand equity					2		3		5
Total	10	3	7	2	16	3	24	7	77

Note: Y (Yes) = significant COO effects on brand perception; N(No)= insignificant COO effects on brand perception

COO and Brand Evaluation

The country-of-origin effect was found to be more positive for products originating from developed countries than those coming from emerging countries (i.e. Chao and Rajendran, 1993; Haubl, 1996; Agbonifoh and Elimimian, 1999; Magnusson *et al.*, 2001; Sohail, 2005; Pecotich and Ward, 2007; Koubaa, 2008; Josiassen, 2010). For example, Agbonifoh and Elimimian (1999) found that Nigerian consumers evaluate cars and electronics from technologically more advanced countries (UK and USA) more favourably than those from technologically less advanced countries (Ghana, Taiwan and Nigeria). Furthermore, Sohail (2005) studied Malaysian adults' perception of household cleaning products, food products, personal care items, clothing/footwear, furnishing items, electrical appliances and electronics and found that developed country products (Germany) were much more appreciated than developing country products (Malaysia). The study conducted by Pecotich and Ward (2007), with the purpose of investigating the decision-making process of the Australian consumers with respect to a well-known foreign computer brand (IBM) and a not so familiar brand (Osborne Computers), with

237

different countries of origin (Australia, USA, France, China and Morocco), suggested that both novices and experts in the field exhibited a degree of developed country preference. Experts used the COO information as a summary construct while the novices used the COO information as a halo, regardless of brand name and quality.

Thanasuta *et al.* (2009) quantified the effect of COO and brand names in monetary units, using multiple car brands in Thailand, cars coming from Germany, Sweden, France, Japan, Korea, Malaysia and the USA and found that the German brands are ranked the highest, with Mercedes at the top, BMW second and Audi in third position; the Japanese brands present the same valuation ranges as their American competitors; and finally the luxury car segment has high entry barriers as seen by the positive relationship between market share and the price premium rankings of the top two brands, Mercedes and BMW.

Liu and Johnson (2005) conducted an experiment on US consumers and tested whether Chinese and Japanese country stereotypes can be activated through the presence of COO information and what effects it could have on how consumers perceive multiple computer brands. The result suggested that the participants' categorisation decision was accurate due to the use of the country stereotypes that were activated by the COO cue, while the COO effects occurred without the participant's intention or control.

COO was also found to affect different dimensions of consumer knowledge. The studies of Schaefer (1997) and Phau and Sunttornnond (2006) showed that brand familiarity and objective product knowledge have a significant effect on the use of the COO cue in product evaluation, while subjective product knowledge and personal experience with a brand were not found to have a significant effect on the use of COO in product evaluation. Kumara and Canhua (2010) conceptualised a COO expectation attribute scale in the evaluation of foreign products by Chinese students and found that the derived model of COO expectations was divided between four dimensions: economic, information, conviviality and personality.

In the case of services, Paswan and Sharma (2004) investigated the relationship between COO image and the brand's country of origin from the perception of Indian consumers concerning franchising firms originating in the USA, Germany, Japan and South Korea and found that the accuracy of brand–COO knowledge influences the COO image and helps a brand dominate the consumers' cognitive brand set domain. On the other hand, inaccurate brand COO knowledge leads to a negative image about the COO. Antecedents like social class, education and travel abroad positively influence brand –COO knowledge.

In addition, in the case of low involvement products, there is evidence that COO has an impact on the consumers' perception of products and brands. For example, Ahmed *et al.* (2004) conducted a study on Singaporean students concerning 2 low involvement products (coffee and bread), and found that COO appeared to affect the Singaporean consumers' evaluation of coffee and bread brands, and that developed countries of origin (Switzerland and France) were perceived more favourably than emerging countries of origin (Singapore, Indonesia and Malaysia).

Contrary to the above, some scholars argue that COO has less of an impact on the consumers' overall brand perception (Chao and Gupta, 1995; Ettenson, 1993; Zbib *et al.*, 2010; Bruwer and Buller, 2012). For example, Chao and Gupta (1995) found in a study on US car buyers, involving multiple car brands that COO effects are not present prior to searching for information about a car. On the other hand, COO information proved to be product specific and vehicle category specific, where cars from developed countries, like the USA and some European Western countries, were evaluated more favourably than the ones from emerging economies, which at that time was Japan. Ettenson (1993) found in his study of Polish, Russian and Hungarian TV consumers that brand names and the interaction between COO and brand name recognition played less of a role in consumers' making process. But the study also showed that Polish and Hungarian consumers have a preference for Western TVs over the local ones.

Bruwer and Buller (2012) investigated the COO effect on the Japanese consumers with the 8 best-selling wine brands in Japan and found that the top five cues ranked by the Japanese consumers were taste, style, colour, price and recommendations from friends and family ranking, while COO ranked only seventh. The study also showed that consumers with higher levels of objective knowledge do not use the COO cue more than consumers with lower knowledge. Finally, female consumers were found to be the main wine purchase decision-makers. Similarly, Zbib *et al.* (2010) studied the COO effect of the Lebanese consumers of potato chips from Lebanon, Egypt, Belgium, and the Kingdom of Saudi Arabia, and found that the evaluation of specific attributes did not vary by country of origin. In addition to this, there were no differences in the overall quality perceptions by country of origin. The same authors studied the effect of COO on the Lebanese shampoo consumers of Pantene, Sunsilk, and Palmolive, and found again that there were neither difference in the quality perceptions of the product nor the attribute evaluation of shampoos sourced from different countries.

Country of brand, which is the country where a brand is originally developed, was found to have a higher impact than the actual country of origin. Lim and O'Cass (2001) examined the role of origin on the Singaporean consumers' perception of different fashion clothing brands (Culture-of-brand –origin[3]). The results suggested that Singaporean students can better identify the cultural origin of the brands rather than their actual country of origin, and this is due to the consumers' perception of how well they are acquainted with the brand. Jin *et al.* (2006) investigated whether consumers use brand origin rather than COO cues in evaluating a brand. The brand origin was found to be an identifiable feature for Indian consumers; they have associated the brands with countries where the brands are originally developed rather than with countries in which the products are currently produced. Higher income groups were found to show preference towards foreign brands and those brands originating from a developed country (UK) were perceived to be superior to those from a less developed country (India).

To sum up, there is conflicting evidence of the relationship between COO and brand evaluation. The majority of the articles, which included both products and services in their study, stated that the COO effect has a positive impact on brand perception and that the country-of-origin effect is more positive for products originating from developed countries than those coming from emerging countries (i.e. Haubl, 1996; Agbonifoh and Elimimian, 1999; Magnusson *et al.*, 2001; Sohail, 2005; Pecotich and Ward, 2007; Koubaa, 2008; Josiassen, 2010). On the other hand, Chao and Gupta (1995), Ettenson (1993), Zbib *et al.* (2010) and Bruwer and Buller (2012) argue that COO has less of an impact on the consumers' overall brand perception, mainly due to the fact that consumers identify the cultural origin of the brands instead of their actual country of origin, and this is due to the consumers' perception of how well they are acquainted with the brand. A possible explanation for these two contradictory views lies in the

---

[3]The culture-of-brand-origin becomes available to consumers due to exposure to marketing activities of the brand. Consumers attach certain cultural traits to a brand when information about the foreign country is not available Lim and O'Cass, 2001)

fact that the perceived country of brand is of greater importance for the consumers than the country of origin, usually identified by the country of manufacture. Furthermore, the methodological differences seem to influence the inconclusive evidence since a reliance on a small convenient sample of students, rather than a meaningful consumers sample may lead to biasing the outcome between the research setting and real life situations (Saran and Gupta, 2012).

COO and Purchase Intention

Many of the reviewed articles studied the effect of summary attributes such as brand name and COO on purchase intention and behaviour (Lundstrom, *et al.*, 1998; Knight and Calantone, 2000; Ahmed and d' Astous, 1993; Lee and Lee, 2011). For example, Lee and Lee (2011) examined the impact of the COO image (China and USA) on the Taiwanese consumers' perception of computers and how to establish a successful brand redeployment strategy for the Lenovo brand after Lenovo acquired IBM. They studied 5 redeployment brand options: (1) as a new brand, (2) as IBM, (3) as solely Lenovo, (4) as IBM-Lenovo, or (5) as Lenovo-IBM). The results showed that the COO image (general country attributes and general product attributes) has a positive and significant influence on purchase intentions after the acquisition. General product attributes were found to play a mediating role between general country attributes and purchase intentions. Ahmed and d' Astous (1993) conducted a study on Canadian and Belgian consumers of cars with the aim to investigate the effects of 3 COOs (Japan, Canada and Russia), 3 brand names (Toyota, Ford, and Lada) and 3 levels of price and service on the consumers' purchase value and found that brand name and COO showed a significant impact on the consumers' overall perception of the brand and their purchase intention.

242

Miranda and Parkvithee (2013) investigated the evaluation and purchase intention of the middle class and working class consumers in Thailand with regard to Thai branded low-fashion apparel made in three Asian countries representing different manufacturing competences. The results showed that if a low involvement product (i.e. t-shirts) with high brand equity is sourced from a developing country of origin, consumers would evaluate higher-end fashion products more favourably than its standard apparel.

Other studies focused mainly on low involvement products (Almonte *et al.*, 1995; Bailey and Gutierrez de Pineres, 1997; Kwok *et al.*, 2006, and Kumar *et al.*, 2009). In a study conducted on Chinese consumers, Kwok *et al.* (2006) investigated the impact of the COO of different grocery brands on consumer purchase behaviour and found that Chinese consumers prefer buying local Chinese grocery brands rather than foreign ones. Their preference for local brands was mainly due to the fact that the Chinese consumers did not know the true origin of the brands.

Almonte *et al.* (1995) and Bailey and Gutierrez de Pineres (1997) studied Mexican consumers' evaluation of food products from the USA and tested whether the *malinchismo* effect, i.e. the preference to buy American products, was predominant among the interviewed Mexicans. They found that Mexican consumers perceived the Mexican salsa more favourably than the US one. In another study conducted by Bailey and Gutierrez de Pineres (1997), the results showed that there was a tendency for upper-class Mexican consumers to be manifest malinchismo (i.e. a strong preference for U.S. products over local ones). Another factor which was studied in connection to the consumers' purchase intent was the need for cognition (Karunaratna and Quester (2007) and the need for uniqueness and self-concept (Kumar *et al.*, 2009). The need for cognition denotes "a need to structure relevant situations in meaningful, integrated ways" (Cohen *et al.*,

1955: 291), it is actually a tendency for people to engage in and enjoy effortful cognitive activities. Karunaratna and Quester (2007) examined how the need for cognition of Australian consumers influences the degree to which the purchase intention of 3 car brands, Holden, VW and Mazda is influenced by COO components. The results suggested that nationalism influenced the way the consumers evaluated product components for Australian car components. Despite the fact that Holden has a foreign owned status, the brand was still closely associated with the Australian psyche and was the most powerful influencer of purchase intention. The Mazda brand was preferred over VW (which increases as NFC increases), but for every other component system, German components were viewed as superior. Kumar *et al.* (2009) examined the Indian consumers' perception of local and US clothing brands (Levi's) and found out that need for uniqueness and self-concept have an indirect effect on the Indian consumers' purchase intention. The notion of need for uniqueness and self-concept is based on the psychological notion that individuals wish to see themselves as different from others and that certain individuals have a "need for separate identity" or a "need for uniqueness (Kumar *et al.*, 2009: 512).

As in the case of product evaluation, COO seems to have an impact on purchase intention when it comes to services. For example Kabadayi and Lerman (2011) examined the moderating effect of trusting beliefs of US students about a toy store on the effect of two countries of origin, China and Germany. It was found that COO affects product evaluation and purchase intention, in the sense that consumers give less weight to negative COO (China) in the presence of strongly positive trusting beliefs, and on the other hand that the effects of specific beliefs depend on the level of perceived manufacturer risk. In a study conducted by Lin and Chen (2006) the country-of-origin image was found to have a significantly positive influence on the Taiwanese consumer purchase decision of insurance and catering services and that the congruency between country-of-origin image and product knowledge have a significantly positive influence on consumer purchase decision under different product involvement levels. Jimenez and Martin (2012) studied the mediating role of trust in the relationships between a firm's reputation and COO, purchase intention and consumer animosity. The study suggests that COO significantly impacts a firm's reputation and that animosity towards a country can reduce trust towards that country's firms and products, while trust emerges as a stimulating factor in the purchase behaviour of products from emerging markets.

In contrast to the arguments above in favor of the positive relationship between COO and purchase intentions, there is also some evidence showing that COO has insignificant impact on purchase intention (Johansson *et al.*, 1994; Aiello *et al.*, 2009; Diamantopoulus *et al.*, 2011). Johansson *et al.*(1994) conducted a qualitative study that explored the effect of the COO association on the buying decision of a product from a controversial country. 43 US farmers were interviewed about their buying intention of a new Russian tractor brand, the Belarus, in comparison with other well-known tractor brands from the USA, Canada, Germany, Italy, Finland, South Korea and Japan. The results showed that there were no strong COO effects for the new brand since the farmers relied more on specific product attributes of the new tractor brand. Aiello *et al.* (2009) examined the influence of three different countries of origin (Italy, France and UK) in connection to multiple luxury brands, like Cartier, Chanel, Dior etc., on the consumers' brand perception and purchasing behaviour. They found that in the case of luxury goods, the brand has a much higher influence on product evaluation and purchase intention than the COO. Diamantopoulus *et al.* (2011) found that COO – as reflected both in country image (CI) and product category image (PCATI) perceptions – does not directly impact the UK consumers' intentions to buy a Whirlpool or Haier refrigerator, but CI and PCATI strongly influence purchase intentions through their impact on brand image.

To sum up, the existing empirical research on the relationships between COO and purchase intentions has produced contradictory results. Some studies have shown positive and significant impacts of COO effects on purchase intentions of both high and low involvement products (Lundstrom *et al.*, 1998; Knight and Calantone, 2000; Ahmed and d' Astous, 1993; Almonte *et al.*, 1995; Bailey and Gutierrez de Pineres, 1997; Kwok *et al.*, 2006, and Kumar *et al.*, 2009; Lee and Lee, 2011). Also COO seems to have a positive and significant impact on purchase intention and evaluation of services (Kabadayi and Lerman, 2011; Lin and Chen, 2006; Jimenez and Martin, 2012).In contrast, other studies have shown that the impact is not significant (see Johansson *et al.*, 1994; Aiello *et al.*, 2009; Diamantopoulus *et al.*, 2011). The explanations given by authors of these studies for the weak impact is that consumers tend to rely more on specific product attributes than on the origin of the product in the investigations that they conducted.

Multiple countries of origin

A new strand of country-of-origin research based on the decomposition of product images into relevant COO dimensions emerged in the 1990s. Scholars such as Nebenzahl and Jaffe (1996), Ahmed and d'Astous, (2007) and Essoussi and Merunka (2007), have argued for the decomposition of manufactured product images into country of design (COD), country of assembly (COA), and country of origin of parts (COP).

Among the reviewed articles there is quite a high number of scholars who studied the perception of brand image when the production is sourced multi-nationally (Ahmed and d'Astous, 1995, 1996; Nebenzahl and Jaffe, 1996; Hamin and Elliott, 2006; Essoussi and Merunka, 2007; Fetscherin and Toncar, 2010; Chen and Su, 2012; Moradi and Zarei, 2012; Sinrungtam, 2013).

While testing the impact of COD and COA on brand perception, some scholars found that these COO sub components tended to produce more significant effects than the brand names. For example, Ahmed and d'Astous (1995) examined the impact of COO on Canadian household and organisational buyers' product perception (computer systems, fax machines, cars and VCRs), by looking at the COD and COA. The results suggest that COD is more important in organisational purchases than COA and brand name. In the case of household buyers, COD and COA are equally important, but brand name appears more important than COO. In 1996 the same authors investigated how consumers react to hybrid products in the presence of brand name and other product cues and found that COD and COA information has a stronger impact than brand name on the Canadian consumers' evaluation of quality and purchase value of cars, VCRs and shoes. Similarly, Nebenzahl and Jaffe (1996) conducted a study on VCRs and microwaves with US students in order to measure how the perception of brand image changes when the production is sourced multi-nationally. The results show that the perceived value of a product is a weighted average of its perceived brand and "made-in" country values and the value can be higher or lower than the value of the brand without reference to the made in country.

In a developing market context, Hamin and Elliott (2006) investigated the effects of COA, COD and consumer ethnocentrism (CE) on the Indonesian consumers' quality, price and value perception of airline travel brands, and found that COO was more important than price for both high and low ethnocentric consumers. The high CE respondents preferred the

247

domestic brand over the foreign ones and vice versa. Moradi and Zarei (2012) explored what kind of effects country of brand (COB) and country of manufacture (COM) have on the brand equity formation of Iranian students, concerning laptops and mobile phones from Japan, the USA, Finland, China and Malaysia. They found that those products made in industrial countries with lots of experience are considered to have a higher quality compared to countries that have little experience or those that have just joined the group of industrialised countries.

When testing the effect of the COO sub-components on brand perception, scholars found positive effects either on purchase intentions (Sinrungtam (2013) or brand equity (Chen and Su, 2012). Fetscherin and Toncar (2010) tested the impact of the country of origin of a car brand and the effect of the COM on the US consumers' brand personality perceptions of a US car brand and a Chinese car brand. The COM of a car was perceived to be of a higher influence than the COB. It was found that the US car made in China had a lower brand personality than the Chinese car made in the USA.

Some studies found no significant effect of COO sub-components on consumer product assessment or purchase intentions (Hui and Zhou, 2003; Hamin and Elliott, 2006; Wong *et al.*, 2008; Ahmed *et al.*, 2011). Wong *et al.* (2008) for example, examined the extent to which COD, COA and COM affect quality perceptions and purchase intentions of Chinese students studying in different Australian Universities, for high involvement products such as cars and digital cameras. The results showed that there is no direct effect of the three COO sub-components on consumer product assessment or purchase intentions for the two high involvement products. Ahmed *et al.* (2011) also examined how Canadian consumers perceive bi-national products (one congruent with Denmark and one not congruent with Denmark).

They found that product country congruency has a greater impact on consumer evaluations than COO. Hamin and Elliott (2006) found that brand is the most important factor, followed by COA and COD, while investigating the effects of COA, COD and consumer ethnocentrism (CE) on Indonesian consumers' quality, price and value perception of TV brands (Sony and Polytron). Hui and Zhou (2003) examined the impact of COM on the US consumers' perception of brands (Sony and Sanyo) and brand equity and discovered that COM does not have a significant effect on brand evaluation, when the information is congruent with the brand origin.

To sum up, the reviews show that the available evidence on the impact of multiple COOs on brand perception and consumer behaviour is inconclusive. While some studies found a positive impact of multiple countries of origin on brand perception, others found no significant effect of COO sub-components on consumer product assessment or purchase intentions.

COO and Consumer Ethnocentrism

Previous research on the COO effect on consumer behaviour also introduced the term of consumer ethnocentrism(CE) as being the cause of its appearing, thus presenting a close relationship between the two terminologies. CE represents an individual tendency to view the purchasing of imported products as wrong as it hurts the domestic economy (Shimp and Sharma, 1987). It may lead to overestimating the quality of locally made products while underestimating the quality of foreign-made products. This perspective has been confirmed in a number of the studies reviewed (see Huddleston *et al.*, 2001; Erdogan and Uzkurt, 2010). Ethnocentric perceptions also influence consumer behavioural tendencies not only towards local and foreign products in general but also towards brands (Kaynak and Kara, 1997; Vida and

Damjan, 2001; Kinra, 2006; Liu *et al.*, 2006; Chryssochoidis *et al.*, 2007; Zolfagharian and Sun, 2010). For example, Kinra (2006) investigated the Indian consumers' attitudes towards local and foreign brands, by looking at the COO effect and ethnocentric tendencies. The findings suggested that foreign brands were perceived by Indian consumers as being more reliable and safe than their local brands. COO credibility was rated high for foreign brands, particularly for consumer durables. With regard to the ethnocentricity level, Indian consumers were not prejudiced against foreign brands; they evaluated them higher on quality, technology, status and esteem than Indian brands.

In a similar context, Liu *et al.* (2006) examined how CE relates to the Chinese consumers' brand evaluation across 3 brand naming strategies of a store sign: Chinese name, English and Chinese name and English and Chinese name with the brands' COO, and found that a high ethnocentric level has a negative impact on the evaluation of a store sign containing a foreign brand name and a foreign COO. Thus, the interaction between COO and CE on foreign brand evaluation was proven to be significant when the COO was the USA, but insignificant when the COO was Australia.

Also in the case of low involvement products CE affects consumer beliefs, culminating in the appearance of COO-effects (Chryssochoidis *et al.*, 2007).The authors evaluated the level of ethnocentrism of Greek consumers, and investigated the CE-COO effect relationship and implications for consumers' perceptions of imported food products, like beer, ham and cheese. The results showed that CE affects consumer beliefs and how the perceived quality of domestic and foreign products are evaluated, culminating in the appearance of COO-effects. Vida and Damjan (2001) studied the factors underlying consumer choice of domestic vs. foreign products of Slovenian consumers.

Their resuts suggested that the relationships between ethnocentric attitudes, familiarity with global brands and consumer domestic purchase decisions of the merchandise was significant.

There were few studies of services in the review. But the available evidence shows relationships between COO attributes and consumers' service evaluation. For example, Ferguson *et al.* (2008) conducted a qualitative study of stakeholders of higher education services in Burkina Faso, Ghana, Ivory Coast, Mali and Nigeria. The results showed that personal characteristics, such as motivation and ability to process information on the one hand, and ethnocentrism and culture orientation on the other, tend to influence the use of COO attributes in evaluating a service.

Some scholars suggested that CE has no influence on the COO effect (Yagci, 2001; Cumberlan *et al.*, 2010; Sharma, 2011). For example, Sharma (2011) investigated the role of CE in COO effects for consumers from the USA and the UK with regards to cars and found that ethnocentrism does not interact well with COO and has a weak negative effect on the consumers' product evaluation and behavioural intentions for imported products. Cumberlan *et al.* (2010) suggest that for Polish consumers, the impact of CE is minimal regarding two Danish brands. Yagci (2001) examined whether brand image overrides the effects of CE under different COOs. Brand image was found to be the most important variable in predicting the consumers' attitude toward the product, quality perception, and purchase intention. The findings showed that CE affects brand evaluations when the product is manufactured in its home country (i.e., BMW in Germany). In the relationship between CE and COO, consumer ethnocentrism becomes a significant predictor only when the product is manufactured in a less-developed/liked country (i.e. S. Korea). It was found that CE has a greater importance than COO.

All in all, the reviewed articles that studied the link between COO and CE and their effect on brand perception also produced some inconclusive results. Scholars like Kinra (2006), Liu *et al.* (2006), Chryssochoidis *et al.* (2007), Ferguson *et al.*(2008), Zolfagharian and Sun (2010) found that in connection with the country-of-origin effect, the ethnocentric perceptions indeed showed an influence on consumer behavioural tendencies, not only towards local and foreign products and services in general, but more specifically towards brands. On the other hand, some scholars suggested that CE has no influence on the COO effect (Yagci, 2001; Sharma, 2011), and consumer ethnocentrism becomes a significant predictor only when the product is manufactured in less-developed/liked countries. The main reason behind this contradictory evidence may lie in the differences in product involvement. Studies which included low involvement products showed a greater relationship between CE and COO, than studies which used high involvement products.

COO and Quality Assessment

Studies have also been conducted to see the effect of COO on the perceived quality of different products and brands (Lin and Sternquist, 1994; Kaynak *et al.*, 2000; Pecotich and Rosenthal, 2001; Ahmed *et al.*, 2002; Chu *et al.*, 2010). The results generally showed that COO has a positive and direct influence on quality perception. Chu *et al.* (2010) conducted a study on Taiwanese students to determine whether brand image could counter a negative COO of Chinese and Taiwanese laptops. They found that, taken separately, brand and COO are important determinants of consumers' perceptions of quality and favourability and the COO effect was stronger when consumers were exposed to joint evaluation than when they were exposed to separate evaluation processes.

252

Pecotich and Rosenthal (2001) studied the impact of COO on quality, purchase intentions and price perceptions when CE is manipulated in the presence of brand information. The results showed that although COO had no effect on the respondents' perception of price, their ethnocentricity and purchase intention (when the brand information was available), it had a very strong effect on quality. Furthermore, the COO cue was found to have a significant effect when it was presented together with a strong national brand image. Similarly, Kaynak *et al.* (2000) examined the impact of multiple developed and emerging COOs on quality perception of general food products, electronics and household goods of Bangladeshi consumers. They found that COO positively influenced quality perception; products from developed countries were rated much more favourably than those originating in developing countries. That is, electronic goods from Japan, Germany and the USA were rated most favourably. Food products from the USA, Germany and England were ranked as top choices. Fashion merchandise from the USA, Germany and England were the three top choices. In the case of household goods, the USA, Germany and England were ranked first, and Italy, Japan and Sweden as second and Korea as third choice. Products in general from the USA, Germany and Japan tied for first place, England as second and Sweden as their third choice.

Lin and Sternquist (1994) examined the effects of COO on the Taiwanese consumer perception of product information cues concerning jumpers. COO was found to positively influence the consumers' product quality. The sweater which was labeled "Made in Japan" received the highest evaluation and the one labeled "Made in Taiwan" the lowest.

Balestrini and Gamble (2006) examined the behaviour of Chinese wine consumers towards COO effects and found that COO is more important when the wine is being purchased for special occasions than for their private consumption. Similarly,

Speece and Nguyen (2005) studied the importance of COO and individual brand perception and whether price cuts influence negative perceptions of Vietnamese consumers concerning TVs. The results show that brand is the most important in the quality segment, moderately important in the value segment and lowest in the price segment. Sony is the top brand, and its quality is much more appreciated than its price, and people with stronger quality orientation will choose Japanese brands. In the case of services, Ahmed *et al.* (2002) investigated the impact of COO and brand on the Singaporean consumers' quality perception and purchase intention of services, i.e. cruise lines. The results suggested that the COO effect was a more important informational cue than the brand effect for quality or attitude ratings, while brand was more positively correlated with purchase intentions.

To sum up, the findings of the relationship between COO and quality perception have produced fairly conclusive results and show that COO has a positive and direct influence on quality perception, where products and services from developed countries are rated much more favorably than those originating from developing countries.

COO and Brand Equity

Through stereotyping, consumers associate different countries with intangible attributes like "reliability" and "durability" (Pappu *et al.*, 2006).Researchers have argued that these country-of-origin associations of consumers influence the brand equity dimensions of a brand from a specific country (Pappu *et al.*, 2006, 2007; Yasin *et al.*, 2007; Baldauf *et al.*, 2009; Sanyal and Datta, 2011; Parkvithee and Miranda, 2012). According to Aaker (1991), brand equity is defined as "the value consumers associate with a brand, as reflected in the dimensions of brand awareness, brand associations, perceived quality and brand loyalty". For brands like

Sony or Toyota, which are available to consumers all over the globe, the country of origin, Japan, definitely influences consumer-based brand equity in a positive way, since Japan is regarded as a high technology country with a world renowned high quality production history of electronics and automobiles.

Studies by scholars such as Pappu *et al.*, (2006, 2007), Yasin *et al.* (2007) and Sanyal and Datta (2011) have shown that there is a positive relationship between COO and brand equity. For example, Pappu *et al.*, (2006) examined the relationship between COO and brand equity in an Australian context using TV and car brands and found that consumer-based equity of a brand made in a country with stronger product category-country associations (e.g. Japan), was significantly higher than that of the same brand made in a country with weaker product category-country associations (e.g. China/Malaysia). In the same context, Pappu *et al.*, (2007) examined whether there is a relationship between macro country image, micro country image and consumer-based brand equity, and whether these relationships are consistent across different product categories. The results suggested that there is a significant relationship between consumer-based brand equity dimensions and both macro and micro country images of the brand. For TVs, brand associations had a stronger impact than perceived quality and brand loyalty. Yasin *et al.* (2007) also examined the effects of country-of-origin image on the development of brand equity, and found that brand distinctiveness, brand loyalty and brand awareness/ associations have significant impact on brand equity and COO image significantly impacts brand awareness/associations.

The effect of COO, brand equity and purchase intention on consumers' evaluation of products was also tested by Parkvithee and Miranda (2012), who found that if a low involvement product (i.e. T-shirts) with a high brand equity is sourced from a country of origin of perceived low competence, the superior reputation of the brand encourages consumer partiality to the apparel's quality and purchase inclination. A brand of modest equity, manufactured in an under-developed economy, is capable of gaining greater consumer support for its higher-end fashion products than for its standard apparel.

Finally, Baldauf *et al.* (2009) assessed how ceramic tiles brands are perceived by Austrian retailers (defined as retailer-perceived brand equity–RPBE), by investigating the effect of COO as a driver of RPBE. The results show that there is a positive relationship between product country image and RPBE, and that there is a positive effect of RPBE on brand profitability performance which supports the notion that brand equity is an important intangible firm asset.

In summary, the evidence generally corroborates earlier studies that found a positive relationship between COO and brand equity, i.e. that brand distinctiveness, brand loyalty and brand awareness/associations have a significant impact on brand equity and that COO image has a significant effect on brand awareness/associations.

Summary and Directions for Future Research

The 77 papers reviewed above have covered the following 6 issues: (i) COO and brand evaluation, (ii) COO and purchase intention and brand perception, (iii) multiple countries of origin and brand perception, (iv) COO and CE and brand perception, (v) COO and quality assessment, as well as (vi) COO and brand equity. The available body of empirical knowledge provided by the articles only provided conclusive support for 2 of the 6 issues studied. Generally, the studies found positive and strong associations between COO and quality assessment, as well as COO and brand equity. The evidence for the 4 other issues were inconclusive, but the majority of the articles found that the COO effect has a positive impact on brand perception. COO effect was also found to be more positive for products originating from developed countries than those coming from emerging countries (i.e. Haubl, 1996; Agbonifoh and Elimimian, 1999; Magnusson *et al.*, 2001; Sohail, 2005; Pecotich and Ward, 2007; Koubaa, 2008; Josiassen, 2010).However, Chao and Gupta (1995), Ettenson (1993), Zbib *et al.* (2010), Bruwer and Buller (2012) argue that COO has less of an impact on the consumers' overall brand perception, mainly due to the fact that consumers identify the cultural origin of the brands instead of the country of origin of the actual finished product. This partly depends on how well they, as consumers, are acquainted with the brand.

With regard to COO and purchase intentions, it was found that the COO image has a positive and significant influence on purchase intentions when considering high involvement products (Lundstrom *et al.*, 1998; Knight and Calantone, 2000; Ahmed and d' Astous, 1993; Lee and Lee, 2011), and low involvement products (Almonte *et al.*, 1995; Bailey and Gutierrez de Pineres, 1997; Kwok *et al.*, 2006, and Kumar *et al.*, 2009). In addition, in the case of services, COO seems to have an impact on purchase intention and product evaluation (Kabadayi and Lerman, 2011; Lin and Chen, 2006; Jimenez and Martin, 2012). That said, other scholars provide evidence indicating a weak relationship between COO and purchase intention (Johansson *et al.*, 1994; Aiello *et al.*, 2009; Diamantopoulus *et al.*, 2011). These studies suggest that brand has a much higher influence on product evaluation and purchase intention than the COO, partly because consumers rely more on specific product attributes than on the origin of the products.

Another issue that has attracted substantial empirical research attention is the impact of multiple countries of origin on brand perception. These studies broke down manufactured product images into country of design (COD), country of assembly

(COA), and country of origin of parts (COP) in order to study their impact on brand perception. Contributors to this strand of research include Ahmed and d'Astous (1995), (1996), Nebenzahl and Jaffe (1996), Hamin and Elliott (2006), Essoussi and Merunka (2007), Fetscherin and Toncar (2010), Chen and Su (2012), Moradi and Zarei (2012), and Sinrungtam (2013). The results of these studies have found a significant and positive association between multiple countries of origin and brand perception. That said, there are also some studies which found no significant effect of COO sub-components on consumer product assessment or purchase intentions (Hui and Zhou, 2003; Hamin and Elliott, 2006; Wong *et al.*, 2008; Ahmed *et al.*, 2011), because other cues like product country congruency showed a greater impact on consumer evaluations than the COO effect.

There have also been studies examining the links between COO and the ethnocentric orientations of consumers (see Kaynak and Kara, 1997; Vida and Damjan, 2001; Kinra, 2006; Liu *et al.*, 2006; Chryssochoidis *et al.*, 2007; Zolfagharian and Sun, 2010). Some studies suggested that CE has no influence on the COO effect (Yagci, 2001; Cumberlan *et al.*, 2010; Sharma, 2011), and consumer ethnocentrism becomes a significant predictor only when the product is manufactured in a less-developed/liked country.

As stated before, the relationships between COO and quality assessment, and COO and brand equity were found to be conclusive stating that COO has a positive and direct influence on quality assessment (Lin and Sternquist, 1994; Kaynak *et al.*, 2000; Pecotich and Rosenthal, 2001; Ahmed *et al.*, 2002; Chu *et al.*, 2010) and brand equity (Pappu *et al.*, 2006, 2007; Yasin *et al.*, 2007; Baldauf *et al.*, 2009; Sanyal and Datta, 201; and Parkvithee and Miranda, 2012).

All in all, what emerged from the literature review was how contradictory the knowledge of the impact of the COO effect on brand perception actually is, suggesting that a great deal of cross cultural quantitative verification is still needed and further consumer behavioural studies need to be undertaken in the 4 areas.

Another issue that emerged from the 6 research topics identified through the literature review is that researchers' choice of methodology has impacted their investigations. For example, most of the qualitative studies consistently showed no strong COO effects on brand perception (Johansson *et al.*, 1994; Aiello *et al.*, 2009; Ahmed *et al.*, 2011), while the quantitative studies on the same issue produced conflicting results. A possible explanation for this result could be that when employing quantitative techniques, the research presents a predetermined limited set of categories that the respondent has to choose from, and such a method could be viewed as an inadequate process by which to measure such an wide concept as country image (Dinnie, 2004).

The literature review showed that only 12 of the 77 papers reported studies on multiple countries of origin and brand perception and 10 papers reported empirical investigations on country of origin and consumer ethnocentrism. These areas therefore appear to be under-researched and require greater attention in future research. The review has also shown that most of the studies are of single country types and limited to specific periods of time. That is, researchers have not shown very much interest in comparative and longitudinal studies. Wong *et al.* (2006) also made a similar observation and called for more cross-cultural or regional studies, since consumers' perceptions concerning different brands can differ across cultures. According to Wong *et al.* (2006), it would be useful to place a greater emphasis on longitudinal studies and find out whether consumers perceive brands differently on the basis of products' country of origin, and if so, what has triggered their change in perception.

Future research should also take into consideration other elements of decision-making such as the consumers' demographic profiles and their effect on brand perception when COO information is available. There are very few studies of this type among the reviewed articles and they have produced contradictory results. In the case of gender, Samiee *et al.* (2005) argued that women are more prone to rate foreign products more favourably, while while men exhibited more ethnocentric tendencies, and had more biased perceptions of foreign products. On the other hand, the research conducted by Ahmed *et al.* (2004) and Vida and Damjan (2001) found no significant differences between males and females in their likelihood of purchasing each product from different countries. Studies which focused on evaluating the role of age, suggested that older people are more strongly influenced by country-of-origin effects (Schellinck, 1989; Wall *et al.*, 1991; Schaefer, 1997), while others suggested that younger consumers exhibited a greater COO effect (Insch and McBride, 2004). For the level of education, previous studies have suggested that if the consumer's income is high, the probability of buying domestic products is lower. However, McLain and Sternquist (1991) found no such relationship between the income level and product brand perception. Since demographic factors form the core of consumer market segmentation, further research is needed into whether country-of-origin effects operate differently in terms of socioeconomic or psychographic characteristics.

The evidence reported in this review also reveals other under-researched areas that should receive attention in future research effort. For example, most studies have focused attention on very well-known brands from developed countries. Some scholars have argued that products from developing (emerging) economies experience the effects of negative country images that adversely affect their evaluation by both Western and non-Western consumers (Chu *et al.*, 2010). Some studies have also suggested that favourably perceived brand names can help mitigate a negative country image (Speece and Nguyen, 2005; Kabadayi and Lerman, 2011). The available amount of knowledge on the issue, however, remains scarce. That said, in the light of the fact that an increasing number of firms from developing countries are entering the global market scene (usually with little-known brands), research into the COO effects on these unknown brands will provide companies in developing country with a stronger knowledge base for their international marketing strategy formulation (Lin and Chen, 2006; Wong *et al.*, 2007). It will also widen the available amount of academic knowledge in the field.

Some scholars have called for additional research into the COO phenomenon in Central and Eastern European (CEE) countries due to the dynamics of economic activities in the region. For example, an increasing number of these countries have joined the EU, and Western European companies are aggressively marketing their products to consumers in the CEE. At the same time, some previous research has shown that these consumers are exhibiting an increasing degree of ethnocentricism that is disturbing to Western European marketing managers (Beverland, 2001; Pecotich and Rosenthal, 2001; Dmitrovic, Vida and Reardon, 2009). Apparently, the transition from a centrally-planned system to a free market economy in the countries of Central and Eastern Europe (CEE) has not translated fully into a total eradication of the communist ideology in the mental fabric of the citizens of these countries. Recent research suggests that an increasing number of citizens in these societies yearn for the return to the communist era and nationalistic tendencies seem to manifest themselves in consumer preferences (Gellner, 1993; Verdery, 1993; Molchanov, 2000; Demirbag *et al.*, 2010;

Siemieniako, 2011).There is therefore a need for further empirical investigations into how the changing of both the political landscape and "communist nostalgia" impact brand perception and purchase behaviour of consumers with different demographic profiles (see Gellner, 1993; Verdery, 1993; Molchanov, 2000; Demirbag *et al.*, 2010; Siemieniako, 2011 for similar arguments).

One possibility would be to approach the issue of the COO effect considering more factors of a psychological, political and technological nature, such as the influence of ideology on the country-of-origin effect and consumer ethnocentrism, for brands from either emerging or developed countries (Chryssochoidis *et al.*, 2007).

As mentioned earlier, research into the impact of multiple countries of origin on brand perception is another interesting area for further research. A number of scholars argue that future research should explore the relationship between country image and brand perception in greater detail, given that each brand is associated with a certain country. According to Wong *et al.* (2006) and Diamantopoulus *et al.* (2011) there is a growing need to study the impact of hybrid products, i.e. products with a different country of design (COD), country of assembly (COA), and country of parts (COP), on the consumers' perception of brands. Thus, one area of interest would be to study the impact of multiple countries of origin of a product with Western and non-Western countries of origin, by providing additional insights into the relative influence of the three sub-components on the consumers' evaluation of high involvement products.

The articles reviewed have also suggested that consumers' responses to the brand personality may have been influenced by their individual differences with regard to purchase intention, product attitude, or consumer ethnocentrism (Fetscherin and Toncar, 2010, Souiden *et al.*, 2011). Some scholars have criticised the previous studies on the grounds that they have examined each of these constructs separately and call for the application of an integrated framework for the COO effect on purchase intention and purchase behaviour of brands (Chryssochoidis *et al.* 2007; Chu *et al.,* 2010).

Conclusions

In the face of the extensive amount of literature on the country-of-origin effect, this chapter has made an attempt to shed some light onto how the link between the COO effect and brand has been discussed in the literature over a twenty year period (1993 - 2013). The aim is to examine issues that have received research attention, the compelling nature of the empirical evidence generated, and to highlight the research gaps and future research possibilities that there are in the field.

In total, 77 articles were reviewed and several important contributions emerged from this study. To the best of my knowledge, this is the first academic article to review the literature of COO effects on brand perception in a systematic way. The review has shown that the empirical evidence remains unsettled with regard to a number of issues. I have outlined four issues that manifest conflicting views and that require additional research interest. These are: the relationship between COO and brand evaluation, COO and purchase intention and brand perception, multiple countries of origin and brand perception, and COO and CE and brand perception. Specifically, the low number of empirical investigations on two of the four topics (multiple countries of origin & brand perception, and COO and CE & brand perception) require a great deal of attention in future research. The complexity of the phenomenon provides scholars in the field of Marketing and Business studies ample scope for further research.

References

Agarwal, S. & Sikri, S. 1996, "Country image: consumer evaluation of product category extensions", *International Marketing Review,* vol. 13, no. 4, pp. 23-39.

Agbonifoh, B.A. & Elimimian, J.U. 1999, "Attitudes of developing countries towards "country-of-origin" products in an era of multiple brands", *Journal of International Consumer Marketing,* vol. 11, no. 4, pp. 97-116.

Ahmed, S.A. & d Astous, A. 1996, "Country-of-origin and brand effects: A multi-dimensional and multi-attribute study", *Journal of International Consumer Marketing,* vol. 9, no. 2, pp. 93-115.

Ahmed, S.A. & d Astous, A. 1995, "Comparison of country-of-origin effects on household and org", *European Journal of Marketing,* vol. 29, no. 3, pp. 35.

Ahmed, S.A. & d Astous, A. 1993, "Cross-national evaluation of made-in concept using multiple", *European Journal of Marketing,* vol. 27, no. 7, pp. 39.

Ahmed, S.A. & d'Astous, A. 2008, "Antecedents, moderators and dimensions of country-of-origin evaluations", *International Marketing Review,* vol. 25, no. 1, pp. 75-106.

Ahmed, S.A. & d'Astous, A. 2004, "Perceptions of countries as producers of consumer goods: A T-shirt study in China", *Journal of Fashion Marketing and Management,* vol. 8, no. 2, pp. 187-200.

Ahmed, S.A., d'Astous, A. & Halima Benmiloud Petersen 2011, "Product-country fit in the Canadian context", *The Journal of Consumer Marketing,* vol. 28, no. 4, pp. 300-309.

Ahmed, Z.U., Johnson, J.P., Chew, P.L., Tan Wai Fang & Ang, K.H. 2002, "Country-of-origin and brand effects on consumers' evaluations of cruise lines", *International Marketing Review,* vol. 19, no. 2/3, pp. 279.

Ahmed, Z.U., Johnson, J.P., Yang, X., Chen, K.F. &*et al.* 2004, "Does country of origin matter for low-involvement products?", *International Marketing Review,* vol. 21, no. 1, pp. 102-120.

Aiello, G., Donvito, R., Godey, B., Pederzoli, D., Wiedmann, K., Hennigs, N., Siebels, A., Chan, P., Tsuchiya, J., Rabino, S., Ivanovna, S.I., Weitz, B., Oh, H. & Singh, R. 2009, "An international perspectiveon luxury brand and country-of-origin effect", *Journal of Brand Management,* vol. 16, no. 5-6, pp. 323-337.

Almonte, J., Falk, C., Skaggs, R. & Cardenas, M. 1995, "Country-of-origin bias among high-income consumers in Mexico: An empirical study", *Journal of International Consumer Marketing,* vol. 8, no. 2, pp. 27.

Bailey, W. & Gutierrez de Pineres, S.A. 1997, "Country of origin attitudes in Mexico: The malinchismo effect", *Journal of International Consumer Marketing,* vol. 9, no. 3, pp. 25-41.

Balabanis, G., Mueller, R. & Melewar, T.C. 2002, "The human values' lenses of country of origin images", *International Marketing Review,* vol. 19, no. 6, pp. 582-610.

Balabanis G, Diamantopoulos, A. 2008, "Brand Origin Identification by Consumers: A Classification Perspective", *Journal of International Marketing,* vol. 16, no. 1, pp. 39-71

Baldauf, A., Cravens, K.S., Diamantopoulos, A. & Zeugner-Roth, K.P. 2009, "The Impact of Product-Country Image and Marketing Efforts on Retailer-Perceived Brand Equity: An Empirical Analysis", *Journal of Retailing,* vol. 85, no. 4, pp. 437-452.

Balestrini, P. & Gamble, P. 2006, "Country-of-origin effects on Chinese wine consumers", *British Food Journal,* vol. 108, no. 5, pp. 396-412.

Booth, A., Papaioannou, D. and Sutton, A., 2012. "Systematic Approaches to a Successful Literature Review", *SAGE*, ISBN: 0857021346

Bruwer, J. & Buller, C. 2012, "Country-of-origin (COO) brand preferences and associated knowledge levels of Japanese wine consumers", *The Journal of Product and Brand Management,* vol. 21, no. 5, pp. 307-316.

Chao, P. & Gupta, P.B. 1995, "Information search and efficiency of consumer choices of new cars: Country-of-origin effects", *International Marketing Review,* vol. 12, no. 6, pp. 47.

Chao, P. & Rajendran, K.N. 1993, "Consumer profiles and perceptions: Country-of-origin effects", *International Marketing Review,* vol. 10, no. 2, pp. 22.

Chattalas, M., Kramer, T. & Takada, H. 2008, "The impact of national stereotypes on the country of origin effect", *International Marketing Review,* vol. 25, no. 1, pp. 54-74.

Chen, Y-M., & Su, Y-F. 2012, "Do country-of-manufacture and country-of-design matter to industrial brand equity?",*Journal of Business & Industrial Marketing,* vol.27, no. 1, pp- 57-68.

Chryssochoidis, G., Krystallis, A. & Perreas, P. 2007, "Ethnocentric beliefs and country-of-origin (COO) effect", *European Journal of Marketing,* vol. 41, no. 11/12, pp. 1518-1544.

Chui Yim Wong, Polonsky, M.J. & Garma, R. 2008, "The impact of consumer ethnocentrism and country of origin sub-components for high involvement products on young Chinese consumers' product assessments", *Asia Pacific Journal of Marketing and Logistics,* vol. 20, no. 4, pp. 455-478.

Diamantopoulos, A., Schlegelmilch, B. & Palihawadana, D. 2011, "The relationship between country-of-origin image and brand image as drivers of purchase intentions", *International Marketing Review,* vol. 28, no. 5, pp. 508-524.

Erdogan, B.Z. and Uzkurt, C. (2010), "Effects of ethnocentric tendency on consumers' perception of product attitudes for foreign and domestic products", Cross Cultural Management: An International Journal, vol. 17, no. 4, pp. 393-406.

Essoussi, L.H. & Merunka, D. 2007, "Consumers' product evaluations in emerging markets: Does country of design, country of manufacture, or brand image matter?", *International Marketing Review,* vol. 24, no. 4, pp. 409-426.

Ettenson, R. 1993, "Brand name and country of origin effects in the emerging market economies of Russia, Poland and Hungary", *International Marketing Review,* vol. 10, no. 5, pp. 14.

Ferguson, J.L., Dadzie, K.Q. & Johnston, W.J. 2008, "Country-of-origin effects in service evaluation in emerging markets: some insights from five West African countries", *The Journal of Business & Industrial Marketing,* vol. 23, no. 6, pp. 429-437.

Fetscherin, M. & Toncar, M. 2010, "The effects of the country of brand and the country of manufacturing of automobiles", *International Marketing Review,* vol. 27, no. 2, pp. 164-178.

Garbarino, E., Lee, J.A., Lerman, D. & Horn, M. 2001, "The influence of uncertainty avoidance on country of origin stereotypes", *American Marketing Association.Conference Proceedings,* vol. 12, pp. 399.

Gillian Sullivan Mort, Hume Winzar & Han, C.M. 2001, "Country image effects in international services: A conceptual model and cross national empirical test", *American Marketing Association.Conference Proceedings,* vol. 12, pp. 43.

Hamin & Elliott, G. 2006, "A less-developed country perspective of consumer ethnocentrism and "country of origin" effects: Indonesian evidence", *Asia Pacific Journal of Marketing and Logistics,* vol. 18, no. 2, pp. 79-92.

Haubl, G. 1996, "A cross-national investigation of the effects of country of origin and brand name on the evaluation of a new car", *International Marketing Review,* vol. 13, no. 5, pp. 76-97.

Huddleston, P., Good, L.K. and Stoel, L. (2001), "Consumer ethnocentrism, product necessity and Polish consumers' perceptions of quality", International Journal of Retail & Distribution Management, Vol. 29, No. 5, pp. 236-246.

Hui, M.K. & Zhou, L. 2003, "Country-of-manufacture effects for known brands", *European Journal of Marketing,* vol. 37, no. 1/2, pp. 133-153.

Hwei-Chung Chen & Pereira, A. 1999, "Product entry in international markets: the effect of country-of-origin on first-mover advantage", *The Journal of Product and Brand Management,* vol. 8, no. 3, pp. 218-231.

Jalali,S. and Wohlin, C., 2012. "Systematic literature studies: Database searches vs. backward snowballing", *Conference paper: 6th ACM-IEEE International Symposium on Empirical Software Engineering and Measurement,* ESEM; pp.29-38

Javalgi, R.G., Cutler, B.D. & Winans, W.A. 2001, "At your service! Does country of origin research apply to services?", *The Journal of Services Marketing,* vol. 15, no. 6/7, pp. 565-582.

Jesson, J.K., Matheson, L., and Lacey, F.M. 2011, Doing your literature review: Traditional and systematic techniques", SAGE Publications, ISBN: 978-1-84860-153-6.

Jiménez, N. & Martín, S.S. 2012, "Emerging Markets Commerce: The Role of Country-of-Origin and Animosity in Purchase Intention", *International Journal of Business and Management,* vol. 7, no. 17, pp. 34-42.

Johansson, J.K., Ronkainen, I.A. & Czinkota, M.R. 1994, "Negative country-of-origin effects: The case of the new Russia", *Journal of International Business Studies,* vol. 25, no. 1, pp. 157.

Jorgensen A.W., Hilden J., and Gotzsche P.C., 2006. „Cochrane reviews compared with industry supported meta-analyses and other meta-analyses of the same drugs: Systematic review". *British Medical Journal,* vol. 333, no. 782.

Josiassen, A. 2010, "Young Australian consumers and the country-of-origin effect: Investigation of the moderating roles of product involvement and perceived product-origin congruency", *Australasian Marketing Journal,* vol. 18, no. 1, pp. 23-27.

Jyh-shen Chiou 2003, "The impact of country of origin on pretrial and posttrial product evaluations: The moderating effect of consumer expertise", *Psychology & Marketing,* vol. 20, no. 10, pp. 935-954.

Kabadayi, S. & Lerman, D. 2011, "Made in China but sold at FAO Schwarz: country-of-origin effect and trusting beliefs", *International Marketing Review,* vol. 28, no. 1, pp. 102-126.

Karunaratna, A.R. & Quester, P.G. 2007, "Influence of cognition on product component country of origin evaluation", *Asia Pacific Journal of Marketing and Logistics,* vol. 19, no. 4, pp. 349-362.

Kaynak, E., Kucukemiroglu, O. & Hyder, A.S. 2000, "Consumers' country-of-origin (COO) perceptions of imported products in a homogenous less-developed country", *European Journal of Marketing,* vol. 34, no. 9/10, pp. 1221-1241.

Kinra, N. 2006, "The effect of country-of-origin on foreign brand names in the Indian market", *Marketing Intelligence & Planning,* vol. 24, no. 1, pp. 15-30.

Knight, G.A. & Calantone, R.J. 2000, "A flexible model of consumer country-of-origin perceptions A cross-cultural investigation", *International Marketing Review,* vol. 17, no. 2, pp. 127-145.

Knight, J.G., Holdsworth, D.K. & Mather, D.W. 2007, "Country-of-origin and choice of food imports: an in-depth study of European distribution channel gatekeepers", *Journal of International Business Studies,* vol. 38, no. 1, pp. 107-125.

Koubaa, Y. 2008, "Country of origin, brand image perception, and brand image structure", *Asia Pacific Journal of Marketing and Logistics,* vol. 20, no. 2, pp. 139-155.

Kumar, A., Youn-Kyung, K. & Pelton, L. 2009, "Indian consumers' purchase behavior toward US versus local brands", *International Journal of Retail & Distribution Management,* vol. 37, no. 6, pp. 510-526.

Kwok, S., Uncles, M. & Huang, Y. 2006, "Brand preferences and brand choices among urban Chinese consumers", *Asia Pacific Journal of Marketing and Logistics,* vol. 18, no. 3, pp. 163-172.

Lee, H.-M.& Lee, C.-C. 2011, "Country-of-origin and brand redeployment impact after brand acquisition", *The Journal of Consumer Marketing,* vol. 28, no. 6, pp. 412-420.

Liefeld, J.P. 2004, "Consumer knowledge 'and use of country-of-origin information at the point of purchase", *Journal of Consumer Behaviour,* vol. 4, no. 2, pp. 85-96.

Lim, K. & O'Cass, A. 2001, "Consumer brand classifications: an assessment of culture-of-origin versus country-of-origin", *The Journal of Product and Brand Management,* vol. 10, no. 2, pp. 120-136.

Lin, L. & Sternquist, B. 1994, "Taiwanese consumers' perceptions of product information cues: Country of origin and store prestige", *European Journal of Marketing,* vol. 28, no. 1, pp. 5.

Liu, F., Murphy, J., Li, J. & Liu, X. 2006, "English and Chinese? The Role of Consumer Ethnocentrism and Country of Origin in Chinese Attitudes towards Store Signs", *Australasian Marketing Journal,* vol. 14, no. 2, pp. 5-16.

Liu, S.S. & Johnson, K.F. 2005, "The Automatic Country-Of-Origin Effects on Brand Judgments", *Journal of Advertising*, vol. 34, no. 1, pp. 87-97.

Long-Yi, L. & Chen, C. 2006, "The influence of the country-of-origin image, product knowledge and product involvement on consumer purchase decisions: an empirical study of insurance and catering services in Taiwan", *The Journal of Consumer Marketing*, vol. 23, no. 5, pp. 248-265.

Lundstrom, W.J., Lee, O.W. & White, D.S. 1998, "Factors influencing Taiwanese consumer preference for foreign-made white goods: USA versus Japan", *Asia Pacific Journal of Marketing and Logistics*, vol. 10, no. 3, pp. 5-29.

M Sadiq Sohail 2005, "Malaysian Consumers' Evaluation of Products Made in Germany: The Country of Origin Effect", *Asia Pacific Journal of Marketing and Logistics*, vol. 17, no. 1, pp. 89-105.

Magnusson, P., Westjohn, S.A. & Zdravkovic, S. 2011, ""What? I thought Samsung was Japanese": accurate or not, perceived country of origin matters", *International Marketing Review*, vol. 28, no. 5, pp. 454-472.

Miranda, M.J. & Narissara Parkvithee 2013, "The influence of social class on the perceptions of country of origin", *Marketing Intelligence & Planning*, vol. 31, no. 4, pp. 388-404.

Mohammad Ali Zolfagharian & Sun, Q. 2010, "Country of origin, ethnocentrism and bicultural consumers: the case of Mexican Americans", *The Journal of Consumer Marketing*, vol. 27, no. 4, pp. 345-357.

Moradi, H. & Zarei, A. 2012, "Creating consumer-based brand equity for young Iranian consumers via country of origin sub-components effects", *Asia Pacific Journal of Marketing and Logistics*, vol. 24, no. 3, pp. 394-413.

Narissara Parkvithee & Miranda, M.J. 2012, "The interaction effect of country-of-origin, brand equity and purchase involvement on consumer purchase intentions of clothing labels", *Asia Pacific Journal of Marketing and Logistics,* vol. 24, no. 1, pp. 7-22.

Nebenzahl, I.D. & Jaffe, E.D. 1996, "Measuring the joint effect of brand and country image in consumer evaluation of global products", *International Marketing Review,* vol. 13, no. 4, pp. 5-22.

Norjaya Mohd Yasin, Mohd Nasser Noor & Osman Mohamad 2007, "Does image of country-of-origin matter to brand equity?", *The Journal of Product and Brand Management,* vol. 16, no. 1, pp. 38-48.

Okechuku, C. 1994, "The importance of product country of origin: A conjoint analysis of the United States, Canada, Germany, and the Netherlands", *European Journal of Marketing,* vol. 28, no. 4, pp. 5.

Pappu, R., Quester, P.G. & Cooksey, R.W. 2007, "Country image and consumer-based brand equity: relationships and implications for international marketing", *Journal of International Business Studies,* vol. 38, no. 5, pp. 726.

Pappu, R., Quester, P.G. & Cooksey, R.W. 2006, "Consumer-based brand equity and country-of-origin relationships", *European Journal of Marketing,* vol. 40, no. 5/6, pp. 696-717.

Parameswaran, R. & Pisharodi, R.M. 2002, "Assimilation effects in country image research", *International Marketing Review,* vol. 19, no. 2/3, pp. 259.

Paswan, A.K. & Sharma, D. 2004, "Brand-country of origin (COO) knowledge and COO image: investigation in an emerging franchise market", *The Journal of Product and Brand Management,* vol. 13, no. 2/3, pp. 144-155.

Pecotich, A. & Rosenthal, M.J. 2001, "Country of Origin, Quality, Brand and Consumer Ethnocentrism", *Journal of Global Marketing,* vol. 15, no. 2, pp. 31-60

Pecotich, A. & Ward, S. 2007, "Global branding, country of origin and expertise", *International Marketing Review,* vol. 24, no. 3, pp. 271-296.

Petticrew, M. and Roberts, H., 2008. "Systematic Reviews in the Social Sciences: A Practical Guide", *John Wiley & Sons,* ISBN: 1405150149

Phau, I. & Vasinee Suntornnond 2006, "Dimensions of consumer knowledge and its impacts on country of origin effects among Australian consumers: a case of fast-consuming product", *The Journal of Consumer Marketing,* vol. 23, no. 1, pp. 34-42.

Chu, P.-Y., Chang, C., Chen, C-Y., C. & Wang, T. 2010, "Countering negative country-of-origin effects", *European Journal of Marketing,* vol. 44, no. 7/8, pp. 1055-1076.

Samantha Kumara, P.A.P. & Canhua, K. 2010, "Perceptions of country of origin: An approach to identifying expectations of foreign products", *Journal of Brand Management,* vol. 17, no. 5, pp. 343-353.

Samiee, Saeed, Terence A. Shimp, and Subhash Sharma. 2005. "Brand origin recognition accuracy: its antecedents and consumers' cognitive limitations." *Journal of International Business Studies,* vol. 36, no. 4, pp. 379-97

Sanyal, S.N. & Datta, S.K. 2011, "The effect of country of origin on brand equity: an empirical study on generic drugs", *The Journal of Product and Brand Management,* vol. 20, no. 2, pp. 130-140.

Schaefer, A. 1997, "Consumer knowledge and country of origin effects", *European Journal of Marketing,* vol. 31, no. 1, pp. 56-72.

Sharma, P. 2011, "Country of origin effects in developed and emerging markets: Exploring the contrasting roles of materialism and value consciousness", *Journal of International Business Studies,* vol. 42, no. 2, pp. 285-306.

273

Shimp, T. and Sharma, S. (1987), "Consumer Ethnocentrism: Construction and Validation of the CETSCALE", Journal of Marketing Research, Vol. 24, No. 3, pp. 280-289.

Sinrungtam, W. 2013, "Impact of Country of Origin Dimensions on Purchase Intention of Eco Car", *International Journal of Business and Management,* vol. 8, no. 11, pp. 51-62.

Souiden, N., Pons, F. & Mayrand, M. 2011, "Marketing high-tech products in emerging markets: the differential impacts of country image and country-of-origin's image", *The Journal of Product and Brand Management,* vol. 20, no. 5, pp. 356-367.

Speece, M. & Duc Phung Nguyen 2005, "Countering negative country-of-origin with low prices: a conjoint study in Vietnam", *The Journal of Product and Brand Management,* vol. 14, no. 1, pp. 39-48.

Strutton, D. & Pelton, L.E. 1993, "Southeast Asian consumer perceptions of American and Japanese imports: The influence of country-of-origin effects", *Journal of International Consumer Marketing,* vol. 6, no. 1, pp. 67.

Thanasuta, K., Patoomsuwan, T., Chaimahawong, V. & Chiaravutthi, Y. 2009, "Brand and country of origin valuations of automobiles", *Asia Pacific Journal of Marketing and Logistics,* vol. 21, no. 3, pp. 355-375.

Uddin, J., Parvin, S. & Rahman, M.L. 2013, "Factors Influencing Importance of Country of Brand and Country of Manufacturing in Consumer Product Evaluation", *International Journal of Business and Management,* vol. 8, no. 4, pp. 65-74.

Wang, X. & Yang, Z. 2008, "Does country-of-origin matter in the relationship between brand personality and purchase intention in emerging economies?", *International Marketing Review,* vol. 25, no. 4, pp. 458-474.

Yagci, M.I. 2001, "Evaluating the effects of country-of-origin and consumer ethnocentrism: A case of a transplant product", *Journal of International Consumer Marketing,* vol. 13, no. 3, pp. 63-85.

Yi-Min, C. & Yi-Fan, S. 2012, "Do country-of-manufacture and country-of-design matter to industrial brand equity?", *The Journal of Business & Industrial Marketing,* vol. 27, no. 1, pp. 57-68.

Zbib, I.J., Wooldridge, B.R., Ahmed, Z.U. & Sarkis Benlian 2010, "Selection criteria of Lebanese consumers in the global snack food industry: country of origin perceptions", *The Journal of Consumer Marketing,* vol. 27, no. 2, pp. 139-156.

Zbib, I.J., Wooldridge, B.R., Ahmed, Z.U. & Yeghig Benlian 2010, "Purchase of global shampoo brands and the impact of country of origin on Lebanese consumers", *The Journal of Product and Brand Management,* vol. 19, no. 4, pp. 261-275.

Zeugner-Roth, K.P., Diamantopoulos, A. & Montesinos, M.Ã. 2008, "Home Country Image, Country Brand Equity and Consumers' Product Preferences: An Empirical Study", *Management International Review,* vol. 48, no. 5, pp. 577-602.

Zhang, Y. 1996, "Chinese consumers' evaluation of foreign products: the influence of culture, product types and product presentation format", *European Journal of Marketing,* vol. 30, no. 12, pp. 50.

Zhongqi Jin and Bal Chansarkar & Kondap, N.M. 2006, "Brand origin in an emerging market: perceptions of Indian consumers", *Asia Pacific Journal of Marketing and Logistics,* vol. 18, no. 4, pp. 283-302.

CHAPTER NINE

Country of origin effects on consumer brand perception of familiar vs. unfamiliar brands of technological complex products in a developed market setting

Jeanne S. Bentzen and Andreea Iacob

Abstract.

The purpose of this paper is to extend the knowledge of the effect of brand familiarity on how Country of Origin influences brand perception in a developed country. We used a 2x2 factorial experimental design to test the effects of COO with two levels of sourcing location – Czech Republic and Romania- on a technologically complex product (cars), represented by 2 brands, one familiar brand (Skoda) and one unfamiliar brand (Dacia). Data were collected using a questionnaire which was administered to respondents, with diversified demographic characteristics, in 4 large cities in Denmark with 205 usable questionnaires. We used ANOVA to test our hypotheses. The findings suggest that country of origin has a significant positive impact on the consumers' perception of the Czech manufactured Skoda Fabia, representing the familiar brand, and a significant negative impact on the consumers' perception of the Romanian manufactured Dacia Sandero, representing the unfamiliar brand.

Keywords: *Country of origin, country of manufacture, brand perception, Denmark, brand familiarity*

Introduction

Globalization has led to the exposure of products from different countries to consumers all over the world, and thus made the country of origin cue, that is, how consumers perceive a product from a specific country, more noticeable (Shankarmahesh *et al.*, 2006; Samiee *et al.*, 2005; Ghalandari and Norouzi, 2012). Empirical studies have shown that while products from industrialized countries generally enjoy positive country image both at home and abroad, products from the emerging market economies suffer liabilities of negative country image (Chao 1989; Zhang, 1996; Okechuku and Onyemah, 1999; Kaynak *et al.*, 2000). However, offshore outsourcing of manufacturing to less developed countries has changed the perceptions of foreign-made products based on their country of design, country of parts, and country-of assembly (Chao, 1993). The COO effect has shown to be much more complex than was originally assumed and empirical research has often shown conflicting results (Verlegh and Steenkamp, 1999; Phau and Suntornnond, 2006). Multiple country affiliations are one of the issues that are creating challenges. Many studies focus on the situation where brands from developed countries are produced in less developed countries. Although this has been the most common construction we also see that many developing countries or countries that have until recently been categorized as developing are selling their products in the Western world. In Europe we see this development especially related to the Eastern European countries. These countries have gone through a tremendous development since the mid-1980s, and although some have changed faster than others there is still a question of whether the stereotypes related to former East Block countries are still playing a role in the way consumers perceive the products and brands originating from these countries; especially if these products are technologically complex; a factor that is often seen to play a role in the influence of the COO effect (Verlegh and Steenkamp,1999). Due to historical reasons these countries although geographically close to the rest of Europe have been separated from the rest of Europe for many years causing the flow of products across borders to be limited compared to the rest of Europe. The familiarity and accustumization with the products from these countries are thus not corresponding with the geographical closeness.

It is a well-known fact that consumers develop stereotypical beliefs about products from other countries. These stereotypical belief may represent a knowledge structure that are less accurate and often biased, however, they play an important role in complex decision settings (Taylor, 1981; Hong and Wyer, 1989,1990; Maheswaran, 1994)

It is widely acknowledged that the research on COO is extensive, but it appears, however, that previous research has not paid too much attention to finding out the effect that country of origin plays for consumers from old developed countries, when facing a familiar versus unfamiliar brand from new markets (developed or less developed countries) (Schaefer, 1997; Hui and Zhou, 2003, Phau and Suntornnond, 2006). We do know that when a known or unknown branded product is manufactured in a developing country or a country with a less favorable image, then country of manufacture presents a different impact on global product attitude (Hui and Zhou, 2003). One key brand association is the country from which the brand has originated, for example the brand origin of Sony is Japan (Thakor and Kohli, 1996). However, when the product is manufactured in a developing country, as opposed to a developed country, which is the country of the brand origin, the information about country of manufacture produces a negative effect on product assessment (Schaefer, 1997). Hui and Zhou (2003) state that the effect of country image on brand image is moderated by both brand and country reputation, that is, the brand image of a well-known brand of a given product produced in a country famous for that product is likely to be affected differently from the brand image of a well-known brand produced in a country unknown for this and vice-versa. However, the case here is that the brand originates from the countries that possibly carry a less favorable image in regards to the specific product category.

Country image is a construct that is referred to in relation to COO. Laroche *et al.* (2005) find that this is a three dimensional concept which consists of cognitive, affective and conative elements. This corresponds with Verlegh and Steenkamps (1999) understanding of mechanisms related to the COO effects. They refer to the affective elements as consisting of emotion, identity, pride and autobiographical memories, illustrating that a lot more than factual knowledge about a country's economy, political and cultural situation can be affecting the COO effect. This suggests that privious events and experiences related to a country and its products involving affective reactions can affect the country's image later on.

The two countries used in the present study are the Czech Republic and Romania. The Czech Republic is a member of OECD, characterized as a developed country by e.g. OECD and the World Bank, and is thus on of the Eastern European countries that has gone through a transition faster and has sold their products in Western Europe longer, assuring more familiarity with their products among Western European consumers. This status could potentially influence the perception of the Western European consumers of the country and the spillover effect on products produced in the country. Romania on the other hand is not on the list of developing countries and could thus suffer from the effect known of developing countries. The two countries both have a long history of producing cars and they have also both been former members of the Comecon with the negative perceptional cues that could provide in Western Europe. In the developed market setting where the empirical research is carried out, which is Denmark, many consumers may have memories about the cold war period and recollections about the perception and attitude towards cars from the Comecon countries at that time, providing an effect similar to the bad image effect known from developing countries – especially related to technological complex products (Verlegh and Steenkamp, 1999). This could thus potentially serve as a negative image provider in spite of both countries history with producing cars.

The present study contributes to the research stream on brand familiarity and COO effects and attemts to fill the research gap of COO effects on familiar vs. unfamiliar brands of highly complex technological products from new developed or less developed countries in developed markets. We examine the country of origin effect of both familiar (Skoda Fabia) and unfamiliar (Dacia) brands in a developed country (Denmark). The rest of the chapter is structured as follows. In section 2, we shortly reviewed the extant literature on country of origin, country of manufacture and brand perception in order to develop a conceptual model for the present study. We then, formulate hypotheses for the empirical investigation in section 3, again drawing on knowledge from the existing literature. This is followed by a presentation of the methodological approaches used for the empirical investigation and data materials in section 5. Afterwards the results of the empirical analyses are reported and finally the findings are discussed, noting their implications for marketing strategy formulation as well as limitations in the present study and their implications for subsequent studies in the field.

Literature Review and Model Development

When reviewing the literature on COO effects, one can acknowledge that there exists a huge body of empirical research. Schooler (1965) was the first to conduct an empirical study about COO and proved that consumers rate identical products based on their country-of-origin. Previous research depicted that COO has an impact on brand/product perceptions (Etzel an Walker, 1974; Han and Terpstra, 1988; Leonidou *et al.*, 1999; Paswan and Sharma, 2004), beliefs and attitudes (Lee and Ganesh, 1999;

Knight and Calantone, 2000), perceived quality (White and Cundiff, 1978; Han and Terpstra, 1988; Teas and Agarwal, 2000; Balduaf *et al.*, 2009) and evaluations (Hong and Wyer, 1989; Roth and Romeo, 1992). COO has also been shown to influence consumer preferences (Knight and Calantone, 2000) and purchase intentions (Roth and Romeo, 1992; Nebenzahl and Jaffe, 1996; Ghalandari and Norouzi, 2012).

The country of origin effect of products on consumer perception has been well studied (Klein *et al.*, 1998; Balabanis and Diamantopoulus, 2004; Liu and Johnson, 2005; Verlegh *et al.*, 2005; Hong and Kang, 2006; Maheswaran and Chen 2006; Pappu *et al.*, 2007). According to Han and Terpstra (1988) country-of-origin (COO) is defined as "the country of manufacture or assembly" identified by "made in" or "manufactured in" labels. But due to the growth of multi-national companies into trans-national companies and the emergence of hybrid products coming from different countries, the image of the made-in label has been blurred (Baker and Michie, 1995; Ahmed *et al.*, 2004). According to Johansson *et al.*, (1985), the country of origin effect can be observed in two ways: halo effect and summary construct. Halo effect comes into play when consumers are not familiar with the products of a country, then the country image acts as a "halo" that directly affects consumers' beliefs about these products. This means that stereotypes about that specific country come into the consumer's mind. A general understanding provided by the extant literature is that economic, social, and cultural systems of countries as well as their relative stage of economic development are used by consumers as stereotypical cues in their evaluation of products and choice behaviour (Bilkey and Nes, 1982; Tse and Gorn, 1993). On the other hand, when consumers are familiar with a country's products, the summary construct model operates in which consumers infer a country's image from its product information, which then indirectly influences brand attitudes

(Han, 1989).

From an information-processing perspective it is argued that consumers evaluate a product based on both intrinsic cues (e.g., taste, design, and other product features) and extrinsic cues (price, brand, and warranty) (Ahmed & d'Astous, 2008). As an extrinsic attribute, COO is used by consumers in the absence of information about tangible attributes (Han, 1989; Han and Terpstra, 1988). Some previous studies have shown that consumers typically view products made in developing countries less favourably than the ones manufactured in developed countries (Cordell, 1992; Lin and Sternquist, 1994; Kinra, 2006; Hu *et al.*, 2008; Wang and Yang, 2008).

In recent years, business scholars have shown some interest in the country of manufacture effect of known vs unknown products (Schaefer, 1997; Hui and Zhou, 2003; Phau and Suntornnond, 2006). Phau and Suntonnond (2006) stress the importance of recognizing that different dimensions of consumer knowledge affect COO. One dimension is brand familiarity. Schaefer (1997) also distinguishes between general product class knowledge and brand familiarity. Brand familiarity refers to: *"Consumer knowledge regarding the brand that exists in a product category"* (Phau and Santornnond, 2006: 35) This means that consumers with expert knowledge about a product category can still be unfamiliar with a specific brand, which could potentially mean that COO will play a different role in brand perception. Phau and Santornnond (2006) argue that familiarity and experience with a country's products moderate the COO effects. They find that there is a COO effect on familiar brands, but not on unfamiliar brands – a finding contrary to immediate assumptions. Previous studies have been focused on the relative salience of the information on country of manufacture and brand name as determinants of product assessment and willingness to buy it. These studies have shown mixed results, for example Tse and

Gorn (1993), showed that even a well-known brand such as Sony was unable to reduce the impact of unfavourable country of manufacture effect on product evaluation. The study conducted by Hui and Zhou (2003) indicated the fact that the information about country of manufacture does not produce a significant effect on the evaluation of a branded product when the information is congruent with the brand origin. These authors have also come to the conclusion that when a branded product is manufactured in a less developed country, or a country with a less favourable image than the country of brand origin, then the information produces significant negative effects on product evaluation.

Based on the discussions above, we propose a conceptual model to test whether a newly developed country or less developed country of origin information for a familiar as well as for an unfamiliar brand has an impact on brand perception.

Figure 2: Conceptual Model

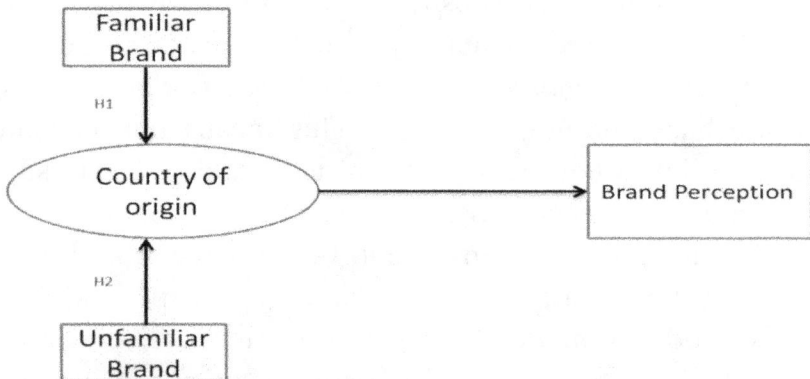

Hypotheses

Country of origin effect of familiar vs. unfamiliar brands

As indicated above previous studies have found that consumers can be expected to rely more on country of origin in product evaluations if the brand name of the product is not known, whereas, if the brand is known, they are more likely to base their evaluations on the known attributes of the brand (Hui and Zhou, 2003). Phau and Suntornnond (2006) also assume the effect but find in testing it that COO effects have more influence on familiar brands. Eroglu and Machleit (1989) state on the one hand that consumers will use country of origin to infer product quality if they know little else about the product and/or product class, on the other hand they also find that product knowledge facilitates the use of extrinsic cues such as country of origin. Maheswaran (1994) found that experts rely on attribute information when evaluating motor cars, whereas novices rely on country of origin information when attribute information is unambiguous. However, if attribute information is ambiguous both novices and experts use COO in their evaluations but in different ways. In other words consumer expertise functions as a moderator of COO. Sadrudin *et al.* (2011) reported that consumers are less concerned with country of origin if they are familiar with a brand. Based on this, we conclude that when a branded product is manufactured in a less developed country, or a country with a less favourable image than the country of brand origin, the information produces significant negative effects on product evaluation. When consumers are confronted with a familiar brand name they tend to reach evaluations quickly (Chattalas and Takada, 2008) because they are familiar with the brand's attributes. Thus consumers who are familiar with a particular brand will have a positive perception of country-of- origin information in evaluating that brand (Schaefer, 1997).

H1: For a familiar brand, the country of origin information will produce a positive significant effect on the consumer's brand perception.

H2: For an unfamiliar brand, the country of origin information will produce a negative effect on the consumer's brand perception.

Methodology

Survey Instrument

Data were collected using questionnaires consisting of 13 item scales scored on 5-point Likert-type scale relating to the brand perception of two car brands – Skoda Fabia (known brand) and Dacia Sandero (un-known brand). Skoda has been present on the Danish market for many years also during the cold war, so this is a brand that Danes are very familiar with. Dacia on the other hand was just entering the Danish market as this research was done, and although a few Danes have heard about the brand, they cannot be said to be familiar with it.

Firstly the respondents were asked to state their overall knowledge about cars and car brands. Secondly, to express their overall feeling about the Skoda Fabia car and the Dacia Sandero, by showing them pictures of the two cars, consisting some technical details. Third we asked the respondents to present their purchase intentions before and after having the information that Skoda is manufactured in the Czech Republic and is a subsidiary of Volkswagen; and Dacia cars are being manufactured in Romania, under the Renault Group. The final section of the questionnaire represented the demographic characteristics.

Data Collection Process

The questionnaire was first written in English and then translated into Danish by a Danish professor at Aalborg University and then back-translated to English by another Danish speaking academic. It was then finally translated to Danish. These back-translations were considered necessary to ensure that all idioms and Danish expressions were correct. It was then pretested on Danish students studying at Aalborg University. The questionnaire was then administered to respondents at pre-selected central locations (e.g. shopping malls), thus making use of the mall intercept approach, which has been used in a number of previous country-of-origin studies (Saffu and Walker, 2006). The collection of the questionnaires occurred in Copenhagen, Aarhus, Odense and Aalborg – the Capital and the three largest cities in Denmark. The sample consisted of 205 respondents, varying in gender and age (see Table 1). In attempt to avoid bias resulting from differences in nationality (Parameswaran and Pisharodi, 2002), all respondents were Danish citizens. Denmark is appropriate for this kind of research because of its open economy, and because of the sale of Skoda cars and the growing interest in Dacia cars from young Danish consumers on blogs (bilbasen.dk). The data were screened for uni-variate outliers and data editing was performed in order to identify omissions and errors in responses.

Table 1: The percentage distribution of the socio-demographic profile of the 205 respondents

Demographic characteristics	%
Gender	
Women	44.9
Men	55.1
Age in years	
≤ 25	45.4
26 - 45	41.0
≥ 46	13.7
Education	
Gymnasium	18.5
Short higher education	7.8
Medium long higher education	40.5
Long higher education/PhD	33.2
Occupation	
Employed	32.7
Students	62.4
Unemployed	4.9
Income in DKK	
< 20.000 DKK	20.2
≥ 20.001	38.8

Data analysis and results

The data analysis was performed in two steps. Firstly, the 5- point scale responses to brand perception were subjected to scale reliability analysis. Secondly, a descriptive analysis is carried out to gain an overview of how the respondents perceive the two car brands and their respective countries of origin (Czech Republic for Skoda Fabia and Romania for Dacia Sandero). Thirdly, we conducted an Analysis of variance (ANOVA) to investigate the specified hypotheses. All analyses were done using the SPSS version 22.

Scale analysis of the measures

A measure of the respondents' perception of the familiar and unfamiliar car brands, used a five-point bipolar scale. The reliability analysis was performed for the scales and the Cronbach's alpha coefficients were 0.709 for the brand perception of the Skoda Fabia and 0.800 for the brand perception of the Dacia Sandero, which denote a high reliability ($\alpha > 0.7$). The average mean were 3.23 for the brand perception of the Skoda Fabia and 3.37 for the brand perception of the Dacia Sandero (see Table 2).

Table 1: Measures of the five point scale analysis

Scale	Items
Brand perception (Skoda Fabia) (α = .709; M = 3.23; SD=2.66)	Good fuel economy; Exterior styling attractive; Good car equipment; Nice design; Overall good
Brand perception (Dacia Sandero) (α = .800; M = 3.37; SD=2.80)	Good fuel economy; Exterior styling attractive; Good car equipment; Nice design; Overall good
α= Alpha; M=Mean; SD= Standard Deviation	

Consumers' perception towards the brand Skoda Fabia (known brand) and Dacia Sandero (un-known brand)

Five characteristics for the perception of the Skoda brand have been evaluated by the Danish consumers (see Table 3). A total of 83% of the respondents agree that Skoda Fabia offers a good fuel economy, while 28.8% believe that the style and design of the car are attractive. The results further show that 30.8% think that Fabia has a good car equipment and 42.5% of the respondents have an overall good brand perception of the Skoda Fabia.

Table 4 presents the overall evaluation of the Dacia Sandero. The results suggest that 67.8% agree that the car offers a good fuel economy, while 45.4% believe that the style and design of the car are attractive. The results further show that 28.8% think that Sandero has good car equipment and 39.5% of the respondents have an overall good brand perception of the Dacia Sandero. While Dacia scores better than Skoda in terms of exterior styling, the overall brand perception of the Romanian car is slightly lower than the Czech Skoda Fabia.

Table 3: Percentage distribution of respondents scores and mean scores for the Skoda Fabia brand perception (n = 205)

Instrument items [a]	Strongly disagree	Disagree	Neither agree nor disagree	Agree	Stronly agree	M	SD
1. Good fuel economy	0	3.4	24.9	61	22	3.79	.671
2. Exterior styling attractive	6.8	24.9	39.5	28.8	0	2.90	.897
3. Good car equipment	2	11.7	55.6	29.3	1.5	3.17	.722
4. Nice design	8.3	23.9	37.6	28.8	1.5	2.91	.956
5. Overall good	0	5.4	52.2	41	1.5	3.39	.613

M=Mean; SD= Standard Deviation

Table 4: Percentage distribution of respondents scores and mean scores for the Dacia Sandero brand perception (n = 205)

Instrument items [a]	Strongly disagree	Disagree	Neither agree nor disagree	Agree	Totally agree	M	SD
1. Good fuel economy	0	2.9	29.3	49.3	18.5	3.83	.755
2. Exterior styling attractive	2.4	16.1	36.1	42	3.4	3.28	.861
3. Good car equipment	1	8.8	61.5	27.3	1.5	3.20	.650
4. Nice design	2	15.6	40.5	40	2	3.24	.810
5. Overall good	0.5	8.3	51.7	38	1.5	3.32	.666

M=Mean; SD= Standard Deviation

Country-of-origin effect of the brand Skoda Fabia (known brand) and Dacia Sandero (un-known brand)

The country-of-origin effect of the two brands is further presented in Table 5 for Skoda Fabia and Dacia Sandero. The results for Skoda suggest that 25.4% of the respondents have a negative opinion about Skoda Fabia being manufactured in the Czech Republic, while 39% feel that the Romanian country of origin for Dacia Sandero has a negative effect on them.

Table 5: Percentage distribution of respondents scores and mean scores for the country-of-origin effect of Skoda Fabia and Dacia Sandero (n = 205)

Instrument items	Negative effect	Neutral	Positive effect	M	SD
Skoda cars are manufactured in the Czech Republic. How does this information affect your opinion of the brand?	25.4	68.3	6.3	1.80	.531
The Dacia Sandero is manufactured in Romania. How does this information affect your opinion of Dacia	39	56.1	4.9	1.65	.569

M=Mean; SD= Standard Deviation

Results of the Analysis of Variance (ANOVA)

As mentioned earlier, ANOVA models are used to investigate the impact of the country-of-origin effect and demographics on brand perception. The estimated functional form for our models is as follows:

$$Yi = \alpha_0 + \alpha_j Xi + \varepsilon i$$

i represents an individual respondent; Y is a vector of the component factor score for brand perception. The α_0, is the mean of the referenced category, αj are the parameter estimates of the rest of the categories in the group X, and εi the error term assumed to be normally distributed $N(0, \sigma 2)$.

The classified levels of the distribution of respondents and mean estimates of the brand perceptions of the two cars by COO and demographics are presented in Table 6.

The dependent variables (Y-vector) represents how consumers perceive the fuel economy, exterior styling, car equipment and whether they think the car is overall good. The independent variables are country-of-origin.

Table 6: Distribution of respondents and mean estimates of Skoda Fabia and Dacia Sandero brand perceptions by COO and demographics

	Respondents				Brand perception Skoda Fabia (SF)		Brand perception Dacia Sandero (DS)	
	N		%		M	SE	M	SE
	SF	DS	DS	F				
Total	205		100		3.23	.054	3.37	.052
COO effect	SF	DS	DS	F				
Negative	0	19	9.3		-	-	-.869	.222
Less negative	52	61	29.8	8.3	-.167	.137	.097*	.124
Neutral	140	115	56.1	.9	0	.084	.089*	.090
Less positive	12	10	4.9	.5	.682*	.286	.037	.306
Positive	1	0	0	5.4	.466	.989	-	-

*M=Mean; SE= Standard Error; * p< 0.05;*

The results suggested that there was a statistically significant relationship between COO effects and the dependent variable "Brand perception of Skoda Fabia": F = 2,468, p=0.05. The inspection of the means show that the respondents with a positive perception towards the country of origin, Czech Republic, consistently score higher means scores compared to those being negative and neutral to the fact that the Skoda Fabia comes from the Czech Republic. Hypothesis 1 is thus confirmed.

As in the case of the Skoda Fabia, the effect of the country of origin of the Dacia Sandero proved to have a significant relationship with how the respondents perceive the brand: F= 1442.029, P=0.001, eta square= 4.3%. The inspection of the means show that means scores for "Less negative effect" and for "Neutral" are higher compared to the other levels of country-of-origin effect. Hypothesis 2 is in this regard confirmed, since the respondents are more negative than positive or neutral towards the fact that the unknown brand Dacia is manufactured in Romania, although being neutral has also scored higher mean scores than those respondents who perceived Romania as having a negative effect.

Conclusions

The present study empirically tested the link between COO and brand perception of familiar and unfamiliar technologically complex brands from new or less developed counties in a developed market setting. The results show that country of origin has a significant positive impact on the consumers' perception of the Czech manufactured Skoda Fabia, representing the familiar brand, and a significant negative impact on the consumers' perception of the Romanian manufactured Dacia Sandero, representing the unfamiliar brand. These findings show a somewhat different picture than previous studies e.g. Schaefer (1994 and Phau and Suntornnond (2006) given that there is a COO effect on both familiar and unfamiliar brand. As an extension it shows that the effects can be both positive and negative depending on the brand or country of origin. The result could be due to the fact that Skoda has a longer history on the market, they have perhaps overcome their less favorable image and consumers are very familiar with the brand. It is however also possible that the positive effect of Czech Republic country of origin is due to the developed country status, or the fact that more people have direct personal experiences with the country. These findings add to the body of research indicating that consumers use country of origin as an informational cue, and reinforce the notion that country of origin plays an important role in consumer product evaluation; an information of specific relevance for marketing strategy.

This study has some limitations, including the type of product and the research context chosen. Since the effects can be very country and product or at least product category specific it would be interesting to determine the effects of COO for other technologically complex products or even products with lower levels of technological complexity. It would also for the same reason be interesting to test the effects on brands from more countries. Furthermore, even though we collected data from a developed market (Denmark), we cannot conclude that these results are representative of different developed countries, and thus, a replication of this study in other developed countries would be welcomed. Denmark has a special situation being a country with extremely high prices on cars, which could be affecting the buying behavior of the consumers making them more oriented towards lower priced car brands and thus more receptive towards car brand from countries with less favorable COO. Finally, since both car brands are hybrid (have multiple country affiliation): Skoda, although produced and originally from the Czech Republic, belongs to the German VW Group and Dacia, although produced in and originally from Romania, belongs to the French Renault Group, it would be interesting to find out, whether country of brand plays a role in the greater flexibility of brand evaluation, which would be a potential prospect for future endeavors.

References

Ahmed, Z.U., Johnson, J.P., Yang, X., Fatt, C.K., Teng, H.S. and Boon, L.S. (2004) 'Does country-of-origin matter for low-involvement products'.*International Marketing Review*21(1), 102-120

Ahmed, S.A., and d'Astous, A. (2008)'Antecedents, moderators, and dimensions of country-of-origin evaluations'.*International Marketing Review* 25(1), 75-106

Baker, M.J., and Michie, J. (1995)'Product country images: perceptions of Asian cars'. *University of Strathclyde, Department of Marketing, Working Paper Series* 95(3)

Balabanis, G., and Diamantopoulos, A. (2004)'Domestic country bias, country-of-origineffects, and consumer ethnocentrism: A multidimensional unfolding approach'. *Journal of the Academy of Marketing Science*32(1), 80-95

Baldauf, A., Cravens, K.S., Diamantopoulos, A., and Zeugner-Roth, K.P. (2009)'The impact of product-country image and marketing efforts on retailer-perceived brand equity: An empirical analysis'. *Journal of Retailing* 85(4), 437-452

Bilkey, W.J., and Nes, E. (1982)'Country-of-origin effects on product evaluations'. *Journal of International Business Studies* 13(1), 89-99

Chao P. (1989)'The impact of country affiliation on the credibility of product attribute claims'. *Journal of Advertising Research*29 (2), 35-41

Chao, P., and Rajendran, K.N. (1993)'Consumer profiles and perceptions: Country-of-origin effects'. *International Marketing Review* 10(2), 22

Chattalas, M., Kramer, T., and Takada, H. (2008)'The impact of national stereotypes on the country-of-origin effect'. *International Marketing Review* 25(1), 54-74

Cordell, V.V. (1993)'Interactions effects of country-of-origin with branding, price, and perceived performance risk'.*Journal of International Consumer Marketing*5(2), 5-20

Eroglu, S.A. and Machleit, K.A.(1989)'Effect of individual and product-specific variables on utilising country of origin as a product quality cue', International Marketing Review, 6(6), 27-41

Etzel, M.J., and Walker, B.J. (1974)'Advertising strategy for foreign products'.*Journal of Advertising Research* 14(June), 41-44

Ghalandari, K., and Norouzi, A. (2012)'The effect of country-of-origin on purchase intention: The role of product knowledge'. *Research Journal of Applied Sciences, Engineering and Technology* 4(9), 1166-1171

Han, C.M. (1989)'Country image: Halo or summary construct?'.*Journal of Marketing Research*26(2), 222-9

Han, C.M., and Terpstra, V. (1988)'Country-of-origin effects for uni-national and bi-national products'. *Journal of International Business Studies* 19(2), 235-255

Hong, S., and Wyer, R. S. (1989)'Effects of country-of-origin and product-attribute information on product evaluation: An information processing perspective'. *Journal of Consumer Research* 16(2), 175-187

Hong, S., and Kang, D.K. (2006)'Country-of-origin influences on product evaluations: The impact of animosity and perceptions of industriousness brutality on judgments of typical and atypical products'. *Journal of Consumer Psychology* 16(3), 232-239

Hu, X., Li, L., Xie, C., and Zhou, J. (2008)'The effects of country-of-origin on Chinese consumers' wine purchasing behaviour'. *Journal of Technology Management in China* 3(3), 292-306

Hui, M.K., and Zhou, L. (2003)'Country-of-manufacture effects for known brands'. *European Journal of Marketing* 37(1/2), 133-153

Johansson, J.K., and Nebenzahl, I.D. (1985)'Multinational production: effect on brand value'. *Journal of International Business Studies* 17(3), 101-126

Kaynak, E., Kucukemiroglu, O., and Hyder, A.S. (2000)'Consumers' country-of-origin (COO) perceptions of imported products in a homogenous less-developed country'. *European Journal of Marketing* 34(9/10), 1221-1241

Kinra, N. (2006)'The effect of country-of-origin on foreign brand names in the Indian market'. *Marketing Intelligence and Planning* 24(1), 15-30

Klein, J.G., Ettenson, R., and Morris, M.D. (1998)'The Animosity Model of Foreign Product Purchase: An Empirical Test in the People's Republic of China'. *Journal of Marketing* 62(January), 89-100

Knight, G.A., and Calantone, R.J. (2000)'A flexible model of consumer country-of-origin perceptions: A cross-cultural investigation'. *International Marketing Review* 17(2), 127-145

Laroche, M., Papadopoulos, N., Heslop, L.A., and Mourali, M. (2005)'The influence of country image structure on consumer evaluations of foreign products'. *International Marketing Review* 22 (1), 96-115

Lee, D., and Ganesh, G. (1999)'Effects of partitioned country image in the context of brand image and familiarity: A categorization theory perspective'. *International Marketing Review* 16(1), 18-41

Leonidou, L. C., Hadjimarcou, J., Kaleka, A., and Stamenova,G. T. (1999)'Bulgarian consumers' perceptions of products made in Asia Pacific'. *International Marketing Review* 16(2), 126-142

Lin, L., and Sternquist, B. (1994)'Taiwanese consumers' perceptions of product information cues: Country-of-origin and store prestige'. *European Journal of Marketing* 28(1), 5

Liu, S.S., and Johnson, K.F. (2005)'The automatic country-of-origin effects on brand judgments'.*Journal of Advertising* 34(1), 87-97

Maheswaran, D., (1994)'Country of origin as a stereotype: effects of consumer expertise and attribute strength on product evaluations", Journal of Consumer Research, 21(2), 354-65

Maheswaran, D., and Chen, C. (2006)'Nation equity: Incidental emotions in country-of-origin effects'. *Journal of Consumer Research* 33(3), 370-376

Nebenzahl, I., and Jaffe, E (1996)'Measuring the joint effect of brand and country image in consumer evaluation of global products'.*International Marketing Review* 13(4), 5-22

Okechuku, C. (1994)'The importance of product country-of-origin: A conjoint analysis of the United States, Canada, Germany, and the Netherlands'. *European Journal of Marketing* 28(4), 5-19

Pappu, R., Quester, P.G., and Cooksey, R.W. (2007)'Country image and consumer-based brand equity: relationships and implications for international marketing'. *Journal of International Business Studies* 38(5), 726-745

Parameswaran, R., and Pisharodi, R.M. (2002)'Assimilation effects in country image research'. *International Marketing Review* 19(3), 259-278

Paswan, A.K., and Sharma, D. (2004)'Brand-country-of-origin (COO) knowledge and COO image: investigation in an emerging franchise market'. *The Journal of Product and Brand Management* 13(2/3), 144-155

Phau, I., and Suntornnond, V. (2006)'Dimensions of consumer knowledge and its impacts on country-of-origin effects among Australian consumers: A case of fast-consuming product'. *The Journal of Consumer Marketing* 23(1), 34-42

Roth, M.S., and Romeo, J.B. (1992)'Matching product category and country image perceptions: A framework for managing country-of-origin effects'. *Journal of International Business Studies* 23(3), 477-498

Sadrudin A.A., d'Astous, A., and Petersen, H.B. (2011)'Product-country fit in the Canadian context'.*Journal of Consumer Marketing*28(4), 300-309

Saffu, K., and Walker, J. (2005)'The country of origin effect and consumer attitudes to buy local campaign: The Ghanaian case'. *Journal of African Business* 7(1), 183-199

Samiee, S., Shimp, T.A., and Sharma, S. (2005)'Brand origin recognition accuracy: Its antecedents and consumers' cognitive limitations'. *Journal of International Business Studies* 36(4), 379-397

Schaefer, A. (1997)'Consumer knowledge and country-of-origin effects'. *European Journal of Marketing* 31(1), 56-72

Schooler, R.D. (1965)'Product bias in the Central American common market'.*Journal of Marketing Research* 2(4), 394-397

Shankarmahesh, M.N. (2006)'Consumer ethnocentrism: An integrative review of its antecedents and consequences'. *International Marketing Review* 23(2), 146-172

Taylor, Shelley E. (1981): "A Categorization Approach to Stereotyping" in Cognitive Processes in Stereotyping and Intergroup Behavior, ed. Davis L. Hamilton, Hillsdale, NJ: Erlbaum, pp. 83-114

Teas, R. K., and Agarwal, S. (2008)'The effects of extrinsic product cues on consumers' perceptions of quality, sacrifice, and value'. *Journal of the Academy of Marketing Science* 28(2), 278-290

Thakor, M. V., and Kohli, C., (1996)'Brand origin: Conceptualization and review'. *Journal of Consumer Marketing* 13(3), 27-40

Tse, D. K. and Gorn, G. J. (1993)'An experiment on the salience of country-of-origin in the era of global brands'.*Journal of International Marketing* 1(1), 57-76

Verlegh, P.W.J., and Steenkamp, J-B.E.M. (1999)'A review and meta-analysis of country-of-origin research'.*Journal of Economic Psychology* 20(5),521-546

Verlegh, P.W.J., Steenkamp, J-B. E. M., and Meulenberg, M.T.G. (2005)'Country-of-origin in consumer processing of advertising claims'. *International Journal of Market Research* 22(2), 127-139

Wang, X., and Yang, Z. (2008)'Does country-of-origin matter in the relationship between brand personality and purchase intention in emerging economies?'. *International Marketing Review* 25(4), 458-474

White, P.D., and Cundiff, E.W. (1978)'Assessing the quality of industrial products'.*Journal of Marketing*42(1), 80-86

Zhang, Y. (1996)'Chinese consumers' evaluation of foreign products: the influence of culture, product types and product presentation format'. *European Journal of Marketing* 30(12), 50-68

CHAPTER TEN

The Relevance of Culture in International Joint Ventures: An Integrative Approach

Li Thuy Dao

Abstract

This chapter seeks to revisit the question of how much culture has an impact on the operation of international joint ventures. Current understanding is generally split into two opinions: one viewing culture as differences that exert some negative influence on joint venture performance, while the other views culture as emergent in the joint venture's working processes. While the former stream of research still lacks consensus on the degree of impact, the latter stream of research remains underrepresented and uncertain with regard to how culture emerges through the different processes in the post-formation phase. The paper presents a critical review of the two perspectives, argues for the need for an integrative approach based on a dynamic view of culture that allows possible areas of synthesis between the two perspectives, and integrates applicable knowledge from research on related foci.

Introduction

International joint ventures have for the last decades been a popular mode of foreign market entry and collaboration across national borders. Today, while international joint ventures may not be the preferred choice for resource-intensive and internationally-experienced firms, especially given the liberalization of foreign direct investment in many countries, they are still a well-considered strategic option for firms in need of supplementary knowledge or resources in order to operate in foreign markets. The path of success by means of international joint ventures, however, is not straightforward. Indeed, it appears much discouraging if one looks at any effort in revealing statistical evidence of relatively high joint venture failure (e.g. Pothukuchi et al. 2002). Among the most concerned reasons for such failure are

301

factors related to culture, such as culture incompatibility between partners (Cartwright & Cooper, 1993) or simply cultural differences (Parkhe, 1993; Pothukuchi et al, 2002).

There is no doubt that culture has a significant impact on the operation and management of IJVs. Nevertheless, researchers do not seem to have obtained consensus on how much the impact can be, or even whether it is a negative or positive impact. For instance, Beamish and Lupton (2009) registered that seven out of 87 most highly-cited articles studying IJV performance discussed how cultural differences impact IJV performance, yet presenting mixed results. Other studies also hint at the fragmentation of research on culture in IJVs (Teerigankas, 2007; Christoffersen et al 2013). One explanation for this is that culture has been rather loosely conceptualized in joint venture studies, implying potentially diversifying views of culture and thereby diversifying patterns of impact.

Indeed, prior research, fragmented as it can be in terms of outcomes, is likely to be grounded in one of two contrasting views of culture. The first view of culture, represented by the majority of joint venture studies, recognizes culture as comprising some distinct, relatively stable characteristics that determine behaviours of its members. These studies are particularly inspired by Hofstede's (1980, 2001) framework of cultural value dimensions. One notable 'consequence' of the Hofstedian approach is the so-called cultural distance concept which has been widely applied in IJV research since Kogut & Singh (1988) developed the construct in a study on the influence of cultural factors on entry mode selection based on the indices of Hofstede's model. The cultural distance approach has, however, been criticized for the relatively linear and rigid impact of cultural differences on expected outcomes (Shenkar, 2001). Moreover, studies adopting this approach often take for granted its underlying assumption of organisational and societal (national) homogeneity, and no distinction between the home and host environment.

The second view of culture calls for a more dynamic scope of culture as relevant in IJVs, based on the conception of culture as socially constructed by IJV members (Brannen & Salk, 2000). Rather than focusing on the inter-national dimension of IJVs and highlighting cultural differences caused by the partners' national origins, this emergent stream of research has brought IJVs back to the domain of organization theory treating culture as an issue of multi-level diversity. Whereas IJV scholars appear to pay rather scant attention to the organisational culture perspective, their colleagues studying similar inter-firm contexts such as mergers and acquisitions, have been more engaged in this level of culture and spending more effort in conceptualizing cultural diversity on both national and organizational levels (Søderberg et al 2000; Vaara, 2000; Teerigankas, 2007).

In the context of the above mentioned observations, the present paper aims at reassessing the question of how culture influences the operation and management of IJVs in an integrative perspective. It does so by conducting a critical review of prior research on culture and IJVs, discussing an integrated conception of culture as relevant to IJVs, and finally identifying directions for an integrated approach to understanding culture in IJVs. Researchers and students of international business can benefit from the present paper in two ways. First, it provides a literature review that is not biased toward a narrow view of culture that would for any stated research purpose exclude other aspects of culture and thereby impact on an IJV. Second, the integrated approach proposed in the paper serves as a conceptual departure for further investigation in search of a comprehensive understanding of the phenomenon, carrying important managerial implications as well.

The chapter is structured into four main sections. Following this introduction is the literature review section, comprising a sub-section reviewing mainstream studies adopting a functionalist view of culture that emphasizes culture-as-difference, and a sub-section reviewing a small number of studies adopting an interpretive view of culture focusing on culture as "emergent". Section three discusses an integrated conception of culture and potential directions for an integrated approach to studying cultural impact in IJVs. Section four summarizes the paper's contributions and limitations.

Literature review

As earlier mentioned, culture in studies directly dealing with IJVs has been rather loosely defined, even not explicitly defined at all, whereas hundreds of definitions of the concept have been registered in literature. Most definitions, however, can identify themselves with a particular scientific paradigm as a philosophical ground in terms of how social reality and human behavior is to be understood. In this regard, international management scholars generally differentiate between a functionalist perspective and an interpretive perspective of culture (Søderberg & Holden, 2002; Boyacigiller et al. 2004; Sackmann & Phillips, 2004; Fang, 2006). A functionalist perspective of culture treats culture as a relatively stable, internally consistent, homogenous system of assumptions, norms and beliefs as transmitted by socialization to new generations. This conception of culture is said to have emerged from a desire among earlier social anthropologists to adopt a scientific approach to the study of culture in the sense that cultures (or cultural values) can be quantifiable, generalizable and comparable (Peterson, 2007). Meanwhile, an interpretive view of culture basically advocates that culture is socially constructed, and highlights the complexity of the culture phenomenon as a result of identification among culturally unique individual members. Seen in IJV literature, given its emphasis in studying the impact of culture, the former perspective can be described as featuring culture-as-difference, whereas the latter culture-as-emergent.

Culture-as-difference in IJVs

Just like its dominance in international management literature, the functionalist perspective of culture is employed by most IJV studies to date, dealing with the widely accepted assumption that differences between partners' cultural origins can be a challenge for the joint venture management (Beamish & Lupton, 2009). Cultural differences are found on various levels including national, organizational, and professional levels. National culture differences have been the prime focus of IJV studies.

Perhaps most celebrated in this stream of literature is the well-cited work of Geert Hofstede (1980, 2001) with an initial framework of four cultural dimensions and later expanded to IJV settings. In an explicit or implicit way, most scholars following this perspective endorse Hofstede's definition of culture: "the collective programming of the mind which distinguishes the members of one human group from another" (1980:21). Hofstede chooses to focus on the collective programming of societies, defined by national boundaries, and on its expression in values. Based on a survey of IBM employees across 72 nations conducted in the period of 1968-1972, Hofstede identified four cultural values dimensions: Individualism – Collectivism, Power Distance, Uncertainty Avoidance, and Masculinity – Femininity. New dimensions have since been added: Long-term versus Short-term orientation (Hofstede & Bond, 1988), and most recently Indulgence versus Restraint (Hofstede, 2010). Hofstede's model since its birth became quickly popular as it provides culture scores for 53 countries, making the model not only conceptually but also empirically attractive, linking the dimensions to particular research settings.

Apart from those studies adopting Hofstede's dimensions directly, other studies in the stream have relied on a *cultural distance* index, developed by Kogut and Singh (1988) as an aggregate index built on Hofstede's first four cultural dimensions. The cultural distance index in their work originally applied to the choice of entry modes between wholly-owned subsidiaries, joint ventures or Greenfield investments. It has since laid a conceptual ground for studying the impact of cultural differences not only in entry mode studies but also studies focusing on the performance of already-established alliances and joint ventures as well. Having been employed constantly in numerous empirical studies, the cultural distance effect has become the driving construct, if not the driving understanding of cultural impact, in the field.

In most IJV studies, cultural differences or distance, largely inspired by Hofstede's (1980, 2001) dimensions or Kogut and Singh's (1988) composite index, are found to be adversely related to IJV performance. Hofstede in a recent book chapter confirms the significance of cultural differences, besides other factors, in explaining why international alliances fail (Hofstede, 2010). Empirical research has shown that cultural differences influence joint venture stability and longevity (e.g. Li & Guisinger, 1991; Shenkar & Zeira, 1992; Hennart & Zeng, 2002; Sirmon & Lane, 2004), conflict (Swierczek, 1994), control (Cyr, 1997), trust and commitment (Pothukuchi et al. 2002), HRM practices (Lu, 2006). Most studies focus on the impact of national culture, while only few studies claim the impact of organizational culture, and fewer combine the effect of both levels (Meschi & Roger, 1994; Pothukuchi et al. 2002). Recently, professional culture has also been included as a cultural level of impact (Sirmon & Lane, 2004; Mohr & Puck, 2005).

There have been a number of reviews including or particularly focusing on the linkage between cultural differences or distance and IJV performance (Robson et al. 2002; Nippa et al. 2007; Ren et al. 2009; Beamish & Lupton, 2009; Reus & Rottig, 2009; Christoffersen et al. 2013). These reviews show that there is no consistent and statistically significant relationship between cultural distance and joint venture performance (see Table 1). The most recent review by Christoffersen et al (2013) attempted to address possible reasons why empirical evidence studied have not supported the theoretical significance of the relationship. They reviewed a sample of 63 articles published in 15 different journals empirically studying the cultural distance/ performance linkage using regression analysis, where cultural distance was specified either as a control variable, an antecedent variable, or a moderating variable; and performance was measured by either subjective or objective modes. They argue that various attributes on the national culture level as well as on the organizational culture level have different impacts on various performance measures, and those impacts again vary according to the particular national setting under study. Besides, cultural distance measured by subjective managerial perceptions appears relatively more consistently related to subjectively-measured performance, yet subject to certain biases.

Table 1 – Recent reviews of cultural impact on IJV performance

Authors	Focus	Sample	Main conclusions regarding cultural impact
Robson et al (2002)	Drivers of IJV performance	91 empirical studies published by 2000	The impact of sociocultural distance on IJV performance is unclear
Nippa et al (2007)	Success factors, cultural distance as a factor of (mis)'fit'	16 studies on Sino-foreign JVs and 25 on others, published between 1991 - 2005	Mixed results in both samples about the impact of cultural distance
Ren et al (2009)	Drivers of IJV performance	54 studies published between 1999-2009	Cultural distance (national / organisational) produces different effects depending on how it is measured. Partners' cultural sensitivity should be taken into consideration
Beamish & Lupton (2009)	Determinants of IJV performance	86 studies published between 1982 – 2006 (cited 20+ times)	Mixed results on the impact of culture
Reus & Rottig (2009)	Determinants of IJV performance	61 studies of IJVs in China (quantitative analysis)	Objectives measures of cultural distance show a weak positive effect while subjective measures a negative effect
Christoffersen et al 2013	Cultural distance – performance	63 studies with regression analysis of results	Weak empirical support for any systematic relationship between cultural distance and IJV performance

On the conceptual level, cultural distance has been subjected to a number of criticisms that throw some light on the above-mentioned inconsistencies in empirical results. Shenkar (2001) presented a thorough account of the conceptual history of the cultural distance construct back to even before Kogut & Singh (1988). He also pointed to important shortcomings of the underlying approach in terms of conceptual and methodological properties, besides evidencing inconsistencies among studies with regard to the impact of cultural distance on foreign direct investment. The criticized conceptual properties concerned the illusion of symmetry (i.e. no distinction between the home firm and the host environment), linearity, stability, causality, and discordance; all reflecting the relatively linear and rigid impact of cultural distance on expected outcomes. The criticized methodological properties included the assumption of corporate homogeneity (i.e. organisational uniformity), special homogeneity (i.e. national uniformity), and equivalence. The paper also advocated new focus on closing the cultural distance, namely globalization and the perceived consequential convergence, geographical proximity, foreign experience, acculturation, cultural attractiveness, and staffing.

In an effort to divert international management research from the cultural distance metaphor, Shenkar also proposed a new way of thinking of culture in terms of "friction", defined as "the scale and essence of the interface between interacting cultures, and the "drag" produced by that interface for the operation of those systems" (2001:528). By adopting the new metaphor, research is believed to shift from a functionalist perspective of culture to a more dynamic approach, referred to as the social constructionist approach treating metaphors "in a broader context of social relevance and hierarchical encounter" (Shenkar et al. 2008: 911). However, despite a persistent effort in articulating the benefit of the cultural friction metaphor, the proposed construct has not been conceptually elaborated or empirically justified. Drogendijk and Zander (2010) point out that the cultural friction notion still concentrates on dualities and the differences between cultures, thus excluding the possibility of building on cultural similarities and other ways of looking at cultural differences, not as barriers or problems, but as advantages.

To summarize, the dominant thinking in international management literature in general and IJV literature in particular is that culture-as-difference creates problems or barriers for people working together in a collaborative setting across national borders. Joint venture practice has provided mixed evidence, pointing at certain conceptual biases as discussed above. The impact of culture differences at the national level has somehow been over-emphasized whereas its impact on the organizational level and other levels is over-simplified. The nature of cultural impact does not simply reside within a causality relationship with joint venture performance, as a consequence of the dichotomy-based approach to culture, but embraces a more dynamic type that calls for a more dynamic conception of culture. Culture-as-emergent appears to be a response.

Culture-as-emergent and IJVs

Historically, the social constructivist view of culture emerged as an anti-essentialist voice attacking mainstream research in understanding intercultural phenomena. The attack seems to rest on two major weaknesses of mainstream literature. One is the missing dynamics of culture, and the other is the overlooked impact of the individual and the context on culture, as discussed in the previous chapter. In filling these theoretical gaps, social-constructivist scholars have suggested a perspective on culture that can accommodate irregular, ambiguous as well as dynamic aspects of culture.

The social constructivist view of culture can be traced back to the early 1970s research in social anthropology (Geertz, 1973;

Smircich, 1983), a view which has had a great influence on organisational research (Boyacigiller et al. 2004). These studies took an interpretive perspective and shared a common research interest in how organisational participants make sense of their social world, thereby capturing the ongoing process of sense-making and meaning creation instead of seeking predefined patterns of culture (Schultz, 1997). Only recently has the social constructivist view or interpretive view of culture gained widespread acknowledgement within international management research, with an emerging stream of research focusing on intercultural interaction rather than comparison of (mostly national) cultures (Søderberg & Holden, 2002; Boyacigiller et al. 2004). Given this focus, researchers adopt a view of culture as emergent and negotiated between interaction partners (Sackmann & Philips, 2004). Often cited in these studies is, for instance, the inspiring definition of culture by anthropologist Aiwa Ong in her work on the "cultural struggle" of Malay workers in a transition period, namely a culture that is "historically situated and emergent, shifting and incomplete meanings and practices generated in webs of agency and power" (1987: 2). This definition represents a dynamic view of culture that includes aspects of complexity and ambiguity as a result of interaction and negotiation of meanings. This meaning-oriented view of culture was well explicated in the notable work of another anthropologist, Clifford Geertz, in his collection of essays justifying an interpretive theory of culture (1973). It has laid a conceptual foundation for those intercultural interaction studies in search of an emergent culture in IJVs (Kleinberg, 1994; Brannen, 1998; Salk, 1997; Brannen & Salk, 2000; Salk & Shenkar, 2001).

The emergence of a common culture in IJVs is found to occur through a *negotiated order* featuring the construction and reconstruction of meanings and actions by individual actors (Brannen, 1998; Brannen & Salk, 2000). The emphasis here is that the negotiated culture is not merely a blend or hybrid of the cultures of origin; but rather, it contains also some aspects of the venture's own idiosyncratic making (Ibid). Negotiation, in this context, must not be understood as a highly formalized process of negotiations resulting in legally enforceable outcomes. It is rather the informal interactions and communications that people interpret and react to.

The assumptions of the negotiated culture model are as follows (Brannen & Salk 2000).

- The national cultural origins of IJV members serve as point of departure for the members as sources of values, meanings and norms that are brought to the bicultural organisational context (a notion that resonates well with "essentialist" cultural scholars).

- The structure of the IJV, the characteristics of its members, the relations of power and interdependence among them, and the specific issues they face will shape the cultural traits that become salient in the social negotiation of the working culture.

- When members from two distinct national and organisational cultures come together, a 'negotiated culture' emerges.

- The specific attributes of an IJV working culture are emergent and cannot be determined a priori.

- The cultural stances of organisational actors may map into 'issue domains' in unexpected ways.

These basic assumptions are drawn mainly from the works of Brannen (1998), Salk 1997) and Salk and Shenkar (1997). A few remarks should be noted on these assumptions. First of all, as assumption one goes, the negotiated culture approach recognizes the significance of national cultural origins, which, over time, can be combined or modified through ongoing interactions (Brannen, 1998). However, national cultures, as well as any other cultural category that individual members subscribe to can be manifested at different levels among different individuals, ranging from *marginal*, i.e. lack of commitment to the "normal" beliefs, to *hyper-normal*, which refers to those who hold more extreme beliefs, with *cultural normal* in between. These levels are described as a range of personal fit with cultural attributes (ibid). Each *individual cultural stance* is a composite of different levels of personal fit with the cultural attributes of different representative groups, e.g. nation, organisation, profession. When a group of individuals gather in an organisation, they may not equally bring the cultural norms of their macro groups (i.e. nations), which is why organisational culture may not be representative of national culture (Ibid).

Second, the negotiated culture that emerges in the IJV setting is a working culture that centres on the issues which arise during the IJV life, establishing and moderating over time the norms and practices to be shared among members of the organisation. Different organisational issues and events are proposed to evoke different cultural stances on the part of participant individuals. Three major factors influence the negotiated culture: cultures of origin, individual stance-taking, and the IJV context (Brannen 1998, Brannen & Salk, 2000). Drawing on empirical evidence from a German-Japanese joint venture, the authors provide documentation for how the effect of national cultural attributes on organizational culture formation is significantly tempered by the extent to which individual members have internalized national culture norms, which in turn depends on particular organizational issues that arise at distinct stages in the venture's history. Their message is clear: national cultural attributes are not reliable predictors of joint venture issues and differences, as well as the formation of a joint venture's organizational culture, therefore not a strong determinant of joint venture outcomes.

The intercultural interaction stream has with its conceptual emphasis created a linkage between culture and two critical social processes in IJVs, namely power bargaining and identification. According to the interpretive view of culture, power relations between individual actors play a significant role in the construction of culture. Power and control are two classic issues in IJVs (Geringer & Hebert, 1989; Yan & Luo, 2001). One partner can gain relative bargaining power if they contribute critical resources and knowledge to the joint venture, or attach less strategic importance (dependence) to the partnership (i.e. in a way their exit option is higher). This power asymmetry is often well reflected in the initial structural arrangements of the joint venture, and subject to change over time as knowledge is transferred and shared. However, power in IJV studies concerns primarily the organizational level of interaction, whereas power in the construction of culture relates to the individual level. The linkage is, yet, still loosely conceptualized.

The second linkage is between culture and identity. Some scholars have noticed the dynamic impact of culture in a so-called process of social identification in IJV settings (Salk, 1997; Child & Rodrigues, 1996; Salk & Shenkar, 2001). The phenomenon of social identity is particularly relevant in the case of joint ventures since they bring together different collective entities, existing/ independent (the parent ones) and new/ supposedly mixed (the joint venture) where individual actors have to attach to one entity or another in their decision making process. Drawing on social identity theory, the studies explore processes of social identification and categorization, in which differences between cultures are perceived and utilized as a major source of identification. They suggest that national social identities are the most salient sense-making vehicles used by joint venture team members, despite possible contextual changes that could expectedly favour organisational social identities. The studies also emphasize the role of organisational/structural and environmental contexts as antecedents of social identification. Structural factors refer to organisational design and joint venture dependence on the parents for human and other resources; while environmental influences include the competitive environment of the venture and of each parent, and the degree to which the environment imposes common threats or rewards. Interestingly, their conclusion implies that social identification processes, set early in an IJV's history, tend to mediate the impact of contextual changes on the enactments of the IJV setting and functioning by its members.

Recently, some scholars have incorporated the discussion of cultural impact into an interpretive framework of alliance/ joint venture evolution, namely a sensemaking framework (Clarks & Soulsby, 2009; Das & Kumar, 2010). Building on earlier models of alliance process (Doz, 1996, Ring and van de Ven, 1994), Clarks & Soulsby (2009) propose an integrated model of process sensemaking in IJVs, mapping the evolution of the collaborative process through ongoing adjustment of structural conditions and expectations departing from initial conditions and ongoing assessment of collaborative outcomes in terms of efficiency and equity. Its major contribution lies in the explicit conceptualization of the role of interpretive processes and the indication of two possible sensemaking paths, i.e. *accumulating* or *obsolescing*, leading to a positive or negative joint venture development. The nature of sensemaking here resembles the negotiation and construction of meanings as advocated by the negotiated culture perspective. In case the joint venture falls into an obsolescing bargain, the underlying culture may entail relatively fragmented negotiations that ultimately might lead to venture deterioration or even dissolution. An emergent culture appears to be input as well as outcome of sensemaking. Meanwhile, Das & Kumar (2010) focus on the nature of sensemaking in an alliance context and distinguish between two types of interpretive schemes: *sensemaking of chaos* and *sensemaking in chaos*. Sensemaking of chaos assumes that predictability is and should be the system's operating norm, encourages rational decision making to prevent chaotic situations. In contrast, sensemaking in chaos assumes that chaos is normal, encourages coping with interruptions through experimentation and allows for flexibility in decision making. The authors argued that national cultural backgrounds of alliance partners are a key determinant of choice of interpretive schemes. With regard to the impact of culture, Clarks & Soulsby (2009) do not make an explicit connection to culture, whereas Das & Kumar (2010) adopt a functionalist view of culture with the assumption that culture "shapes the behavior of alliance managers as well as the interpretations imposed by alliance managers on alliance functioning" (p. 25).

In brief, social constructionist studies have contributed to IJV literature by unveiling the dynamic manifestation of culture through joint venture processes and issues, making the discussion of culture directly relevant to joint venture management. In line with the culture-as-difference stream, the culture-as-emergent stream endorses the significance of national culture origins as initial frames of reference for joint venture members' sensemaking, though emphasizing the emergence of an organizational culture over time. Accordingly, the impact of culture on joint venture is complex and not to be captured in any direct or explicit linkage with joint venture performance. On the one hand, this view, while being argued for rendering culture relevant to managers (Holden, 2002), may appear limited in providing immediately useful practitioner/ managerial agendas. But on the other hand, it opens a 'conceptual window' toward studies taking other anchors than a cultural anchor, such as identity, sensemaking, organizational learning, yet sharing the same focus, which is joint venture evolution, thereby integrating the culture puzzle into a broader managerial game where individual perceptions and interpretations are treated as important. The challenge of the culture-as-emergent stream of research remains a big concern, since it is in need of substantial empirical documentation by means of the resource-demanding methodology of in-depth longitudinal case studies involving different national settings.

As a concluding point, both streams of studies point to a need for integrating one another's insights into the various ways culture generates an impact on IJVs. For the culture-as-difference stream, the lack of consensus on the effect of measurable cultural differences on various attributes of joint venture performance indicates that such effect can be more complex and dynamic than a homogenous, value-based conception of culture can handle. For the culture-as-emergent stream, cultural differences as an initial source of identification and sensemaking can be better illustrated with the vast amount of information from the other stream, and any significant link between a particular cultural attribute and joint venture outcomes, such as the one behind the well-documented challenge of a joint venture between a relatively low power distance country partner and a relatively high power distance country partner, provides some hints at what partners should be aware of in order to avoid falling into, for instance, a situation of obsolescing sensemaking caused by negative pre-conceptions. In the following discussion, some conceptual outlines are made for an integrated approach to culture that might apply to IJVs.

Directions for a more integrated approach to culture in IJVs

Obviously, the conception of culture underlying each study differs according to its research purpose, focusing on particular aspects of cultural impact and relying on particular measures of such impact. The current paper challenges IJV researchers with a view of culture as most relevant to the joint venture context. First of all, it should be a view of culture that embraces both the relatively distinct essence and variations and emergent issues in a particular culture. Such a conception of culture may appear inappropriate from a paradigmatic point of view maintaining that paradigms (here referring to functionalism and interpretivism) are incommensurable (Burrell & Morgan, 1979). From a pragmatic point of view, as scientifically advocated by numerous critiques (e.g. Schultz & Hatch, 1996; Morgan, 2007), however, a more holistic conception of culture as both difference and emergence seems justifiable. For instance, Schultz & Hatch (1996) advocated paradigm interplay within organizational culture research in three areas: generality/contextuality, clarity/ ambiguity, and stability/ instability. They argued further that culture-as-pattern may contain inherent inconsistencies and conflicts rather than only consistencies and harmony; that culture-as-essence rather concerns more the expressive layers than the deeper layers (i.e. values of cognition), namely the essence of meanings and practices. In a similar vein, focusing on the national culture level, Fang (2006) discussed a national culture concept as containing co-existing paradoxes, seen through the philosophy of yin and yang, highlighting the dynamic interplays among various cultural groupings within and beyond national boundaries to capture the new identity of national culture in the era of globalization.

Second, to be relevant to the joint venture context, culture should be seen in the context of joint venture processes, including three significant processes: learning, power bargaining and relationship building. Culture in context has been conceptualized in, for example, Bjerregaard et al. (2009) as a summary construct based on a holistic social constructionist philosophy. . By context, the authors refer to social, professional and organisational relationships, or as expressed at other points, social, economic, and power relationships in which culture is situated and generated. The scope of context in mainstream IJV literature mostly refers to the national settings, i.e. economic, socio-cultural, legal, etc., in which a joint venture firm is based. Embedded in this use of context is the assumption of culture as a nation-level construct that is external to individual influence. A more 'advanced' conception of context that appears relevant to IJV settings is that of recent knowledge management literature. In this literature, there seems to be a growing understanding of context as dynamically embedded in and enacted through social interaction (Nonaka & Toyama, 2003). To understand the dynamic side of culture in context, we cannot overlook a process of sharing knowledge and learning among interacting individual actors driving the ongoing construction of the joint venture context.

Culture and learning in IJVs can indeed be two compatible processes. The motive for learning in joint ventures is both competitive and cooperative, and the identification process of joint venture members seems to be related to whether competitive or cooperative learning prevails. In the case of learning to compete, joint venture partners certainly have the tendency to identify themselves with the parents rather than with the joint venture, and thereby justify their identification with cultural differences. In the case of learning in the joint venture's development interests, i.e. cooperative learning, identification will be less focusing on differences or distance but more on a common identity via creating building blocks of a common culture. In the latter case, knowledge from each culture can be utilized as a resource for the joint venture. Child & Rodrigues (2011) discuss organizational learning as the bridging of identity boundaries on a basis that is acceptable to the parties concerned, where the negotiation of an integrating frame of reference is centrally critical. The organizational learning framework offers a critical discourse of cognitive and behavioural processes that can accommodate cultural dynamics, particularly relevant to an IJV context where the critical need of knowledge transfer and sharing explicitly enact such processes.

Another framework that can promise further understanding of the culture phenomenon in IJVs is the sensemaking framework. As reviewed earlier, there has been a modest interest recently in exploiting this framework among IJV studies, notably Clarks &

Soulsby (2009) and Das & Kumar (2010). More work is needed in integrating cultural sensemaking into a framework of alliance evolution. A lot of inspiration can be gained from a rather well-articulated stream of research in mergers and acquisitions taking on a sensemaking perspective (Søderberg & Vaara, 2003; Vaara, 1999; Kleppestø, 1998). Primarily, their attempts have converged on the claim that cultural conceptions in mergers and acquisitions are embedded in complex sensemaking processes and associated with identity construction processes. Partly in line with the negotiated culture perspective focusing on IJVs and the social identity perspective in IJV research, this stream suggests that national stereotypes are usually salient in initial interpretations but are gradually replaced by more refined understandings. The stream also contributes to the promotion of narratives as a sensemaking approach and as a research design for future research with the same focus (Søderberg et al., 2000). Teerigankas (2007) presented a thorough discussion of potential areas for cross-fertilization between IJV research and M&A research with a focus on culture. She suggests joint venture and alliance researchers to learn from how merger and acquisition researchers have studied the domestic organizational culture dimensions of mergers and acquisitions, as regards the way in which organizational culture is defined, how its impact and performance has been studied, how the cultural encounter in mergers and acquisitions has been conceptualized, and how the management of cultural change in mergers and acquisitions has been addressed. Sensemaking is one conceptualization that allows for such cross-fertilization. For instance, whereas the focus of the recent joint venture studies using a sensemaking approach only build on the cognitive side of sensemaking, a framework like that of Vaara (2000) might be useful for exploring not only rational aspects but also emotional and motivational aspects of sensemaking in joint venture settings.

Conclusion

This chapter is perhaps the first to review culture in IJV research not limited to a functionalist perspective of culture, or to the cultural distance notion, like previous reviews did. It offers a more nuanced overview of the relevance of culture in an inter-organisational setting like IJVs, where members coming from various multi-level cultural backgrounds are set into interaction with a view to making the joint venture life function properly. An integration of a culture-as-difference view and a culture-as-emergent view has been argued to better capture the various domains and processes constituting the actual impact of culture in IJVs. Whereas prior research has primarily concerned with a rather linear conceptualization of culture in IJVs and so far produced fragmented results, so much knowledge in organisational learning and social identity theories is available as ideas for conceptual integration and fertilization. In terms of empirical coverage, new studies should represent emergent contexts of IJVs other than the traditional setting of Japanese-American, or more broadly Japanese-Western and more lately Chinese-Western joint ventures. Particularly within the sample of transition economy contexts so far represented by China-based joint ventures, researchers should be encouraged to bring new perspectives of culture, such as the culture-as-emergent perspective, with a view to illuminate the underlying dynamic processes including socio-cultural processes, which might offer a better explanation to cooperative joint venture relationships than the currently over-represented national culture distance thesis.

The chapter is by no means a systematic review of both streams of cultural studies in IJVs. More importantly, it claims the need to adopt an integrated approach in the light of a better understanding of both sides of the culture coin and how they play out in the joint venture process. The paper has neither come with its own integrative concept of culture, nor concrete issues of investigation in different empirical settings open for incorporating such a concept. This is left to be done by future research.

References

Beamish, P.W and Lupton, N.C. (2009). "Managing joint ventures", *Academy of Management Perspectives,* vol. 23, no. 2, p. 75-94.

Bjerregaard, T.; Lauring, J.; and Klitmøller, A. (2009). "A critical analysis of intercultural communication research in cross-cultural management: Introducing new developments in anthropology", *Critical Perspectives on International Business,* vol.5, no. 3, p. 207-228.

Boyacigiller, N.A.; Kleinberg, M.J.; Phillips, M.E.; and Sackmann, S.A. (2004). "Conceptualizing culture: Elucidating the streams of research in international cross-cultural management," in B.J. Punnett and O. Shenkar (Eds), *Handbook for International Management Research,* University of Michigan Press, p. 99-167.

Brannen, M. Y. (1998). "Negotiated culture in binational contexts: A model of culture change based on a Japanese/American organizational experience," *Anthropology of Work Review,* vol. 18, no. 2-3, p. 6-17.

Brannen, M. Y. and Salk, J. E. (2000). "Partnering across borders: negotiating culture in a German-Japanese joint venture," *Human Relations,* vol. 53, no. 4, p. 451-82.

Burrell, G. and Morgan, G. (1979).*Sociological paradigms and organizational analysis: Elements of the sociology of corporate life.* London: Heinemann Educational, 432 p.

Cartwright, S. and Cooper, C.L. (1993)."The role of culture compatibility in successful organizational marriage," *Academy of Management Executive,* vol. 7, no. 2, p. 57-70.

Child, J. and Rodrigues, S.B. (1996). "The role of social identity in the international transfer of knowledge through joint ventures," in S.R. Clegg and G. Palmer (Eds), *The Politics of Management Knowledge*, London: Sage, p. 46-68.

Child, J. and Rodrigues, S.B. (2011)."Social identity and organizational learning," in M. Easterby-Smith and M. A. Lyles (Eds.), *Handbook of Organizational Learning and Knowledge Management*, Chichester: Wiley, p. 305-329.

Christoffersen, J.; Globerman, S.; and Nielsen, B.B. (2013). "Cultural Distance and the Performance of International Joint Ventures: A Critical Assessment of Model Specifications and Variable Measurement," *International Journal of Strategic Business Alliances*, vol. 3, no. 1, p. 93-119.

Clark, E. and Soulsby, A. (2009)."Perceptions of MNC management: Local parent sensemaking in international joint venture process," *Journal for East European Management Studies*, vol. 3, p. 286-309.

Cyr, D.J. (1997). "Culture and control: The tales of East-West joint ventures," *Management International Review*, vol. 1, p. 127-144.

Das, T.K. and Kumar, R. (2010)."Interpartner sensemaking in strategic alliances – Managing cultural differences and internal tensions," *Management Decision*, vol. 48, no. 1, p. 17-36.

Doz, Y.L. (1996). "The evolution of cooperation in strategic alliances: Initial conditions or learning processes?" *Strategic Management Journal*, vol. 17, no. 1, p. 55-83.

Drogendijk, R. and Zander, L. (2010). "Walking the cultural distance: In search of direction beyond friction", in T. Devinney, T. Pederden and L. Tihanyi (Eds), "The past, present, and future of international business and management," *Advances in International Management*, vol. 23, p. 189-212.

Fang, T. (2006). "From "onion" to "ocean": Paradox and change in national cultures," *International Studies of Management and Organisation, vol.* 35, no. 4, p. 71-90.

Geertz, C. (1973). *"The interpretation of cultures,"* New York: Basic Books.

Geringer, J.M. and Hebert, L. (1989)."Control and performance of international joint ventures," *Journal of International Business Studies*, vol. 20, p. 235-254.

Hennart, J.M.A. and Zeng, M. (2002). "Cross-cultural differences and joint venture longevity," *Journal of International Business Studies*, vol. 33, no. 4, p. 699–716.

Hofstede Chair in Cultural Diversity," *International Journal of Cross Cultural Management*, vol. 7, no. 3, p. 359-377.

Hofstede, G. (1980). *Culture's consequences: International differences in work-related values*, Beverly Hills, CA: Sage.

Hofstede, G. (2001). *Culture's consequences.* 2nd ed. Thousand Oaks, CA: Sage.

Hofstede, G. J. (2010). "Why do international alliances fail? Some insights from culture and human social biology," in J. Ulijn, G. Duysters and E. Meijer (Eds), *Strategic alliances, mergers and acquisitions: The influence of culture on successful cooperation*, Northampton, MA: Edward Elgar, p. 30-59.

Hofstede, G.J. and Bond, M.H. (1988). "The Confucius Connection: From Cultural Roots to Economic Growth," *Organizational Dynamics*, vol. 16, no. 4, p. 5–21.

Holden, N. (2002). *Cross-cultural management: A knowledge management perspective*, Harlow: Pearson Education, 328 p.

Kleinberg, M.J. (1994). ""The crazy group": Emergent culture in a Japanese–American binational work group," in S. Beechler and A. Bird (Eds), *Research in international business and international relations*, Greenwich, CT: JAI Press (special issue on Japanese management), vol. 6, p. 1-45.

Kleppestø, S. (1998)."A quest for social identity: The pragmatics of communication in mergers and acquisitions," in M.C. Gertsen, A-M. Søderberg, and J.E. Torp (Eds.), *Cultural dimensions of international mergers and acquisitions*, Berlin: de Gruyter, p. 147-168.

Kogut, B. and Singh, H. (1988)."The effect of national culture on the choice of entry mode," *Journal of International Business Studies*, vol. 19, no. 3, p. 411-432.

Li, J. and Guisinger, S. (1991). "Comparative business failures of foreign-controlled firms in the United States," *Journal of International Business Studies*, vol. 22, no. 2, p. 209-225.

Lu, L-T. (2006). "The relationship between cultural distance and performance in international joint ventures: A critique and ideas for further research," *International Journal of Management*, vol. 23 no. 3 pp. 436-445.

Meschi, P-X.and Roger, A. (1994). "Cultural context and social effectiveness in international joint ventures," *Management International Review*, vol. 34, no. 3, p. 197-215.

Mohr, A. T. and Puck, J. F. (2005). "Managing functional diversity to improve the performance of international joint ventures," *Long Range Planning, vol. 38*, p. 163-182.

Morgan, D.L. (2007). "Paradigms lost and pragmatism regained: Methodological implications of combining qualitative and quantitative methods," *Journal of Mixed Methods Research*, vol. 1, no. 1, p. 48-76.

Nippa, M., Beechler, S., and Klossek, A. (2007)."Success factors for managing international joint ventures in China: A review and integrative framework," *Management and Organization Review*, vol. 3, p. 277-310.

Nonaka, I. and Toyama, R. (2003). "The knowledge-creating theory revisited: Knowledge creation as a synthesizing process," *Knowledge Management Research and Practice*, vol. 1, p. 2-10.

Ong, A. (1987). *Spirits of resistance and capitalist discipline: Factory women in Malaysia,* Albany: State University of New York Press.

Parkhe, A. (1993). "'Messy' research, methodological predispositions, and theory development in international joint ventures," *Academy of Management Review*, vol. 18, p. 227-268.

Peterson, M.F. (2007). "The heritage of cross cultural management research: Implications for the

Pothukuchi, V., Damanpour, F., Choi, R, Chen, C.C. and Park, S.H. (2002)."National and organizational culture differences and international joint venture performance," *Journal of International Business Studies*, vol. 33, no. 2, p. 243-265.

Ren, H., Gray, B., and Kim, K. (2009). "Performance of international joint ventures: What factors really make a difference and how?" *Journal of Management*, vol. 35, p.805-832.

Reus, T. and Rottig, D. (2009)."Meta-analyses of international joint venture performance determinants: Evidence for theory, methodological artefacts and the unique context of China," *Management International Review*, vol. *49, no. 5, p.* 607-640.

Ring, P.S. and Van de Ven, A.H. (1994)."Developmental processes of cooperative interorganizational relationships," *Academy of Management Review*, vol. 19, no. 1, p. 90-118.

Robson, M., Leonidou, L., and Katsikeas, C. (2002)."Factors influencing joint venture performance: Theoretical perspectives, assessment and future directions," *Management International Review*, vol. 42, no. 4, p.385-418.

Sackmann, S.A. and Philips, M.E. (2004). "Contextual influences on culture research: Shifting assumptions for new workplace realities," *International Journal of Cross Cultural Management*, vol. 4, no. 3, p. 370-390.

Salk, J.E. (1997). "Partners and other strangers: Cultural boundaries and cross-cultural encounters in international joint venture teams," *International Studies of Management and Organisation*, vol. 26, p. 48-72.

Salk, J.E. and Shenkar, O. (2001)."Social identities and cooperation in an international joint venture: An exploratory case study," *Organization Science*, vol. 12, p. 161-178.

Schultz, M. (1997).*On studying organizational culture*, Berlin: Walter de Gruyter.

Schultz, M. and Hatch, M.Y. (1996). "Living with multiple paradigms: The case of paradigm interplay in organization culture studies," *Academy of Management Review*, vol. 21, p. 529-557.

Shenkar, O. (2001). "Cultural distance revisited: Towards a more rigorous conceptualization and measurement of cultural differences," *Journal of International Business Studies*, vol. 32, no. 3, p. 1-17.

Shenkar, O. and Zeira, Y. (1992)."Role conflict and role ambiguity of CEOs in international joint ventures," *Journal of International Business Studies*, vol. 23, no. 1, p. 55-75.

Shenkar, O., Luo, Y. and Yeheskel, O (2008). "From "distance" to "friction": Substituting metaphors and redirecting intercultural research," *Academy of Management Review*, vol. 33, no. 4, p. 905-923.

Sirmon, D.G. and Lane, P. (2004), "A model of cultural differences and international alliance performance," *Journal of International Business Studies*, vol. 35, p. 306–319.

Smircich, L. (1983). "Concepts of culture and organizational analysis," *Administrative Science Quarterly*, vol. 28, p. 339-358.

Søderberg, A.-M. and Vaara, E. (2003, eds). *Merging across border: People, cultures and politics*, Copenhagen Business School Press, 281 p.

Søderberg, A-M., Gertsen, M. G. C., and Vaara, E. (2000). *Cultural change processes in mergers: a social constructionist perspective.* København, 42 p.

Søderberg, A-M.and Holden, N. (2002). "Rethinking cross cultural management in a globalizing business world," *International Journal of Cross Cultural Management*, vol. 2, no. 1, p. 103-121.

Swierczek, F.W. (1994). "Culture and conflict in joint ventures in Asia," *International Journal of Project Management*, vol. 12, no. 1, p. 39-47.

Teerigankas, S. (2007) "A comparative overview of the impact of cultural diversity on inter-organisational encounters," in C. Cooper, and S. Finkelstein (Eds), *Advances in Mergers and Acquisitions*, vol. 6, p. 37-76.

Vaara, E. (1999). "Cultural differences and post-merger problems: Misconceptions and cognitive simplifications," *Nordiske Organisasjonsstudier*, vol. 1, no. 2, p. 59-88.

Vaara, E. (2000). "Constructions of cultural differences in post-merger change processes: A sense-making perspective on Finnish-Swedish cases," *Management*, vol. 3, no. 3, p. 81-110.

Yan, A., and Luo, Y. (2001).*International joint ventures theory and practice* (1st ed.), New York, NY: M. E. Sharpe.

CHAPTER ELEVEN

Multi-Cultural Strategizing and Organizing in Pluralistic Context

Marita Svane

Abstract

In this chapter, strategizing and organizing is discussed from a multicultural, pluralistic perspective. According to the assumption of the pluralistic perspective, all organizations are to some extent pluralistic and fragmented, and therefore multicultural. However, in the strategy literature, organizations are often assumed to be coherent wholes. The purpose of this chapter is to throw light upon the role of fragmented cultures and cultural dynamics in the strategizing and organizing processes. A concrete multi-cultural merger is used as an empirical study of this phenomenon. The organizational study is based upon the Heideggerian lifeworld ontology whereas the knowledge creation emerges through a postmodern, dialogical approach.

Introduction

In this chapter, the role of culture is discussed in relation to the strategizing and organizing processes in a concrete cross-cultural merger. The organization of the cross-cultural merger is viewed as a cultural fragmented, pluralistic context within which strategizing and organizing take place. Pluralism is a concept that has been largely ignored in the studies of strategy and only inadequately in organizational studies (Jarzabkowski, Fenton 2006, Denis, Langley & Rouleau 2007). The concept is relevant in a business world where organizations become melting points between different cultures from the near and the far distance. Viewing the organization as a cultural pluralistic context implies that multi-cultural encounters and multi-cultural dynamics are phenomena of everyday organizational life. The pluralistic view adopted in the

329

chapter emphasizes how complex and challenging this multicultural phenomenon can be to strategizing and organizing processes and to the management of these processes.

The theoretical discussion is illustrated by a concrete case of a cross-cultural merger. In the case, the strategizing and organizing processes are challenged by the multicultural diversity to an extent that breakdowns the social relations with a whole department of employees and endangers the future survival of the company.

In the beginning of the chapter, the becoming perspective of strategizing is outlined as well as its underlying ontological foundation. In this account, it is argued that culture and strategy are two mutually entangling processes as opposed to more conventional views on culture and strategy. Next, the pluralistic approach to culture, strategy and organization is thus discussed, thereby developing the conceptual framework to capture the multi-cultural pluralistic perspective on strategizing and organizing process. Finally, the challenges of the pluralistic context are discussed, leading to a conceptual framework that can provide insight into the processes of multi-cultural strategizing and organizing.

Having developed this conceptual framework, it is applied on a case to illustrate the challenges, to highlight the significance of culture to the strategizing process, and to discuss the central implications for the management of these processes.

Cultural Strategizing

In the literature on strategy and organization, the distinction between a "being" and "becoming" perspective (Nayak, Chia 2011, Tsoukas, Chia 2002) has become widely accepted as a way of providing a broad overview of the vast literature within the field. The distinction is useful for discussing the relationship between culture and strategy.

330

Being Perspective on Strategy and Organization

According to Chia and Nayak, a being perspective to organizations is understood in terms of a substance ontology that tends to dominate in traditional organizational and strategy approaches (Nayak, Chia 2011). Substance ontology is related to a being perspective that assumes that the natural state of the world is in equilibrium and stability. Organizations are conceived as stable worlds containing and possessing entities such as things and individuals. It places emphasis on the properties, attributes and characteristics of individuals and organizations.

Thus, substance ontology gives priority to a state of being; to an understanding of organizations as identifiable, stable worlds (Nayak, Chia 2011). Change is understood as a transition phase between two identifiable and fixed states; as a movement from point A to B in order to reach a pre-defined goal. Time is thus understood in terms of spatial moments and end-states (Tsoukas, Chia 2002: 295, Nayak, Chia 2011) assuming a linear time perspective where time is running from past to present to future. Strategy becomes a matter of analyzing the past, monitoring activities, predicting the future, designing representational models of the world, navigating in a known world based upon cognitive maps, pre-defining goals and acting intentionally, purposefully and deliberately based upon a means-end logic (Chia, Holt 2009).

Dating back to Chandler as a founding figure within strategy, this conventional approach to strategy originally assumes strategy to be a matter of rational planning and to drive and determine structures based upon changes in the environment (Carter, Kornberger & Schweitzer 2011). Since Chandler, the strategy field has developed into many different directions; however, many of these directions remain more or less rooted in the rational assumption of strategies being deliberate, intended and planned a priori.

Becoming Perspective on Strategizing and Organizing

Understanding organizations and strategy from a "becoming" perspective implies a fundamental paradigmatic shift away from the substance ontology towards a lifeworld ontology. It is a shift away from understanding the social world as *"ready made"* towards understanding organizations as an ongoing *"world-making"* phenomenon (Nayak, Chia 2011: 282).

The becoming perspective to strategy and organization emphasizes the ongoing "world-making" by referring to processes of organizing and strategizing at the practical, everyday level, where the actual organizational goings-on takes place. The focus is thus shifting towards the micro-level of strategizing and organizing, reflected in process oriented Strategy-as-Practice approaches.

In the practice oriented approaches, the world is conceived as a complex, messy, unknown and ceaselessly changing world, unfolding new possibilities in the passage of moving on. In this type of approach, deliberate actions towards pre-defined goals are not the issue. Instead, focus is directed towards understanding the pragmatic processes of wayfinding, sensemaking and coping in new emerging situations (Chia, Holt 2009). Coping on the way, "knowing as we go" in an unknown world presupposes another way of engagement with the world than the rational engagement with the world at the distance as in the being perspective.

In order to capture the difference between these two ways of engagement with the world in the strategy process, Chia & Holt distinguishes between "Building" and "Dwelling", drawing on Heidegger's reflections on building, dwelling, thinking (Heidegger 1993). Building is related to the "being" perspective and the conscious engagement with the world at the distance. The world becomes an object of our thinking. The strategy is a process of building models of the world, of architectural designs and

332

configurations of the world (Chia, Holt 2009). Building strategy is thus rooted in the subject – object dichotomy.

As a contrast, dwelling is related to the "becoming" perspective and a practical embodied way of engaging in the world. Before making the world an object of our consciousness and reflections (building), we are already in the world (dwelling). The dwelling approach to strategy implies a more primordial encounter with the world in the here and now, where the everyday acts of practical coping takes place and which is the pragmatic everyday basis for strategy-making.

Dwelling is thus a more primordial way of being in the world through practical engagement and interaction. Heidegger does not reject building but highlights the essential relations to dwelling, stating that building and thinking originally belonged to dwelling (Heidegger 1993: 362):

Building and thinking are, each in its own way, inescapable for dwelling. The two, however, are also insufficient for dwelling so long as each busies itself with its own affairs in separation instead of listening to one another. They are able to listen if both – building and thinking – belong to dwelling, if they remain within their limits and realize that the one as much as the other comes from the workshop of long experience and incessant practice.

In the modern world, however, building has become separated from dwelling, as building is aiming at constructing a world based upon a means-end schema (Heidegger 1993). This separation inspires Chia & Holt's distinction between the building and dwelling approaches to the strategy process.

In his work of Being and Time, Heidegger unfolds his understanding of how the processes of practical understanding and reflective interpretations are entangled into each other without leading to the detachment from dwelling in the world.

The dwelling approach to strategy is thus rooted in Heidegger's lifeworld ontology.

The concept of lifeworld relates to Heidegger's irreducible structure of "being-in-the-world" (Heidegger 2008). As "beings", we are part of the world, engaging in it, before we reflect upon it. In our practical engagement, we learn to know it as a world with which we are familiar and within which we feel at home and can dwell. In this bodily engagement, we achieve a practical, cultural sense of the familiarity and the meaningfulness of this world. At a primordial level, this sensing of meaningfulness is a practical understanding of meanings which only becomes object of reflections when being interpreted. Interpretation completes the meaning production by defining, differentiating and conceptualizing meanings (Heidegger 2008). Merged into the practical understanding, it becomes an interpreted understanding. Meanings are thus identified, organized and structured. Through these processes of organizing meanings in terms of similarities and differences, we develop our understanding of the world, construct boundaries, and achieve a sense of who we are in relation to other beings. These processes of understanding and interpretation are relational, as we are in-the-world as Being-with-one-another (Heidegger 2008). Thus the world we share with others is a cultural world. Our processes of practical understanding and reflective interpretations are relational processes through which we socially construct the world, cultural boundaries and identities. As stated by Nayak and Chia:"…everyday acts of practical coping, interpretation and sensemaking are in effect acts of "world-making" and identity construction" (Nayak & Chia 2011:289).

The dynamical relationship between practical understanding and interpretation is a two folded, hermeneutical spiral. Whereas reflective interpretation completes the meaning production of the more primordial, practical understanding arising in an emerging situation, the interpreted understanding becomes the fore-structure (Heidegger 2008) or prejudiced understanding (Gadamer 2013). It becomes part of our past history and may influence the practical understanding of new emerging situations in a world of becoming. The hermeneutical spiral may turn into a closing, reproducing hermeneutical circle in so far as the fore-structured, prejudiced understanding is being reproduced in the sensemaking process of new emerging situations. It may clothe our understanding of the world and of new emerging possibilities of the way of being-in-this-world. It has form-shaping force. However, by being "sentient, embodied, situated, reflexive, and responsive beings" we may become alert to "the incessant creation of novelty" in new emerging situations (Shotter 2011: 9), and open towards a prospective sensemaking of new possible arriving futures.

The structure of "being-in-the-world" thus overcomes the fallacy of the subject-object dichotomy. World and being are in a simultaneous, intertwined process of becoming: "Since the person is a being-in-the-world, the coming-into-being of the person is part and parcel of the process of coming-into-being of the world" (Ingold 2000: 168)

The strategy process cannot be separated from the practical understanding and reflective interpretations of the strategy practitioners. We are historical human beings situated here and now in the historical ongoing process (Gadamer 2013), retrospectively making sense of the past and proactively of the arriving future, thereby creating new possibilities and shaping future (Boje 2014: 14). This retrospective and prospective sensemaking process is at the core of the strategy process. In the becoming perspective, time is not conceived as linear, spatial moments but as a fusion of past and future into the present moment of the here and now.

Turning to the micro-level of new emerging situations, where concrete actions and decision making occur, raises the question, how strategy at all can emerge as a strategic consistent and coherent pattern in the messy streams of actions without purposeful, conscious, deliberate and coordinating strategy and action plans? (Chia, Holt 2006: 635, Chia, Holt 2009: 108, 111). To answer this question, Chia & Holt take their point of reference in culture and the experience-based shared tacit knowledge (phronesis knowledge according to Aristotle) of the strategic practitioner. Culture and phronesis knowledge constitute an internalized modus operandi that predispose human actions and decision making:

> In a very real sense, therefore, in acting purposively one cannot help doing what one does in the way one does it, since doing otherwise runs contrary to our cultivated tendencies and hence creates a dissonance that threatens the very fabric of our identity and selfhood (Chia, Holt 2009:109).

Retrospectively we can draw on our background history and practices, our phronesis knowledge and our cultural modus operandi when reacting in new messy situations spontaneously or unthinkingly. Strategy does not have to be purposeful and deliberate in order to emerge as a consistent pattern.

Thus history and culture becomes an integrated part of strategizing and organizing: "…strategy-making must be construed as a collective, culturally shaped accomplishment attained through historically and culturally transmitted social practices and involving dispositions, propensities and tendencies" (Chia, MacKay 2007: 236), just as our identity and selfhood constructions.

In the above discussion, strategizing is understood based upon lifeworld ontology and a practiced oriented becoming perspective. In this discussion, strategizing, culture and identity constructions are closely interlinked. The practice oriented approach to strategizing goes further as it also links strategizing and organizing closely to each other by conceiving organizations to be "a pattern that is constituted, shaped and emerging from change"(Tsoukas, Chia 2002: 567) in an ongoing process of becoming. The becoming perspective implies that the field of strategy and organization start to merge in practice:

> [T]he two run together as simultaneous activity", "[O]rganizing part-shapes strategizing", "[T]he skills and practices of strategising and organising are so similar and intermingled in action that it is hardly worth trying to tell them apart." (Whittington et al. 2006: 618). Organizing is thus part of world-making.

Multi-Cultural Strategizing and Organizing

The above discussion of strategizing, organizing and culture in a practice and becoming perspective is largely overlooking fragmentation, ambiguity and pluralism and its consequences to strategizing and organizing. The question of consistency in strategic actions (Chia, Holt 2009, Chia 2004) is rooted in an understanding of the strategy to emerge from shared directionality due to the shared cultural modus operandi and shared, phronesis knowledge. This assumption is challenged from the natural dynamics of organizations conceived as fragmented and pluralistic contexts. Pluralism, fragmentation and ambiguity have long been acknowledged within the organizational cultural field (Martin 1992, Martin 2002) but in the field of strategy and organization, further research from a pluralist and fragmentation perspective is needed to provide more insight into the dynamical relations between culture, strategizing and organizing.

Multicultural Pluralism

Using the concept of organizational culture may be associated with an understanding of a unifying, integrating culture, and using

337

the concept of organizational subculture may misleadingly indicate that organizational culture is the "natural" starting point for cultural studies (Alvesson 2013, Parker 2000). Ideally, Martin thus prefers to talk about "cultures in organization" (Martin 2002: 164-165). A unifying organizational culture may emerge if all cultural members experience the same problems, communicate with each other and adopt a common understanding of proper behavior (Alvesson 2013). These conditions would rarely be at place due to the many internal and external sources for cultural diversity that produce us-them cultural borders and identity constructions within the organization. The internal and external sources for cultural diversity are related to the discussion of the cultural relationship between the organization and its environment; that is a macro and a micro view on culture.

A macro understanding views the organizational culture as a reflection of societies and nations and of industrial cultures. This view on culture tends to neglect the internal sources of cultural diversity and solely understand organizational culture as a product of the macro environment. Part of the macro view is the role of ethnic groups, classes, gender and age and other sources of social differentiation in creating local unique cultures within the organization (Alvesson 2013). In a local, micro understanding, the organization is viewed as the macro context for the development of cultures within it. The micro understanding thus tends to view the organizational culture as largely unaffected by the surrounding society (Martin 2002). The internal sources for cultural diversity are among others the organizational segmentation of hierarchical and vertical division of labor, importation of different cultures through mergers, acquisitions and the hiring of specific occupations and the formation of counter-culture movements in the organization (Alvesson 2013). Furthermore, us-them boundaries may occur due to 1) spatial / functional division producing geographical and departmental divides between them over there and us over there, 2) generational division producing age and historical divides between them from that time and us from this time, and finally 3) occupational and professional division consisting of vocational and professional divides between them who do that and us who do this (Parker 2000). According to Parker, these divisions function to classify the identity of self and other.

Acknowledging both the internal and external sources of cultural diversity, Martin conceptualizes organizations as "a nexus in which a variety of internal and external influences come together" (Martin 2002: 164). The dynamic relation between organizations and their environment can be understood as cultural traffic (Alvesson 2013). Cultural traffic is related to organizational demography in terms of recruitment, selection and socialization of newcomers and people leaving the organization. It is also related to organizational members being citizens and thus influenced by societal cultural changes. Cultural traffic[4] counteracts the assumption of culture to be unique and unitary as well as it limits the influence of management on cultural dynamics.

The above discussion addresses an understanding of culture that differs from Chia's idea of a cultural device or modus operandi that creates order and patterns in the stream of actions. This indicates an integration perspective. Instead culture may be conceived as disorder as in the fragmentation perspective or as differentiated subcultures as in the differentiation perspective. In the fragmentation perspective, culture lacks consensus and is not clearly consistent or inconsistent. Interpretations of cultural manifestations, situations and events may be ambiguous, contradicting and incongruent producing uncertainty and tensions between opposites, dynamics and perhaps conflicts. The fragmentation perspective on culture focuses on: "multiplicities of

---

[4] Agri Nord: landmændene som kunder og ejere er stemmer i det omkring liggende samfund som har indflydelse.

interpretation that do not coalesce into the collectivity-wide consensus and that do not create the subcultural consensus" but simply are multiple views of issues and constantly in flux" (Martin 2002: 107). The differentiation perspective focuses on subcultural consensus and on the ambiguity in-between subcultures that may cause cross-cultural conflicts and disputes.

The three perspectives on culture are considered as different worldviews and suggested to be integrated in a three-perspective view on culture (Martin 1992, & 2002). They are all at stake in displaying the culture of the organization. In some situations the organization will be "us", but in other situations, culture may be displayed through "a huge variety of contested "us" and "them" claims" (Parker 2000: 227), thus displaying ambiguity and multiplicity. In his study, Parker found that his three sources of cultural divisions were used by organizational members for different reasons and at different times depending on what issues are being discussed and by whom.

The internal and external sources for cultural diversity referred to above are structural categories that impact on the social construction of local cultures and identities. The structural categories may, however, not sufficiently capture the processes of the cultural dynamics through which local cultures emerge, change and disappear. The processes of the primordial, practical, bodily lifeworld engagement and the hermeneutical circle and spiral may provide an additional useful conceptual framework for this purpose by being combined with Wenger's notion of communities of practice (Wenger 1998).

Cultures in organizations can thus be conceived as local, cultural communities of practices in which participating practitioners develop a familiarity and meaningfulness about the way they practically engage with each other and with things in social practice. In communities of practice, new experiences, knowledge and competences develop, learning takes place, and new understandings and worldviews emerge as well as identity constructions undergo changes (Wenger 1998: 4). Being an active participant by engaging in activities with other people is at the same time to be "active participants in the practices of social communities and constructing identities in relation to these communities" (Wenger 1998: 4). In the communities of practice, the participants organize resources, coordinate their activities and mutual relationships together with colleagues and customers and create meanings and interpretations of the world and practices of what needs to be done in order to fulfill the requirements in a meaningful way (Wenger 1998: 6, 13). As the community of practice is a dynamical community, the organizing and meaning creating processes can be understood from a being perspective and throw further light on the interplay between the "organizing" part of world-making and emerging identity and culture constructions.

Organizations can thus be viewed as constituted by a mosaic of local, cultural communities of practices. Organizational members are fragmented, multicultural human beings as they may participate in many local, cultural communities of practices. Their sense of identity emerges and changes in relation to the various communities of practices in which they participate. As the organization consists of a net of interacting local, cultural communities of practices, a shared organizational identity may develop across the various communities of practice. Thereby, identity may exist at an organizational level, at group / local community level and at the individual level as a self-identity. The relation between culture and identity is a complicated interplay and identity constructions such as "we" and "us-them" may not necessarily follow the cultural boundaries of the local communities of practice. Parker suggests "that organizational cultures should be seen as "fragmented unities" in which members identify themselves as collective at some times and divided at others" (Parker 2000: 1). Thus being a participant in a specific local cultural community of practices, identity constructions at all three levels may occur.

The mosaic of changing cultures, of changing cultural borders and the variety of "we" and "us-them" identifications path the way for a multiplicity of interpretations and ambiguity and thus for both creativity and potential conflicts. Culture can be understood as practical embodied meanings and values which we bring with us as our cultural fore-structured understanding and which may undergo changes due to new experiences in practice and new ways of understanding the novelty in emerging situations. The hermeneutical circle and spiral are useful for understanding the nature of the cultural dynamics. The circle addresses the static, stereotyped and generalized reproduction of cultural boundaries and identifications whereas the spiral refers to the open-ended processes of sensing, understanding and interpreting similarities and differences in new ways, thus changing the cultural borders and the "we" or "us-them" identifications.

Challenges to Multi-Cultural Strategizing and Organizing in Pluralistic Context

In the above discussion, a multi-cultural pluralistic perspective on organization is outlined by combining the differentiation and fragmentation perspectives on culture, communities of practices and the Heideggerian approach to a practical, lifeworld engagement. This conceptual framework contributes to understanding how multi-cultural pluralism may challenge and nuance the assumption of culture as an integrating modus operandi producing order and patterns in the stream of strategic actions. In the discussion below, this cultural understanding is integrated in the pluralistic perspective on strategizing and organizing. Therefore, the dynamical relations between culture, strategizing and organization can be discussed offering further insights into the challenges of this interplay.

According to Jarzabkowski and Fenton, pluralistic organizations are shaped by divergent goals and interest of different groups in the organization. As such they distinguish between organizing pluralism and strategizing pluralism (Jarzabkowski, Fenton 2006).

Organizing is defined as "the creation and use of structural practices and coordination processes by internal stakeholders to enact the identity, culture and interest of the organization" (Jarzabkowski, Fenton 2006:2). However, this organizing process may be challenged by the multiple, fragmented cultures and identity constructions in the company. Thus viewed from the pluralistic perspective, the organizing process is met with multiple, potentially conflicting interests emerging from different organizational groups due to their fragmented organizational identities and cultures. Pluralistic tensions may thus arise in the organizing processes.

Strategizing addresses "those planning, resource allocation, and monitoring and control practices and processes through which strategy is enacted" (Jarzabkowski, Fenton 2006: 2). In a pluralistic perspective, this is a complex and fragmented process as the organization has to develop strategizing processes that enable it to enact multiple, shifting, and potentially conflicting strategic objectives and goals and external demands. Enacting multiple conflicting strategic goals simultaneously may cause tensions, especially if the groups and stakeholders have sufficient power bases to ensure the legitimacy of their goals and interests.

Both strategizing and organizing pluralism may thus create tensions. Even though all organizations to some extent are pluralistic, they may be so in varying degrees just as well as pluralism may be manifested in either the organizing domain or the strategizing domain or in both domains (Jarzabkowski, Fenton 2006).

Practicing leaders and academics therefore need to understand the interplay between strategizing and organizing by paying attention to strategizing pluralism (multiple, fragmented and perhaps conflicting strategic objectives, goals and interests) and to organizing pluralism (divergent organizational groups due to fragmented cultures and identities). Jarzabkowski and Fenton distinguish between three modes of association between strategizing and organizing: interdependent, destructive and imbalanced (Jarzabkowski, Fenton 2006: 13).

In the interdependent mode, strategizing and organizing are mutually reinforcing. Whereas organizing practices are tailored to the demands of different strategic goals, strategizing practices recognize the interests and identities of different organizational groups.

As a contrast to this mode, the destructive mode is concerned with extreme pluralism in both domains. In this mode, the organization is pulled in too many directions disabling it to meet the multiple demands, goals and interests of the divergent organizational groups and stakeholders. The risk is an organizational breakdown.

The imbalanced mode is in between these two modes. It occurs when strategizing practices are in favor of the interests of some parts of the organization at the expense of others thereby creating a conflict between different organizational groups or when organizing practices pursue some strategic objectives and pay less attention to other strategic objectives. The latter may result in conflicts arising between cultures and identities, new strategies being blocked, or new ways of organizing practices not being adopted.

The Story of a Multi-Cultural Strategizing – Organizing Process

The knowledge of the concrete company is created through interviews with the CEO, several managers and employees from the different houses and the different professions throughout a period of one year. The knowledge is created through a localist approach to interviews (Alvesson 2003) within the framework of a dialogical, postmodern study (Deetz 2001). This approach emphasizes that knowledge of the company is emerging in the communication with the company. The interview occurs as a dialogue or conversation during which the researcher and the interviewed person together produce knowledge of the company. The knowledge created in the here and now moment of the conversation is a local, situated knowledge implying that the interview is interpreted in its social context. By interviewing the organizational members at this micro level, multiple worldviews are voiced revealing the dissensus and the fragmentation of the organization. In the postmodern approach to organizational studies, dissensus and fragmentations is assumed to be the natural state of organizations and societies. Theories are used as lenses through which we may start to see what previously was unconscious and hidden before our eyes. As lenses, theories may help new understandings of the empirical phenomenon to emerge. In this concrete study, the pluralistic perspective on strategizing and organizing as well as on culture and identity is used as lenses to understand the fragmentation of the company and the organizational breakdown of relations.

Merger History and the Rise of Counter-Cultures

The company is a small and medium sized agricultural, consultancy association with about 200 employees. It is a non-profit organization which is owned by its customers and which struggle to survive in a difficult and competitive environment. Since the middle of the last century, the agricultural sector has undergone profound structural changes and experienced the impact of several economic and financial crises. As a result, the company faces a market characterized by a continuously decreasing number of customers and consequently by severely intensified competition. As a reaction to this development, the industry shows a long history of mergers between various agricultural actors.

In line with this tendency, the company was established in 2008 as a result of a merger between two fiercefully competing consulting organizations. In their turn, these two organizations also originated from previous mergers. The company is today composed located three consultancy "houses" located in three different cities within the geographical market area: Beta House, Delta House and Alpha House. Beta and Delta House belong to one of the merging companies whereas Alpha House constitutes the other company. All three houses have developed their own cultures. Thus the company is constituted by an organizational mosaic of different cultures related to the many mergers in the history of the company. Both employees and managers address cultural differences between the three houses and the CEO even refers to their internal relations as fights.

The strategic and economic advantages of the merger were clear enough. Due to the merger, the company became the largest consultancy company in its main market area and the fifth largest agricultural association in Denmark. With a presence in the three main cities, the company remains close to the local customers.

346

Despite the obvious strategic and economic advantages, the merger did not make sense to all members of the new organization. At the time of the merger decision, Alpha House had to choose between two competitors. Originally, they tried to merge with another competitor but when that failed, they ended up with Beta/Delta, thereby eliminating one of their biggest competitors. Not all organizational members, customers and owners agreed upon this decision and it was only voted for by a marginal number of voices at the general meeting. The elimination of the competition between the two companies was considered to be a huge advantage, but due to severe conflicts in the past history of the two companies, their relationship was rooted in mutual hatred and hostility, overshadowing the merger advantages. In Alpha House, they referred to the merger as "marrying their worst enemy".

The years following the merger were very challenging due to ongoing disagreements, conflicts and disputes. In two and a half year, the organization thus experienced four different CEOs and a board of directors who discussed their disagreements in the public media. A drop in customer and employee satisfaction reflected the lack of trust in the company and the management. The conflicting, critical voices were raised openly as many employees and customers left the company to join the competitors. The "us-them" cultural and identity constructions were thus reinforced during these years. The tendency continued for some years in the aftermath of the merger and significantly weakened the economic performance of the company. Not surprisingly, this development resulted in a growing deficit from 2008 to 2009 which seriously endangered the continued existence of the company.

This was the situation when the present CEO was hired in 2010 to turn around the company. According to his stories, the previous management was not prepared for the challenges related to the integration phase of the merger, meaning that little or no efforts were made to bridge the cultural gaps or to work with the negative construction of the other in the process of identity and culture formation. Neither did they initiate discussions on the future organization and strategic development of the company. In fact, they ceased to act, hoping that time would help the process of integration.

Consequently, the company can be understood in a cultural and organizational pluralistic context as many cultures have beenimported into the organization through the mergers and provide the bases for counter-cultures and "us-them" constructions to emerge. Thus the foundation for a potential organizational breakdown is at place.

Organizing the Strategizing Processes in a Pluralistic Context

Facing this economic, organizational, and cultural situation of the company, the CEO decided two major interventions. First of all, he took actions to reduce the costs of the company by closing down a fourth house in 2010 belonging to the Beta-Delta organization. He also severely reduced the number of employees and managers, implemented changes to the performance management system and recently made the organization lean. .

The second intervention concerned the strategy process. No effort had previously been made to create a strategy for the merger or for the future development of the company. Thus the organization lacked direction. Considering the different cultures in the organization and hostile us-them identity constructions, the CEO decided to facilitate a multi-participatory, bottom-up strategy process, divided into two steps. In the first step, all managers and employees, many customers and owners and the whole board of directors were asked to participate in the strategy formulation.

As the second step, the employees were invited to participate in the work of implementing the strategy. Strategy project groups were formed in relation to the strategic themes identified in the strategy formulation process. These groups are composed by employees in order to continue the bottom up process. The employees are free to choose the strategic theme that would be of most interest to them and then join this project group as long as they have the relevant competences and skills. They are also not allowed to take part of the implementing process and solely concentrate on their operative activities. In the strategic groups, the employees make sense of the strategic theme by relating the theme to their experiences from everyday life and local knowledge from working together with the customers. This constitutes the pragmatic everyday bases for strategy-making in the strategy groups.

The managers participate in steering groups in order to coordinate resources, ensure sufficient organizational capacity for both development and operations, and to assess new proposals forwarded from the strategic groups. The strategy continues thus to be developed, changed and enacted within the broad frame of the strategy formulation.

Three days each year, all employees and managers are asked to participate in the evaluation of the strategy process. During these days, they make sense retrospectively of the past stream of actions and prospectively towards the future: "We work with it all the time. Every year, we evaluate it; what we are doing, where we are heading, what we need to focus on..." Team leader, AlphaHouse.

All in all, several employees express that they have been part of making the strategy and of the process of implementing and changing it in an ongoing process. Thus, they experience that the strategy is meaningful and makes sense to them. Some employees describe the strategy process as an "ongoing journey" that has provided more directionality and developed a sense of a "we" in relation to the whole organization.

The above description of the strategy process highlights how strategizing occurs at the micro level of the organization within the institutionalized strategy formulation. The strategizing process is facilitated in a way that is flexible to the organizational and cultural pluralism of the company. By organizing the strategizing process in this way, the company can enhance knowledge sharing, dissemination of local expertise and the creation of new ideas for business development. An organizational, culturally pluralistic approach to strategizing may thus create an environment in which new initiatives and new strategies may be proposed and enacted (Jarzabkowski, Fenton 2006) or simply just emerge non-deliberately and unintendedly at the micro level of activities.

The strength of this way of organizing the strategizing process is the structural facilitation of multi-cultural encounters and communication in the strategy process. Participants are deliberately mingled together across the different cultures in the organization. Therefore the organizing process may elicit new relations to emerge or existing relations to change, impacting on the "us-them" constructions.

At a first look, the above discussion of the way of organizing the strategizing process indicates the interdependent mode of associating the interplay between organizing and strategizing. The interdependent mode prescribes that "managers do not think of their organizations as coherent wholes, with a uniform organizational culture and identity bound together around a single strategic goal" (Jarzabkowski, Fenton 2006: 14). Instead the managers need to acknowledge pluralism in order to achieve an interdependent interplay between strategizing and organizing.

However, the interdependent mode is not carried out thoroughly in the company. Organizing pluralism is acknowledged, but it is assumed that the multi-participatory strategy process will create more directionality and shared identities and cultures. The development of one organizational culture and identity is in fact an intended social aim of the process. The assumption of the organization as a coherent whole is thus underlying the strategizing-organizing approach just as the assumption of a single strategic goal: "If they themselves have been part of making the strategy, then they can also subject to it" (the CEO). This quotation indicates the underlying assumption of consensus and shared agreements in relation to the established and distinctive strategy foci of the strategy formulation. Thereby the management is overlooking the fragmentation of the continued strategizing process. Ignoring the significance of the strategizing and organizing tensions and conflicts reinforce the course of events heading towards the organizational breakdown.

Pluralistic Tensions in the Strategizing Organizing Processes

The pluralistic way of organizing the strategizing process created an environment for strategic discussions all over the organization. The process revealed several conflicting strategies, goals and demands for the future development of the company in relation to its difficult and changing environment. Despite the assumed consensus of the strategy formulation, the tensions manifest a profound dissensus, disorder and ambiguity in the understanding of the dynamic relation between the company and the changing environment, in the prospective sensemaking of the possible arriving futures and consequently in the identification of future strategic actions.

The disorder and dissensus manifest in tensions arising from competing, fragmented strategizing processes due to the different interests, cultures and identities in the company. Broadly speaking, one of these tensions concerns two competing strategy worldviews as regard how to survive in a declining market. At the concrete, practical level, these strategy sensemaking processes are more ambiguous than that, but at the abstract, theoretical level of this analysis, the simplification is easier to handle in order to understand how the pluralistic tensions in the company challenge the strategizing and organizing processes of world-making.

The two strategizing processes differ as regard to the growth strategy of the company. One of the strategic directions aims for growth through future merger activities, thereby increasing market shares, eliminating competition and strengthening the market position. The other direction shares this growth strategy but takes it further. Whereas the first direction aims at reinforcing the existing activities and services within agricultural consultancy, the latter aims at expanding the main business operations from offering traditional agricultural consultancy to traditional agricultural customers to offering more general business consultancy to SMEs such as handicraft business, service companies, and small production companies. To perform general business consultancy and to generate business ideas and development within this new business activity, new employees have been selected and hired based upon their business and sales oriented mindset and competences.

Furthermore, strategic actions are taken in order to grow through the development of new consultancy services within real estate, insurance and external HR consultancy. Consequently, employees with competences within these occupational areas are hired, whereby new occupational cultures are imported into the organization. One of these new employees is the team leader of external HR consultancy. Coming from Rumania, he has provided the company with the competences and network for entering the Rumanian agricultural market and thereby the opportunity to grow through internationalization. This strategy is now considered as a new business possibility.

Strategy actions emerging within this type of sensemaking imply changes to the business area and activities that the company traditionally was founded on. Thus in the strategizing process, several strategic actions and decisions emerge in order to develop the market into new customer segments and to offer new consultancy services. These actions change the business profile and identity of the company which is also reflected in the branding of the company and in its way of positioning itself in the market.

The tensions reach deep as it touches upon the survival of the company as a non-profit association or as a private profit-oriented firm. The possible dissolution of the association is not only a matter of the form of enterprise but it also challenges the identity, feeling of belongingness to, the cultural traditions, and the family spirit of a community shared by the organizational constituents through a manifold of years. The consultants and the farmers typically share a history of 20-40 years' of relationship. Furthermore, it challenges the power bases of influence as the farmers are customers, owners and part of the board of directors. Even though the question of the form of enterprise is only vaguely voiced and is reaching far out in the future, the present stream of strategic actions and decisions seem to make the question of the form of enterprise more potential, and certainly it points at a profound business oriented change of the culture and identity of the company.

Tensions also emerge in the interplay between strategizing for further market penetration and cultural organizing. To increase sales and the acquisition of new customers, new initiatives are taken to enhance sales behavior and a business mindset. This implies a cultural change from the more family oriented culture to a more business and sales oriented culture. To support this change, several initiatives have been enacted or proposed such as mandatory courses and training in sales, outreach sales activities, internal referral of customers, and new ways of organizing by centering the customer in the heart of all activities and by working more interdisciplinarily in the approach to the customer.

The multiple strategic actions and changes require resources and put pressure on the capacity of the organization. Tensions thus also arise between the business development of the company and the running of the operative activities.

Multicultural Dynamics in the Interplay between Strategizing and Organizing

The understanding of the tensed interplay between the strategizing and organizing processes in the case can be enriched by looking at the phenomenon through the lenses of cultural pluralism and lifeworld dynamics. The following quotations indicate a dynamic process moving from the "us-them" identification rooted in the hostile construction of the other as the enemy to a "we" indicating a shared feeling of identity and belongingness. Furthermore, the quotations indicate changes in the organizing of practices and relations in the company implying that the strategizing – organizing processes have impacted on the organization.

At that time [before the new CEO], we did not feel that we were one big family. But his way of approaching this [the multi-participatory, bottom up strategy process] made us feel more like being employed in ONE organization. It was a long journey because we had to get used to it but both the social and professional cooperation is much different today.

- John, Delta City, employee.

It has become much better, but to begin with, I think we all were frustrated, because we were used to manage our own little house. And there was a feeling of… did we dare share with the others? Or would they play games with us? That has disappeared today."

- Jill, Delta City, employee.

The positive construction of the change process reflected in the quotation is, however, not shared by all members of the organization. In fact, the whole group of employees in the economic department of Alpha House left the company to work for the competitor and along with them a significant number of customers.

These two polarized movements can be related to the interdependent interplay between strategizing and organizing at the one pole and to the destructive interplay at the other pole which has resulted in the organizational breakdown with the department.

In the beginning of the strategy process, the company was characterized by the hostile "us-them" identifications between the two merged organizations. As the CEO and the head quarter functions were related to Beta House and Alpha House was the smallest organization measured in terms of number of employees, the Alpha organizational members feared that the merger was not a true merger but a take-over. Several of the organization members were thus skeptical towards all strategic decisions and actions and some were unable to overcome this skepticism and refused to use the new name of the merged company when speaking with the customers.

This identity construction was strengthened by the geographical division between the three houses, dividing the company into three different local cultures and "us-them" relations between these three houses as well. As hostility and internal fights characterized their relations, they did not trust each other and aimed at protecting their own existence in the difficult market by maintaining their local cultural communities of practices in relation to their customers. The identity construction and cultural defense of their own community became an obstacle to the enactment of the sales enhancing initiatives of collaborating more across the houses.

The cultural community of practices is further fragmentized by the organizational structure of groups in each house. The organizational members are divided into groups corresponding to their professional disciplines such as crop, cattle, and pigs or functions such as: economic, insurance, real estate. Throughout a long history, these groups have developed their own shared ways of organizing and practicing their professional skills and relations with respect to the requirements of the customers. They have developed their own cultural and professional communities of practices. This way of organizing was not optimal to the customer as the pieces of dvice from the various consultants sometimes were conflicting. Despite that, the members resisted to change their organizing practices and relations in order to work more interdisciplinary or to exchange customers across the houses and across professions even though this implied lost opportunities of sales and ambiguous, confusing consultancy advice. Thus cultural boundaries and professional identities at the professional / occupational level result in "us-them" identifications within the houses. These boundaries counter-acted the changes towards a sales culture.

In the above discussion, the differentiation perspective is used to describe a picture of the multicultural mosaic based upon geographical and professional sources of cultural divisions. The mosaic is, however, more fragmented than this structural differentiation, as issues evolve in new situations and are interpreted by the organizational members in ways that do not follow the structural subcultural boundaries. Instead new cultures are formed centering on the specific issues, creating new subcultural boundaries that are blurred, uncertain, and fluctuating. These issue-specific cultures are related to different world views.

In the merged company, the sales culture implies new ways of behaving towards the customer. Consequently, customer relationship becomes an issue of multiple, ambiguous, and contesting interpretations. The multiple meanings manifest in different ways of invoicing the customers. In the family oriented culture, time is invested in the relationship, sometimes without invoicing the time in the spirit of providing customer service. In the sales oriented culture, all time used on the customers should be invoiced, implying that the price of the invoice increases. Due to the familiarity of 20-40 years of relations with the customers, this transcends the values of some employees in the organization whereas other members in the organization views the sales and business oriented thinking and acting as necessary considering the difficult market and economic situation of the company. Thus new ideas for how to earn money on invested time and still provide customer service emerge through these discussions.

Other ambiguous issues emerge in the interplay between identities and sales culture. The sales culture seems to conflict with identities related to the family oriented culture. According to the CEO, this was a struggle between different identities and self-reflexive understandings: "They said they were not salesmen but consultants. When I started to talk about sales, my head was almost chopped off. We almost had to find a synonym to sales." The CEO came up with "consultative sales" as a new concept. The discussions initiated new sense making processes during which a multiple ways of interpreting a sales behavior in relation to the identity of being a consultant was unfolded and new shared and meaningful self-reflexive understandings emerged with some employees in the company.

Also in relation to the strategic movement of becoming a more business oriented company, ambiguous discussion of issues such as "business" and "strategy" emerged: "Some of them [customers-owners] thought, it was a waste of money [the strategy process]. And some of the customers had a lot of focus on the cost and the usefulness of the process, stating "we are after all just an association of farmers" Lily, team leader, Alpha House. This world view clashes with the world view of the CEO: "We move from being an association to becoming a business". Other members of the organization adopted the ideas of the strategy process and business development and of the new business profile of the company.

Consequently, the merged company is constituted by multiple local, cultural communities of practices which are fragmented, interconnected, and overlapping due to the fluctuating cultures related to specific issues emerging in new situations and which may impact on the organizing and practicing of skills, activities and relations. The cultures are not necessarily in accordance with each other but may act as counter-cultures. Thus, the mosaic of cultures is changing as part of the cultural dynamic.

The fragmentation of the cultures in the organization is one of the sources that drives the cultural dynamics. The internal cultural pluralism increases as newcomers from the surrounding society bring new competences, new organized skilled practices and new world views into the organization. Furthermore, the cultural dynamic is also driven by the surrounding fragmented cultures. In the case of the merged company, the customers are culturally divided as some farmers, typically the younger generation of farmers, are becoming more business oriented resulting in other requirements to the consultancy services of the company. According to some of the more business oriented consultants in the company, this is a challenge to the company if the consultants of the company are stuck in their family oriented cultural community of practices. Thus the sensemaking processes of the cultural dynamics of the organization are driven by both internal and external forces, making the organizational boundaries permeable, corresponding to Martin's concept of the cultural nexus and Alvesson's concept of cultural traffic.

The sensemaking processes in the mosaic of fragmented cultures and identities are important as a way of interconnecting and bridging the strategizing pluralism and organizing pluralism. The culture and identity processes are part of the becoming-into-being of the person. Without considering these processes, the coming-into-being of the world through organizing and strategizing may fail due to the unaddressed human tensions.

This is what happens in the case of the economic department when 32 employees leave the company in order to work for the competitor. This group of employees was not able to identify with, to value and to find the strategizing and organizing actions meaningful. Thus they blocked the enactment of the strategies by maintaining their way of organizing their local cultural community of practices. Their power bases were significant as they were supported by a large group of customers who shared their prospective sensemaking of a strategic course of the company that would eventually fail. Consequently, this group of employees was attractive to the competitor.

In the retrospective reflection of the power struggle within this group of employees, the company's management realizes that the group hardly participated in the strategic groups and therefore never really developed new relations with the other groups of the company. The organizing of the flexible multi-participatory strategy process thus failed its purpose of creating new relations and bridging the multi-cultural tensions with respect to this group.

Furthermore, the CEO and the rest of the organization came to a point where they paid less attention to the critical voices of the group. As communication is closed down and the multi-cultural relations are not developed, the hermeneutical processes of sensemaking are turned into a closed circle as opposed to an open-ended spiral. Being caught in the prejudiced fore-structured understanding of each other, the group of the economic department and the rest of the organization cannot bridge their different ways of making sense of the world-making. They cease trying to understand the other's way of understanding. Consequently, the hostile "us-them" identification, the defense of their cultural community of practices and their resistance against the strategic actions are maintained and cemented leading to the breakdown of relations.

As regard the modes of association between strategizing and organizing, the case illustrates that this interplay is tied up with culture and identity dynamics. The way of organizing the strategizing process enable the organizational constituents to respond to the strategic goals and foci of the strategy formulation but this does not entirely happen without marginalizing the interests of some cultural groups and identities in the company. The organizing practices are not consistent with the identities and interests of all culture and identity fragments. The strategizing and organizing processes are only mutually adjusting in those parts of the organization, where the organizational constituents commit to the vision of the strategic business development as this vision is in line with their prospective sensemaking of the world-coming-into-being. As they are able to see themselves and their role in this future, it is also in line with their coming-into-being as persons.

The processes of strategizing and organizing are unbalanced in other parts of the organization, where organizational constituents do not commit to the goals and foci of the strategy. In the case of the economic department, they choose to resist the strategy by not participating in the strategic groups and by not enacting the organizational strategic decisions in their own department. Defending their own strategy world view, their critical voices turn into counter-power bases supported by many of their customers. Consequently, the association mode moves from an unbalanced to a destructive interplay between strategizing and organizing. As tensions arouse, the confrontations between the competing power positions accelerate, resulting in the breakdown of the relations with the economic department. With the 32 employees leaving the company, the pluralism is less polarized in the company but still tensed due to the persistency of different world views, interests and foci, the pressure on identities and cultures and not least the pressure on capacity as the organization is struggling to catch up with the strategic initiatives.

Conclusions

This chapter contributes by creating insights into the role of culture in producing strategizing and organizing tensions. By adopting the pluralistic perspective, culture and identity are understood as differentiated and fragmented constructs which may be fruitful to the understanding of the tensions of strategizing and organizing. In this perspective, it emphasized how cultural boundaries and the "we" and "us-them" identifications are constructed and reconstructed in organizations depending on the situation, the issue, the position of the participants and the purposes of their actions. The lifeworld perspective contributes by highlighting the dynamics of the hermeneutical spiral of circle in the sensemaking processes of being-in-the-world. The spiraling dynamics may create new cultural boundaries and "we" and "us-them" identifications whereas the circling process only reproduces the prejudiced fore-structured understandings and maintain the already existing cultures and identity constructions. These perspectives provide new understandings of the management of the interplay between the strategizing or organizing processes.

The discussions in the chapter reflect how clashes between cultures and identities contribute in developing tensions related to strategizing pluralism and organizing pluralism. It also enlightens the processes of strategizing and organizing as two essential processes of world-making. However, these processes of world-making cannot be understood in isolation from the processes of culture and identification. The unbalanced processes of culture, identity, strategizing and organizing as well as the management's ignorance of this unbalancing may create tensions between the coming-into-being of the world and the coming-into-being of the person. This may cause problems to the enactment of new strategies and eventually lead to organizational breakdowns.

Pluralism is always present in organizations. Management is thus continuously challenged by the multi-cultural pluralism and its impact on the strategizing and organizing processes. However, even though pluralism is related to challenges and risks of tensions and breakdowns, it is also pluralism that drives the dynamic and creative changes. The management needs to handle this pluralistic challenge by providing the conditions for the hermeneutical spiral and dialogues through which different voices of worldviews can be raised and listened to, enabling different cultural lifeworlds to be accessed and bridged.

Bibliography

Alvesson, M. 2013, *Understanding organizational culture,* Sage.

Alvesson, M. 2003, "Beyond neopositivists, romantics, and localists: A reflexive approach to interviews in organizational research", *Academy of management review,* vol. 28, no. 1, pp. 13-33.

Boje, D. 2014, *Storytelling Organizational Practices. Managing in the Quantum Age,* Routledge, New York.

Carter, C., Kornberger, M. & Schweitzer, J. 2011, *Strategy: Theory and practice,* Sage.

Chia, R. 2004, "Strategy-as-practice: Reflections on the research agenda", *European Management Review,* vol. 1, no. 1, pp. 29-34.

Chia, R.C. & Holt, R. 2009, *Strategy without design: The silent efficacy of indirect action,* Cambridge University Press.

Chia, R. & Holt, R. 2006, "Strategy as practical coping: A Heideggerian perspective", *Organization Studies,* vol. 27, no. 5, pp. 635-655.

Chia, R. & MacKay, B. 2007, "Post-processual challenges for the emerging strategy-as-practice perspective: Discovering strategy in the logic of practice", *Human relations,* vol. 60, no. 1, pp. 217-242.

Deetz, S. 2001, "Conceptual Foundations" in *The New Handbook of Organizational Communication. Advances in Theory, Research and Methods,* eds. F.M. Jabli & L.L. Putnam, Sage Publications, London.

Denis, J., Langley, A. & Rouleau, L. 2007, "Strategizing in pluralistic contexts: Rethinking theoretical frames", *Human Relations,* vol. 60, no. 1, pp. 179-215.

Gadamer, H. 2013, *Truth and Method,* Bloomsbury, New York.

Heidegger, M. 2008, *Being and time,* HarperCollins, New York.

Heidegger, M. 1993, "Building Dwelling Thinking" in *Martin Heidegger, Basic Writings,* ed. D.F. Krell, Harper Collins Publishers, New York, pp. 347.

Ingold, T. 2000, *The perception of the environment: essays in livelihood, dwelling and skill,* Psychology Press.

Jarzabkowski, P. & Fenton, E. 2006, "Strategizing and organizing in pluralistic contexts", *Long range planning,* vol. 39, no. 6, pp. 631-648.

Martin, J. 2002, *Organizational Culture: Mapping the Terrain,* Sage Publications, London.

Martin, J. 1992, *Cultures in Organizations: Three perspectives,* Oxford University Press.

Nayak, A. & Chia, R. 2011, "Thinking becoming and emergence: process philosophy and organization studies", *Research in the Sociology of Organizations,* vol. 32, pp. 281-309.

Parker, M. 2000, *Organizational culture and identity: Unity and division at work,* Sage.

Shotter, J. 2011, *Reflections on sociomateriality and dialogicality in organization studies: from "inter-" to "intra-thinking" in performing practices.* Available: http://www.johnshotter.com/mypapers/Intra-thinking.pdf [2014, April].

Tsoukas, H. & Chia, R. 2002, "On Organizational Becoming: Rethinking Organizational Change", *Organization Science,* vol. 13, no. 5, pp. 567-582.

Wenger, E. 1998, *Communities of Practice. Learning, Meaning, and Identity.* Cambridge University Press, Cambridge.

Whittington, R., Molloy, E., Mayer, M. & Smith, A. 2006, "Practices of strategising/organising: broadening strategy work and skills", *Long range planning,* vol. 39, no. 6, pp. 615-629.

Index

www.ingramcontent.com/pod-product-compliance
Lightning Source LLC
Chambersburg PA
CBHW061124220326
41599CB00024B/4157